THE
AUSTRALI....
RUGBY
COMPANION

For over two decades Gordon Bray has been renowned throughout Australia as the 'Voice of Rugby'. His name is synonymous with televised rugby union and his distinctive commentary style as much a part of the Australian game as a John Eales line-out or a Campese goose-step.

Although skilful enough to make a NSW Combined High Schools squad as a scrum-half, not long after leaving school he decided to stop playing the game seriously and concentrate on a broadcasting career with the ABC. By 1980 Gordon had become ABC TV's first-choice rugby commentator – taking over from the legendary Norman May – and quickly developed a reputation for speed, accuracy and passion. Since then he has called over 200 Test matches, including at all four World Cups, Bledisloe Cups and the former Five Nations in the Northern Hemisphere.

Gordon has been the chief rugby commentator with the Seven Network in Sydney since 1995 and writes a twice-weekly column for the *Daily Telegraph*. He is married with two teenage children and lives in Sydney.

Also by Gordon Bray

From the Ruck
The Rugby Laws Explained (ed.)
*The Spirit of Rugby: A Tribute to Australian
 Rugby Union* (ed.)

THE
AUSTRALIAN
RUGBY
COMPANION

'THE GAME THEY PLAY
IN HEAVEN'

EDITED BY GORDON BRAY

VIKING

Viking

Published by the Penguin Group
Penguin Books Australia Ltd
250 Camberwell Road, Camberwell, Victoria 3124, Australia
Penguin Books Ltd
80 Strand, London WC2R 0RL, England
Penguin Putnam Inc.
375 Hudson Street, New York, New York 10014, USA
Penguin Books, a division of Pearson Canada
10 Alcorn Avenue, Toronto, Ontario, Canada M4V 3B2
Penguin Books (NZ) Ltd
Cnr Rosedale and Airborne Roads, Albany, Auckland, New Zealand
Penguin Books (South Africa) (Pty) Ltd
24 Sturdee Avenue, Rosebank, Johannesburg 2196, South Africa
Penguin Books India (P) Ltd
11, Community Centre, Panchsheel Park, New Delhi 110 017, India

First published by Penguin Books Australia 2002

10 9 8 7 6 5 4 3 2 1

Cover design by Tony Palmer, Penguin Design Studio
Text design by George Dale, Penguin Design Studio
Front cover photograph © AAP
Back cover photograph © Getty Images
Typeset in 10.5/16 pt Melior by Midland Typesetters, Maryborough, Victoria
Printed and bound in Australia by McPherson's Printing Group, Maryborough, Victoria

National Library of Australia
Cataloguing-in-Publication data:

The Australian rugby companion: 'the game they play in heaven'.

ISBN 0 670 04034 7.

1. Rugby Union football – Australia. I. Bray, Gordon.

796.3330994

www.penguin.com.au

Contents

Part 2
All is revealed

John Eales

Foreword

Rugby union has made enormous
strides as a sport in Australia over
the last ten years. In that time
player numbers have been significantly enhanced by around 20 per
cent. The increased interest in the
game has seen the Wallabies generate a world-record attendance
for a rugby international – 109 874
attended the 2000 Bledisloe Cup at
Stadium Australia.

Culturally the code has also gone through a massive
change. It has developed from its origins as an amateur
game to arrive at its current state where it is a fully professional code at the elite level. There is little doubt that
through the innovations of John O'Neill and the Australian
Rugby Union administration (and the success of the Wallabies), rugby can now compete with the heavyweights when
it comes to the corporate environment of sport.

Our code has always prided itself on being a game for
everyone. It caters for all shapes and sizes, for men, women

and children, for amateurs and professionals, and for players and spectators alike.

The Australian Rugby Companion is something of a first for rugby in Australia. No other single publication has accepted the challenge of providing everything you need to know about the game between one set of covers. It is a book for all rugby supporters – for the diehard, lifetime fan as well as the newcomer.

No other book has brought so many aspects of our sport together. To mention just a few of its topics: our glorious past, the future, on-field strategies, background information on all our top players, analysis from the leading coaches, the art of back-line play (is there such a thing?) and forward play (now we're talking!), secrets of television commentary, player superstitions and collecting memorabilia. There's also brilliant simplification of the laws (I could have used this in my playing days) by leading referee Wayne Erickson, and an annotated – and shortened – summary of the laws themselves.

What makes this book unique is that it is part handy reference, part up-to-date guide to the current game, part celebration of our glorious rugby traditions. You'll treasure the sheer joy that shines through the reminiscences of an early-1900s Wallaby, pore over the complete World Cup and Bledisloe Cup results, and chuckle at the casual way my successor, George Gregan, reveals how he first became involved in the game.

A book such as *The Australian Rugby Companion* reminds us of how central the game is to our existence. Beyond my family, rugby has been the biggest influence on my life. When one considers the people one meets, the places one can go and the opportunities it affords, it's easy to see why this is so.

But always at the top of these influences are the people. It may seem indulgent to say so but I believe that, in general, rugby people are *good* people. I have been positively influenced by good people at all levels of the game. From my initiation with the Ashgrove Emus through my school rugby days, my club rugby days and my Test-playing days, it's been the people that have made my experience extraordinary.

My involvement in the game has now changed somewhat. I have gone from being a very active player to being a very active – and vocal – supporter. I will also have ongoing rugby-related roles with both the ARU and Channel Seven. This will all, of course, be quite different from the past decade, but at the same time I'm sure it will be bound together by the common thread of the people of rugby.

For an inexperienced armchair critic such as myself, *The Australian Rugby Companion* will be the perfect guide for what promises to be an exciting journey following Australian rugby. I know you will really enjoy the reading of it.

John Eales played the last of his 86 Test matches on 1 September 2001, leading the Wallabies to a last-second Tri-Nations-clinching win over the All Blacks at Stadium Australia. He retired as the most capped lock in Test history and the sixth most capped international player of all time, in a career spanning 11 seasons from 1991. John led the Wallabies in 55 Tests for 41 wins, played 20 Tests against the All Blacks for 11 wins and is revered as one of the true all-time greats of the game.

Acknowledgements

The structure and content of this book have been designed to strike an enticing balance for both traditional supporters and the growing army of newcomers to the code.

My thanks are especially due to editorial consultant David Salter, a former Head of ABC TV Sport and Executive Producer of *Media Watch*, for his patient and always passionate input into this project.

Researcher and statistician Matt Gray performed an extremely valuable role, helping to coordinate sections of the finished copy.

The project would not have been possible without the enthusiasm and willing input of all specialist contributors. Their support is deeply appreciated.

Thanks also to the International Rugby Board and Strath Gordon from *Australian Rugby* for their unqualified support.

To referees Andrew Cole, Stuart Dickinson, Wayne Erickson, Peter Marshall and Scott Young who all donated their time and knowledge – their generosity and expert contributions are gratefully recognised.

The subtitle of this book is unashamedly taken from former Wallaby front-rower Steve Finnane's original publication *The Game They Play in Heaven* (McGraw-Hill). Steve's inspired stratagem has become an international catchphrase.

To Frank Keating, senior sports columnist with the *Guardian*, heartfelt gratitude is conveyed for permission to revisit his exquisite narrative on Mark Ella from *The Great Number Tens*.

Thanks are due to Jim Tucker, senior rugby writer from the *Courier-Mail*, for his professional input. Mark Kolbe at Getty Images has been an outstanding help with sourcing photographs. Gratitude is also extended to Judy Macarthur and John Mulford from Australian Rugby Archives for their willing support of this project.

Special acknowledgement to the excellent Penguin Books team of senior editor Katie Purvis, design consultant George Dale and publishing director Robert Sessions. All have tackled this project with tremendous enthusiasm and passion.

Appreciation is also expressed to Seven Network colleague Damian Keogh, who enthusiastically backed the project from its inception. A former elite and Olympic athlete, Damian's shrewd insight and constructive advice greatly enhanced the finished product.

Finally to my family – wife Cathy and children Anna and Andrew, who all typed (and typed) diligently whenever called on.

Gordon Bray

Prelude

Maintaining the tradition

The Sydney Mail's *pictorial of New Zealand's win over Australia in the First Test at the SCG in 1938, in which the All Blacks ran in four tries, including two by the flying Charlie Saxton.*

Gordon Bray

Lest we forget

'It is the spirit of rugby, the good fellowship, the unselfishness and the teamsmanship in each player that makes him a man worth knowing. He moves in a game that enjoys international significance and is backed by a wealth of tradition – a game in which the right sort of athlete is moulded – and in which some of life's most solid friendships are made.'

– Harald Baker

The timeless thoughts above were penned almost 80 years ago by former Wallaby forward Harald Baker. Back in 1923 the Corinthian ideals of rugby outlined by Baker were taken for granted. Now, with the sport transformed by almost a decade of professionalism, it's vital that those principles remain as the essential fabric of our code.

Many loyal fans believe that preserving the character, ethics and ideals of the former amateur game may already be a lost cause. I cannot agree. After all, didn't former Wallaby coach Rod Macqueen painstakingly reinforce the game's traditional ethos before proceeding to conquer the modern rugby world?

Surely the challenge for us now is to hold on to our Wallaby heritage in the face of rapid, yet inevitable, change.

There is little point railing against the inevitable. We can't pretend that money is not one of the most powerful influences on the game – but is that influence necessarily a bad thing?

In reality, it is still the players who hold the key. It is the players who will sustain those cherished values that have made rugby the envy of other codes. They retain a very powerful say in the conduct of the game. There is no doubt that our current Wallabies all regularly take the time to re-examine the reasons why they, and their former teammates, have been so successful over the past five years. (They could do worse than start those sessions with Harald Baker's penetrating words.) The Wallabies under Macqueen set an example for others to follow. Their teamsmanship was second to none and their sense of humility and dignity earned widespread acclaim.

Rugby is the quintessential team game. There is no place for individuals who put themselves before the collective cause. Ultimately such people will undermine – and eventually destroy – any team. That's precisely why the Wallabies of 2002 and beyond must never lose sight of their debt to the game and its history.

As the guardians of the Wallaby jumper, our current national team represents a dynasty dating back to 1899. Their position is hard-earned but also highly privileged. They do not own the priceless green-and-gold jersey – it is on loan to them. They carry the torch for generations of distinguished players to come, and in memory of the great Australian sportsmen who have gone before them as Wallabies.

Approaching the 2003 World Cup, the test for new coach Eddie Jones is to strike the right balance between 'player power' (for want of a better phrase) and the level of authority and leadership required from a coach and his management.

It's an issue not confined to the Wallaby camp. Without question, the All Blacks mishandled this aspect of their off-field conduct in the domestic Test matches. Coach Wayne Smith allowed his players too much leash. In the end, that policy alone ensured his ultimate demise. The new NZ boss, John Mitchell, appears to have learned from those mistakes. Mitchell is now firmly back in charge of the national team and the players are happy with the arrangement.

One of Macqueen's greatest strengths was his willingness to listen to a wide variety of knowledgeable people within the Wallaby framework. Final decisions were based on carefully measured input across the board. The upshot was that Macqueen and his support team, including the selectors, rarely got it wrong. In his team manager, John Mackay, he had an able lieutenant who could always pick up any slack in player–coach relations. New manager Phil Thompson is highly respected by the players, but he must also be sufficiently detached to help Eddie Jones make the tough decisions that will contribute positively towards the long-term big picture. Eddie, too, should not be blinkered in his consultations with players and staff. It will be crucial for him to spread his net wide because every decision from now on will be vital to our successful World Cup defence.

We must also concede that what worked in the Macqueen era may not necessarily yield the same results during Jones's stewardship. At the same time, the point should not be lost that although the game has moved on, its *raison d'être* remains the same.

As coach of the ACT Brumbies, Jones was both an

innovator and a perfectionist. His work ethic astounded all who came in contact with him. He was his own person, and an inspiring commanding officer. Australian rugby fans expect more of the same from the man entrusted to guide our elite players along the path to further World Cup glory. The boss has to make the hard and responsible decisions. Jones is *The Man*. John Eales has already described him as the best all-round coach he's ever played under.

On the broader stage, it's heartening to note the enormous growth in prestige and public attention that Australian rugby has enjoyed since the advent of real professionalism. A decade ago the season's end always brought a string of media stories reporting the 'defection' of prominent players to rugby league; now the traffic is in the other direction. Talented footballers such as Mat Rogers and Wendell Sailor have switched to rugby union because the code offers them a better platform to express their full abilities – and the incentive of earning genuine international honours.

So, in many significant ways, the 'new' mood of rugby is just a modern restatement of the cherished Wallaby spirit espoused back in 1923 by Harald Baker. I'm confident that today's players will recognise that connection and play their part in preserving those traditions.

Long live the Wallaby dynasty!

OPPOSITE *Wallaby back-rower Greg Cornelsen scored four tries in his 25-Test career – all in the same game! His record haul against the All Blacks at Eden Park, Auckland, in September 1978 inspired an upset 30–16 victory for the Wallabies.*

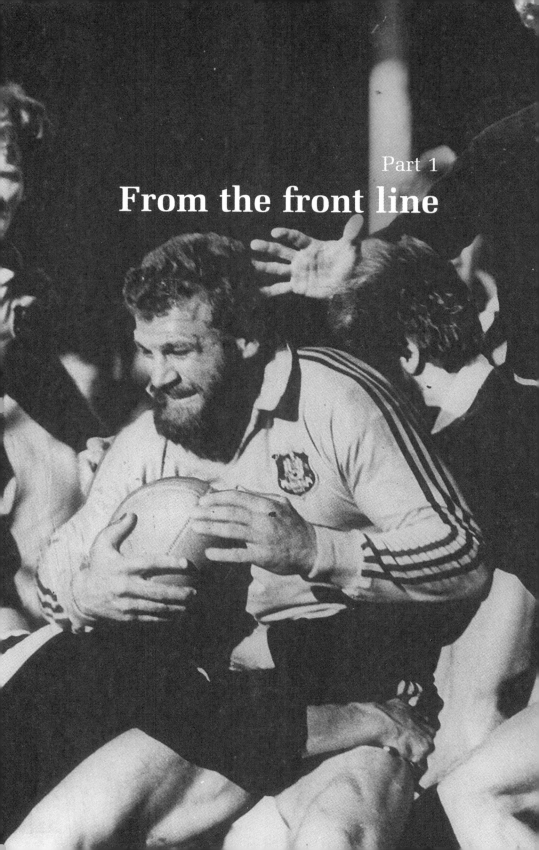

Part 1

From the front line

George Gregan

So you want to be a Wallaby?

Our new skipper traces his journey to the top job in Australian rugby

'Great things are done when men and mountains meet;
This is not done by jostling in the street.'

– William Blake

As a youngster I had no particular aspiration to play sport for Australia. What did appeal to me, though, was the idea of playing sport for a living. Getting paid to do something you absolutely love was something I often thought about.

Although I was born in Zambia, my family arrived in Canberra when I was just two years old so I have no memories of my birthplace. My grandfather played soccer for Rhodesia but apart from the odd backyard game with the round ball, my first serious football was rugby league.

Cricket was my first passion. As kids we played in a narrow side street with a host of local rules for things like 'hitting the fence on the full' and 'landing in the garden patch'. In winter it was rugby or soccer. I always enjoyed being active.

OPPOSITE *Wallaby skipper George Gregan, who is regarded as the best scrum-half in world rugby, always plays well above his weight. A tenacious, confrontational approach is the hallmark of his intensity in both attack and defence.*

I can also remember staying up in the early hours of the morning watching the 1984 Grand Slam telecasts on the ABC. There was something really exciting about being up late and watching the Wallabies beat the Home Countries at all those famous rugby grounds. Mark Ella was like a beacon on that tour with his inspirational play. I guess he was my first rugby idol. That Wallaby team was a role model for the emerging generation of young players. Those memories are still vivid and in hindsight only served to fire my growing passion for rugby.

My own playing only really developed once I went to St Edmund's College in Canberra. My hero there was Ricky Stuart, who was an incredible player. As a youngster I watched him for three seasons in our 1st XV, dominating opposition teams. My early school days at 'Eddy's' were spent at fly-half before I moved to scrum-half in the under 14s. Subconsciously I'm sure I modelled a lot of my play on Ricky. He made a huge impression on me.

It is fair to say that my love of rugby was kindled at St Edmund's. The school has a rich rugby heritage and I quickly became aware of the importance of representing the school and performing well as a team. Rugby is a character-building exercise for young schoolboys, that's for sure.

St Edmund's also afforded my first taste of leadership. I tended to be captain in the rugby teams and vice-captain of the cricket sides, but cricket was probably still my first love. At the risk of being accused of name-dropping, I played against quite a few future Test cricketers when representing in the ACT under-age teams. Players that stick out in my memory are Ricky Ponting, Adam Gilchrist and Shane Lee.

Probably my biggest claim to fame on the cricket field

was being run out by Ponting. I wasn't happy at the time, but can laugh it off now when quizzed about my cricket exploits. I was lucky enough to play a few games for the ACT senior side after some success at grade level as a middle-order batsman.

Golf also became a strong interest. After taking up the game at 11 years of age I was really bitten by the golf bug. It was never a serious career option, although I can authenticate Gordon Bray's claim in commentary that I shot a one-over-par 73 in the 1994 Coolum Classic. My current handicap supposedly sits around six or seven, but sadly it's rarely challenged.

My boyhood dream of becoming a professional sportsman probably took its first serious steps back in 1992 when I was offered a rugby scholarship with the Australian Institute of Sport. My acceptance of the scholarship virtually decided my sporting career path. Although I was still passionate about cricket, I soon discovered that the demands of an AIS training program left insufficient time for any other serious sporting activity. It was impossible to juggle my cricket commitments and train properly for rugby. Funnily enough, though, I didn't see my first Test match in the flesh until 1992. Before that, everything had been witnessed on television with friends and family.

My big chance with the Wallabies came in 1994 when I made my Test debut against Italy at Ballymore. It's still a bit of a blur because I received a nasty head wound and was forced off the field. That wasn't the way the script was meant to go!

People often ask what has been the most significant point of the Wallaby experience for me. Without doubt it goes back to 1998 when we finally turned things around against the All Blacks, winning the series 3–0. We'd really struggled against New Zealand since 1995, so it was deeply satisfying to finally shake the monkey. That series was the springboard for a very successful period in Australian rugby, culminating in our 1999 World Cup victory.

At a provincial level, the Brumbies experience under Eddie Jones was also very rewarding. We had enjoyed great success under Rod Macqueen, but when Eddie first took over in 1998 we really struggled. It forced us to reappraise what we were doing. We hung onto a few things but basically redeveloped the way we played. That was the exciting part, because we were able to turn things around and win the Super 12 for the first time the following year, with new methods and a new strategy. An enormous amount of work went into developing that new approach, nearly three seasons to be exact – a fact that the general public is probably not aware of. Everyone involved in the Brumbies campaign knows how much hard work went into that success, which is why it was such a special experience.

The World Cup triumph was a different form of elation. It's a very tough tournament to win. The team worked extremely hard beforehand and we were good enough to peak just at the right time. With that kind of match schedule you do need a bit of luck but, more importantly, everyone has to be performing well at the business end.

Taking over from John Eales was always going to be a big challenge, and it will continue to be. I'm excited by the prospect. My initial impressions of the role of captain were much as I'd expected. It's quite challenging, and puts more demands on my time. I'm in a situation where people ask

OPPOSITE *George Gregan listens intently to his illustrious predecessor at the 1999 Rugby World Cup. John Eales excelled as a supportive leader whereas Gregan favours a more direct style.*

my opinion on things more than they have in the past.

On last year's European tour I don't believe we played and performed as well as we would have liked. That wasn't a reflection on the work we were doing off the field; we really 'put in'. It may sound like a cliche, but it all comes down to performing well on the day. When you're playing big matches it's absolutely crucial to execute the basics well. We let ourselves down a bit in that area. The tour of Europe was labelled a failure, but frankly it won't be the last time we lose a game or two. Even in our most successful periods over the years we've dropped games. It's just how you bounce back from those losses and make sure that if you are put in similar situations you don't repeat the same errors. I think that is the most important part of a good team. We took lessons out of those defeats that will hold us in good stead, I'm sure, for the future. There's a strong belief within the team that we are on the right track.

Looking towards next year's World Cup, it's safe to say this one will be the hardest to win. It's the nature of football at the moment that teams are getting better and better. The research and homework that everyone does on each other has intensified to the point where it becomes a very small margin between success and failure, especially when you talk about the top teams. It will be simply a matter of believing that when we are in a situation under pressure we can still execute our game well. Any good team must be able to do that – it's what a successful side thrives on.

As defending World Cup champions we are in a phase where the team is expected to be successful. People believe we can win all the time, which is a slightly unreal expectation. Losing is part of the true nature of sport. That said, it's also an expectation the team puts on itself that we should be able to win each time we step out.

Someone once said that experience is recognising the same mistake second time around. We will continue to grow as a team and learn from our setbacks. That's why I believe this current Wallaby team will always rebound strongly.

George Gregan succeeded John Eales as Wallaby captain on the 2001 tour of Britain and Spain. He is Australia's most capped scrum-half, playing his 72nd test against Wales at Cardiff on 28 November 2001. He won the international players' award for Most Outstanding Performer in 2000–01. A successful businessman, he and his wife, Erica, run four 'By George' coffee shops in Sydney. George and Erica's first child, Max, was born in June 2001.

Immortal number 9s

Australia has a proud tradition of producing brilliant scrum-halfs, and for many, Ken Catchpole remains the greatest of all. But can you remember how his illustrious career came to its premature end?

It was the 24th minute of the second half of the First Test in 1968, against New Zealand at the SCG. With Australia trailing 3–10, Catchpole was dragged by one leg from a ruck by Colin Meads, suffering a horrific groin injury. A then-new ruling by the International Rugby Board permitted replacements for injured players, and at that moment, as one magnificent Test career was ending, another began. Twenty-year-old **John Hipwell** came on to replace Catchpole. It would be the first of his splendid 35 caps.

More than two decades later, the Wallaby production line produced another champion number 9. **Nick Farr-Jones** (below) from Sydney University is widely regarded as the finest player of his era. His electrifying combination with fly-half Mark Ella on the 1984 Grand Slam tour of Britain and Ireland is etched into rugby folklore. In 1991 the Sydney lawyer led the Wallabies to World Cup glory – and remains the only national rugby captain to have chatted stark naked for a full 15 minutes to a British prime minister! (John Major visited the Australian change room at Twickenham after the Final. Nick's main recollection of their happy, animated conversation is that his glasses kept fogging up in the steam.)

Rod Macqueen

Back to the future?

Altering rugby's landscape to the vision splendid

'The greatest truths are the simplest.'
– Augustus Hare

Rugby's time-honoured charter stipulates that the code should cater for all shapes and sizes. This noble ideal must always be preserved, because it provides a warranty that all facets of play will remain a true contest for possession.

There should be room in our great game for the long and the short, the large and the small. To give a few of the more obvious examples:

- A scrum should always need powerful props who can hold the scrum up in order to ensure a good controlled contest for the ball.
- Similarly, in the line-out, strong, agile players who can really leap for the ball have become all-important. Big games are increasingly being decided by crucial line-out wins. It's hardly surprising that tall, athletic forwards have become prized possessions.
- Every competitive team needs players who are good in the air at restarts – and that doesn't necessarily translate just

17

to forwards. Multiskilled backs can often outjump many of their taller teammates on the run.

In any contest for possession, the emphasis is not just on winning or losing the ball. First and foremost it is about gaining *quality* possession. Unlike rugby league, where every tackle results in an uncontested play-the-ball, the same situation in union provides a genuine contest. That's precisely why powerful, compact foragers have come into their own.

To complement all of these ball winners, a team also needs those players who can both make and set up breaks – ball runners who can beat opponents man-on-man, and ball players whose passing and handling abilities make space and create openings for their teammates.

Given this necessity for various body shapes and types, the parallel requirement emerging strongly in the modern era is the need for greater all-round fitness and skill levels. Because the ball is now in play longer, any team member short on the necessary skills will quickly be exposed.

Here's an example. As players are now so much fitter, the attacking team will often direct its more adept athletic runners to seek out the less athletic defenders. Teams in possession will aim to uncover weaknesses in the opposition defensive line by varying their play and focusing on ball control and continuity until the opportunities arise. This approach places a much heavier emphasis on defence. It also encourages big, rugby-league-style 'hits'. These, in turn, have led to some hasty decisions by the law-makers. To my mind, their reaction has provoked an alarming threat to the essential fabric of the game. The sheer joy of rugby can only shine through when its key strengths – simplicity, continuity, flair and a positive style of play – are encouraged and rewarded.

Recent law revisions seem to be promoting an opposite approach. Two prime examples: the current blitz on so-called decoy runners, and the active discouraging of 'pick-and-drive' by attacking players. In both cases this has been a response to supposed obstruction implications. As a consequence, attacking depth is disappearing and so is angled running – among the most attractive features of our game. The obstruction law has always existed to cover blatant and accidental offences. Directing referees to target crossovers has been an overreaction that has effectively stripped the game of a crucial attacking element in its structure.

Historically, angled running, support-in-depth and pick-and-drive have been distinctive aspects of the game since its inception. Yet under the current strict dictum, if a player wants to pass the ball to the wings the only option is to offload laterally, which automatically limits space 'out wide'. In practice, the attacking team needs to go forward to attract numbers of defenders in order to create space on the wings. There is nothing terribly magic about this ploy: it's designed as a basic way to drag in opponents and eventually give the fast outside backs their space and opportunity.

By stipulating that players from the attacking team cannot be positioned between the ball carrier and the tackler, the law-makers have drastically altered rugby's landscape. Cutting down these attacking options is making it far easier for the defence. I believe the strategy is basically flawed because the subtleties of angled running, attack-in-depth and support running off the ball are being squeezed out of the game. Instead, one-off running is encouraged because

spreading the ball wide now has such limited scope. Under this highly literal interpretation of the obstruction law, opponents are not being committed in numbers around the middle of the field, so there are no wide-open spaces for the attacking side to exploit. The soul-stirring spectacle of a great back line in full flight has become increasingly rare at Test level. Ironically, the very things we are trying to eradicate from the game – defence-oriented teams – are actually being strengthened by this latest shift in emphasis from the law-makers.

The other anomaly stifling the game is the inconsistency of interpretation at the breakdown and tackle. Strictly speaking, in normal passages of play you could penalise teams either way at every breakdown. Interestingly, the laws governing this facet were originally framed to cover a ruck or maul. But in practical terms, a ruck rarely occurs in modern play. Instead, mauling is now back in focus because it is the only other ball-in-hand way to go forward. In their attempts to address this troublesome area the law-makers have added new words, but the reality is they have only made the breakdown even more complicated. The unwanted outcome is that referee interpretations of this phase of play can now totally dictate the shape of a game.

It would be ideal if we could persuade all whistlers to adopt the approach of English referee Chris White, who had charge of last year's match between the Wallabies and the Barbarians in Cardiff. He rewarded the skills of the attacking team, but he also rewarded the team trying to be positive. The clear difference in that game was that the referee was someone who *conducted* rather than dictated.

The charter of rugby states that we must reward skills that aim to keep the ball alive. It is the rapidly unfolding,

OPPOSITE *The fairytale is complete: John Eales (centre) triumphantly bids farewell after the 2001 Bledisloe Cup clash at Stadium Australia. It was also Rod Macqueen's last match, capping an incredible record as Wallaby coach.*

unpredictable nature of the code that gives rugby so much of its unique appeal. However, in practice it is patently clear that we are no longer rewarding this spirit of continuity. As a consequence the skills of the game have started to diminish.

Of course there must be a genuine contest at the breakdown, but there must also be tangible rewards for positive skills rather than for those teams who are being negative and trying to kill the ball. That's where the forager can come into play in a positive way. If the open-side flanker on the defending team can arrive quickly and get his hands on the ball while still on his feet, he becomes a trump card. Significantly, this ploy also favours another body shape vital to the game's future prosperity.

We must ask ourselves *what is happening to our game?* It's clear to many rugby supporters that the code needs to find a completely different shape at the breakdown. There is widespread confusion and inconsistency. As a great believer in simplicity, I strongly feel that the tackle law should be stripped back to the bone. Instead of allowing the game to evolve naturally in these rapidly changing rugby times, we have continually tinkered with the breakdown in an unproductive way. It's of paramount importance that we now develop a clear, clean interpretation so that referees, players – and, most important of all, the long-suffering fans – have firm understanding of the law. It's also time to adopt a commonsense approach and go back to the original interpretation of obstruction. In other words, attacking teams need to be aware of the clear difference between running someone as *interference* – which is blatant obstruction – and legitimate angled running and deception. The deployment of decoy runners falls into the same category.

Our critics keep asking why flair is disappearing from the game, but nobody has really put their finger on the cause. By suppressing flair and innovation you are automatically supporting negativity and defence. I believe the subtle change of emphasis I've suggested would help reintroduce that flair and intelligence to rugby as we strive to find ways of overcoming the tight defences now dominating the game. At the moment, ball-in-hand attack is restricted to lateral passing and mauls. For rugby's sake, these issues need urgent recognition from the custodians of the code.

We are not too far away from having a truly great game. That's why it's imperative we all have a common vision for the future prosperity of rugby.

Rod Macqueen is the most successful Wallaby coach in history. Under his guidance Australia won every international trophy in existence, culminating in the thrilling series win over the British and Irish Lions in 2001. Rod's bestselling book, One Step Ahead, *which traces his career as a high-achieving sportsman, businessman and coach, has been enthusiastically received by fans of all sports. Test record: played 43, won 34, drawn 1, lost 8.*

The 21st-century forward

The skills we develop today are for the vision of the game tomorrow; we can only speculate as to where the game will be in the next few years. However, here are Rod Macqueen's thoughts on the types of skills required.

Front row   Scrums make an enormous difference because if you're getting bad ball it makes it very difficult to develop a potent attacking platform. Props must be able to take the weight in the scrum but also to run and pass effectively. After having the necessary attributes to dictate at the scrum, every additional skill a prop has is a bonus to the team. The ability to play on both sides of the scrum also gives an enormous advantage. Agility, power and mobility are essential attributes in defence.

Hooker   There is an emerging trend for the hooker to be interchangeable with a prop forward. It would be ideal to have a hooker with the skills and work rate of a flanker but, like their fellow front-rowers, a hooker's first obligation must be to the ball-winning parts of the game. In modern rugby, with the adoption of support in line-outs, the skill requirements of the line-out throw have doubled. A strong organisational ability rounds off the hooker's role. (Mind you, there is no reason why the hooker should have to be the one to throw the ball in.)

Lock/Second row   We will always need athletic players who can get up in the air. Greater emphasis is now being placed on running skills, and this needs to be encouraged even further. Teams have experimented with a blind-side flanker in the lock position, but that ploy is usually only successful if the player is very good with the ball in the air. The modern lock also needs to be a thinker who is rock solid on his own line-out ball and can second-guess the opposition's line-out calls to pilfer opposition throws.

Open-side flanker Ideally this player is very quick, built low to the ground, with an ability to pressure opposition ball at the breakdown. The more speed and ball skills he has, the greater the options. He can make up for lack of height by having every other skill available. With the increased strength requirements, backs will now be a possibility for this position.

Blind-side flanker This position caters ideally for the 'harder' players – those who can make a real impact around the field in attack and defence. They are required to get up in the air as well and to have the ability to jump well without assistance. Because we need to be taking teams on down the centre of the field, players who can offload in the tackle are critical.

Number 8 Like the blind-side flanker, ball in the air and the ability to jump well with assistance are important ingredients. An ability to work forward from the back of the scrum is essential, as are the skills to off-load safely and run with the ball. Perhaps, in scrums, shifting an open-side flanker to number 8 will be an option because he has similar qualities to a scrum-half. It would be great to have three running back-rowers, but the downside of this is that ball-winning ability in the line-out would be drastically reduced.

The final word

The most important ingredient for any team is having a good combination – players with skills that complement each other. Providing it doesn't affect the ball-winning parts of the game, all these positions are interchangeable and the different skills can therefore be used to achieve different defensive and attacking options.

The pursuit
of rugby excellence

It all starts at school

**An insight into the rugby and educational
mind of Brother Anthony Boyd, coach of
St Joseph's College (Sydney) 1st XV**

*'Education is an admirable thing, but it is well to remember from
time to time that nothing that is worth knowing can be taught.'*

— Oscar Wilde

Q *What is your rugby
philosophy for schoolboys?*

A Rugby is a wonderful vehicle for
schoolboys. Here at the college we
treat it as another classroom and
we'd like to think that all concerned
approach the sport in a professional
way. As coaches we are expected to
be thorough and accurate, as if we
were teaching an academic subject.

As a game, we find that rugby helps develop character
and confidence. Self-confidence is a very important issue
for young men, as is self-knowledge. After taking up the
challenge of playing rugby, the boys learn something about
themselves that might not have been otherwise available to
them. From our point of view, that's the real value of the
whole exercise.

26

The pursuit of rugby excellence

A winter Saturday at 'Joey's' is a pretty important day because you have up to 40 teams playing rugby against other schools. Because of our tradition there is a special feeling about having the opportunity to uphold the honour of your school, no matter what the level.

I recently had an encounter with a Chinese boy who played in the 14Fs. He came to me to discuss his sporting activities. The lad also played basketball in the summer. I asked him if he had a preference and he said he much preferred the rugby. That took me a little by surprise, so I asked why. He replied with a comment that reinforced what we are trying to achieve: 'Although I'm only in the 14Fs, rugby makes me feel important.' I'm elated if a boy feels important no matter what team he plays in. That's marvellous.

It's also important that they learn how to handle situations when things don't go well. They have to learn to deal with failure, and realise that to be successful you don't always have to win. At the same time, if you're *not* successful that's not fatal either. Striving, working with others and building a team spirit through concerted effort takes on greater importance at schoolboy level. In fact, I think the kids have this type of concept more in perspective than many adult players.

Q *How much importance is placed on the team aspect in your coaching approach?*
A The game caters for all sizes and abilities. Some of the best games of rugby I see, in terms of quality and sheer effort, come from our seventh-grade team playing against, say, the fifths from another school. The intensity of the open grade is not there, but they have a good level of skill and a real sense

of flair about their approach to the game. Occasionally there's a big hit, but essentially it's just about throwing the ball around, having fun and dictating a hectic pace. The boys are really just expressing themselves individually and collectively, and experiencing the joy of a team sport that is played in a similar way at the same age the world over.

In a team situation, you actually see the boys gain in confidence during a season and often change their attitude as well. Away from rugby, you may get a boy who feels he has to be aggressive and boss others around. Once he gets into the team situation, that sort of self-centred attitude is knocked out of him. He realises he doesn't have to act that way to gain respect. In that sense, rugby is an ideal vehicle to mould the desired character of young men. The whole idea of self-discipline in a team structure is to put yourself out for your teammates. The team must always come first, and that's one of the little lessons we learn in life.

Q *You talk of rugby as a classroom exercise. In what sense is the preparation put in place within that context?*

A It's a classroom in the sense that we approach it in a professional way. Rugby isn't unique in that regard at the school. We apply the same principles to rowing, cricket, basketball and the other sporting activities.

Obviously we tackle rugby more intensely at senior levels because the younger boys just aren't ready for that full intensity. But with the bigger kids, we make sure that any boy who feels capable of playing in the 1st or 2nd XV the following year is on a special program, whether it be weights or extra skill and fitness work. We don't force the boys to do

29

OPPOSITE *One of 'Joey's' favourite sons, Waratah skipper Matthew Burke. Here he tries to evade the tackle of Lions winger Jason Robinson in Sydney 2001 (above) and shares the high emotion of the Third Test triumph with jubilant fans.*

these things. It's up to them to demonstrate how serious they are about being a contender for our top teams. I'm always very keen for our senior players to tackle other sports rather than just focusing on rugby. Boys who make the 1st XV in Year 11 are usually in rowing boats, or cricket, athletic and basketball teams during the summer. Normally I don't start looking at these particular kids until after Easter. That's when we have internal trials, minus the boys engaged in athletics.

In our open age group we have a couple of hundred boys to work through, so it's pretty difficult. You can never get it exactly right. When the athletes return from track and field, you put them into the melting pot and pick the initial teams. That's when we start playing trial games against other schools. After those trials we select our sides for the GPS [Greater Public Schools] competition. It's an exhaustive selection process and the teams remain fairly stable barring injuries.

As coaches, we're constantly monitoring what the professional teams such as the Waratahs, Brumbies, Reds and Wallabies are doing. We then incorporate that knowledge into our own programs.

Q *What are the key ingredients for putting together a successful rugby team?*

A It definitely varies from year to year depending on what sort of talent we have available at the school. Ideally, we look for a good mobile front row, boys who are quick around the field but strong enough to hold up the scrum. You want a bit of height in your locks. They don't have to be tall, as long as they can jump and get around the field. And speed is all-important in the back row. If you haven't got speed, that determines the type of game you'll have to play. I'm not afraid to convert players from other positions. There have been instances of back-rowers moving to the front row. In 1990 I shifted David Kellaher from the backs to open-side flanker and the following year I did the same thing with John Isaac, who is now playing outstanding rugby as an inside centre with Biarritz. Both David and John went on to play Australian Schools in the back row. It's good for boys to learn new positions and we're always watching out for kids with the ability to adapt.

In the backs, in the half/five-eighth combination we want a number 9 who has quick service and doesn't muck around. He needs to be at breakdowns quickly and have the ability to pass off the ground. He doesn't have to have a long pass, providing he can get rid of the ball quickly. The scrum-half also has to be able to put his hands into 'rubbish' – particularly these days, when there are a lot of body pile-ups at the breakdown. A lot of schoolboy half-backs tend to stand back and watch. We want someone who can get in there and get his hands on the ball and then clear it. Good, crisp presentation to supports is imperative.

The fly-half must have good hands and an ability to read the game. Because he has a number of runners in support he needs to be able to choose the right one for the offload.

We look for solidity in the centres – ideally a number 12 with ball-playing flair and also an ability to get over the advantage line if necessary. If you like, a Nathan Grey type but with a bit more of the fly-half skills. That's the ideal, but you don't always get it.

Pace on the wings is essential but they also have to be able to tackle. There's no point in scoring two tries and then letting one in. Defence is very important for our wingers.

Again, the full-back must have pace, an ability to counter-attack and a desire to join the back line effectively at every opportunity.

In summary, talent is a wonderful thing but it's more important that all our players are team men. The boys must be 'coachable' and their consuming attitude must be for the team. With those ideals I've found that the boys listen and respond, and consequently are able to enjoy a degree of success.

Q *You mentioned the honour of playing for the school. Could you give us an insight into the degree of motivation involved for the boys?*
A It's enormous, and difficult to describe. For many of the boys who arrive at St Joseph's in Year 7 it becomes one of their aspirations to represent the school 1st XV at rugby. Some of them express that desire, others harbour it privately, and there are also the boys who are aware of the heritage but don't have it as a major focus.

Sometimes a boy comes along who is a late developer. Ben Peterson is a good example – he didn't play in the As until making the 1st XV. Much of the time he was back in the Cs and Ds in the various age groups. He was a quiet boy who started to grow late and also gained speed. We gave him a trial in the 1st XV and he stayed there for the whole season, then went on to play for the NSW under 21s. So there was a lad who played in lower age groups with a secret desire to represent St Joseph's College 1st XV, a classic example of a young boy who realistically thought he would never make the top but never gave up hope. As he grew and filled out, his dream was suddenly within his grasp.

It's unfortunate that all our boys can't make the 1st and

OPPOSITE *Brother Anthony Boyd (above left) conveys his vast rugby knowledge and passion to students at St Joseph's College, home of many champion teams through the years, such as the 1904 team seen here.*

2nd XVs, because they all put a huge amount of effort into the pursuit of that supreme honour.

Q *Is 'fear of failure' a relevant issue for you as a coach?*

A I've always believed it's important to have a bit of that 'fear of failure' complex. At the same time it's also paramount to have a burning desire to win. Back in 1987 in the World Cup I remember hearing Wayne Shelford, the All Black skipper, mention the fear of failure. New Zealand had just beaten Wales in a quarter-final at Ballymore. Wayne's post-match interview went along the lines that the team was very disappointed in the result because they hadn't played well due to the fact that they didn't have the fear of failure. In other words, they had taken a complacent attitude into the Test match.

Subsequently I had the opportunity to meet up with Shelford and sought further explanation. He pointed out that as captain he always made sure the All Blacks had a fear of failure and totally respected the opposition. At the same time, that burning desire to win was all-encompassing. He said that the fear of failure is what helps you make that desperate tackle – like George Gregan's effort on Jeff Wilson in 1994.

I think there's a lot of truth and relevance in Wayne's philosophy. It's so important to keep your feet on the ground as a team and maintain a proper perspective.

Q *What is the best piece of advice you have been given?*

A It happened in my first year of coaching the 1st XV at Joey's and came from a gentleman named John Healey, who was our conditioner. We were playing Sydney Grammar and were down 0–10 at half-time. John's advice to me was: 'There are a few things that have to happen here. Firstly, you've got to forget the score. We don't want to be in the position of playing catch-up rugby. Secondly, we have the advantage of a strong wind in the second half. Don't kick for touch – kick downfield and chase and keep the ball in play.'

It was all very simple and it worked. We got back into the game and eventually finished on top. It was the best bit of advice because that same scenario happens all the time in schoolboy rugby. I remember being in a similar situation as a member of the Gordon coaching staff in a semifinal against Randwick back in 1995. David Campese had killed us in the first half and we trailed 9–19 at the break. As we moved across to the huddle, John Langford made the observation that Randwick hadn't scored for 20 minutes. I took that on board because we'd kicked three penalties during that time. The message to the team was therefore to keep doing the little things well because they were working, to be patient and the breaks would assuredly go our way – and they did. In rugby, simple advice is usually nine parts in ten.

Brother Anthony Boyd has coached the St Joseph's College 1st XV to seven GPS premierships. The famous rugby nursery has produced 51 Wallabies over the last 100 years. During a brief sojourn in the mid-1990s, Brother Boyd also co-coached the Gordon Highlanders (under Chris Hawkins) to a 1st-grade premiership.

The Australian Schools rugby team

For decades, the sports-minded teaching staff in Australia's rugby-playing states had dreamed of the formation of a national schools' team open to students from all secondary schools in Australia.

The impetus to form an organisation to achieve that goal came in 1969 through the foresight of Dr Danie Craven, president of the South African Rugby Board and a former Springbok legend. He invited the Australian Rugby Union to send an Australian Schools team to South Africa for fixtures against most provinces in the Republic. Most importantly, Craven and the SARB provided $50 000 to support their invitation.

That tour was an outstanding success from the rugby as well as the educational and social points of view. In their report to the ARFU (now the ARU), the tour manager, Brother Gerald Burns, and coach, Bill Toft, recommended the formation of an Australian Rugby Football Schools' Union – with state unions providing the effective infrastructure.

The details of that first historic tour make fascinating reading for those with an interest in the way rugby has developed over the intervening generation.

Tour record: inaugural Australian Schools, South Africa 1969

v. Northern Transvaal at Pretoria won 11–8

v. Western Province at Capetown won 10–3

v. Eastern Province at Port Elizabeth won 29–5

v. Border at East London won 27–3

v. Orange Free State at Bloemfontein drew 11–11

v. Griqualand West at Kimberley lost 10–19

v. Transvaal at Johannesburg won 37–0

Tour squad

Backs Russell Fairfax (Matraville High), Robert Forsberg (Epping Boys High), Timothy Rowlands (The Scots College), Graham McPhail (Brisbane State High), Malcolm Jack (Balgowlah Boys High), Timothy Clementson (Newington College), Ronald Taylor (Barker College), David Giles (Hurlstone Agricultural High School), Robert Armstrong (Epping Boys High), James Hindmarsh (The Scots College), Peter Robinson – captain (Epping Boys High), Andrew Strathopoulos (Cranbrook School), John Babister (Sydney Grammar School)

Forwards Peter Fleming (Ashgrove Marist), Richard Allen (Trinity Grammar School), Peter Bull (Newington College), Gregory Cornelsen (The Armidale School), Brian Hayward (The Armidale School), Alan Coutts (Epping Boys High), Alister Robinson (Hurlstone Agricultural High School), Steve Finnane (Vaucluse Boys High School), Louis Slaughter (The Scots College), Timothy Wardle (St Ignatius College), Charles Horder (Shore School), Sean Mooney (Epping Boys High)

Manager Brother Gerald Burns (St Joseph's College)

Assistant Manager (coach) Bill Toft (James Ruse Agricultural High School)

On tour in South Africa in 1969 with the inaugural Australian Schools rugby team, future Wallaby prop Steve Finnane (left) offloads a pass to a teammate at training in Durban.

The art of winning
The psychology of successful coaching

World Cup-winning coach Bob Dwyer discusses his approach to achieving desired goals

'Winning isn't everything – it's the only thing.'
                                        – Anon.

Q *What are your basic philosophies as a coach for winning?*
A What the game consists of is winning the ball and advancing it towards the opposition try line and, at the same time, not losing the ball. Conversely, you want to make it as difficult as possible for the opposition to win the ball, advance it and retain it.

My philosophy of coaching a team to win perhaps comes from the result I'm looking for. I'm looking for people to play to their capacity physically and to the capacity that the laws of the game allow. The way we have decided to do it at the Waratahs is to make sure that all the basic skills are available to the player and he is physically ready to execute those skills, and to educate him further in combination plays that put into effect those basic skills, then let him go out and play – and not restrict him by fear of mistake or of failure. We want to let players know that we think it's

38

within their capacity, once they are prepared, to *play*. We also want to let them know that they can make their own decisions without fear of criticism by the coaching staff or anyone else.

I have a strong belief that the biggest impediment to making good decisions is fear of failure. That fear is strengthened by criticism of a player's decision-making. I frequently tell players that they will never make a bad decision: they will either make an OK decision, a good decision, a very good decision or an excellent decision. The only time the decision-making process will be a failure is if they *don't* make a decision.

Q *What is more important – day-to-day preparation or making adjustments during the game?*
A Your day-to-day preparation should allow you to have all the options available during the game. Deciding to discard some predetermined options and pick up on some that maybe you hadn't thought to use in this particular game can certainly be a factor. Most experienced teams very easily say, 'Well, we've tried them on A and B and we're meeting some stiff resistance. I think we should now try C and D.' Good teams can do that. I think adjustments during the game are not things we even need to discuss. They should flow naturally if the preparation is correct.

Q *What are the key ingredients of a champion team?*
A The person who assembles the team has to have some accurate ideas of what level of performance will be required to be successful. Sometimes inexperienced people don't have the ability to accurately view and assess a level of

performance. They can be training the team well but not being nearly as demanding as they need to be in order to get the winning performance. It's about being exposed to – and understanding – and therefore having good retention of what level of performance is needed. It's also important to know the level of performance you can realistically aspire to, and whether or not that level is sufficient in the competition in which you play. The good coaches can certainly see that and they are far more demanding. They want more and more from their players in terms of performance.

Q *Aside from raw talent and personnel, was there a common thread in your champion teams?*
A You need players with raw talent, and you need players with the required level of hand–eye coordination, reflexes and agility, vision and physicality, because you just can't win without them. I figure that the best teams have always had roughly five 'world XV' choices, five genuine international players and five players who can handle themselves at that level but that's all. Five 'world XV' choices is quite a lot. It's like saying you have a third of that world team even though you're obviously not a third of the major rugby-playing nations. But the best teams always have those five. The average team has ten genuine international players; it's those five world-choice players that get you there. If you haven't got them, you're going to struggle. You've got to die trying to find them. I certainly believe that if you've got a player who is playing to the level of his ability but not to the level that *you* know will be required to be successful, then you have to find someone else. Even if another player hasn't quite reached that level yet, if you believe that possibly he

could go to that level then you have to replace the high-performing player with the lesser-performing player. I think that's very much been a factor in the success of the teams I've coached.

Q *What's your view on motivation as a key factor?*

A There's no doubt that the motivation for success – or the fear of failure, which is another form of motivation – is absolutely necessary. The real key is how *sustained* that motivation can be over a long period of time so that people are motivated in their base preparation, their skill preparation and their fine-tuning preparation and then motivated for performance. Motivation is essential and unless your players are naturally motivated, driven sorts of people, they won't succeed for any length of time. A player might be a naturally talented superstar, but he'll only succeed for a little while unless he also has that drive and motivation.

Q *Have motivational techniques changed due to professionalism in rugby? Is burnout a new factor coaches have to confront?*

A I think properly prepared players can last longer. It's that word 'properly' that takes a lot of our time. Players can be burnt out. If they are overtrained then they can certainly struggle. I know that each year when I coach the Barbarians team the top players say, 'If we could train like this all the time we could play for another five years'. It's the training that gets them. But over a three-month or six-month period, unless you do some heavy training, your fitness drops right off.

Q *How important is loyalty in a team, both to the coach and to your teammates?*
A Essential. You have to have a real desire to work together to achieve the goal. Generally speaking, working hard to strive for success together creates loyalty. If you do the hard yards together you form a bond with one another. That feeling of loyalty when times are tough is essential.

Q *Are you a believer in the old adage that teams should train as they play?*
A Certainly parts of your preparation need to be performed at the intensity of the game so that the players' minds understand and can accurately predict what is expected of them. The preparation will hopefully ensure their bodies can feel the same way and understand what is happening so they're not suddenly confronted with this horrible feeling in their body that they're not used to. The old adage that you don't win the Melbourne Cup in June also applies. You don't win the game on Tuesday afternoon, but Tuesday afternoon is there for a reason. It's there to put stress on the body so the bodily systems will respond to the pressures put on them and restore energy in preparation for upcoming games.

Q *How important is the delegation of authority in developing a winning staff?*
A Essential. Just as you can only allow a player to get the best out of himself if you give him the freedom to make decisions under pressure and then to reflect on those decisions and improve, the same applies to staff. The support-team staff have to go out armed with all the information, make their own decisions and come back and reflect on how

well they've gone. That's the only way they'll be able to show their true value. If they're always concerned about who's looking over their shoulder, they won't have the freedom of expression necessary for them to do their best.

Q *What is the best advice you've given?*
A A recently appointed national coach asked me what advice I could give him. I said, 'Trust your judgement. Just make your decision and trust it.' The best advice I can give a player is: 'When you go on the pitch, don't think, just *play*. Do all your thinking when the game has stopped, none of your thinking when the game is played. Just play. Let your eyes see and your ears hear – and your hands and feet follow.'

Q *How long does the agony of defeat weigh with you?*
A Well, it's important that you don't let success go to your head, and equally important that you don't let defeat go to your head. If you're searching for perfection, as most people are, the way to get it is to exclude all those bits that are less than perfect, or improve those bits and move them towards perfection. The elements in your defeat that caused you not to be perfect are the ones you have to concentrate on. You have to understand what you're doing well and keep that going. At the same, time the coach's role is almost always to accurately assess the cause and effect. The effect might be, for example, 'We're not making any line breaks'. The cause might be 'The recycle of ball is too slow'. Instead of dropping the guys who are supposed to be making line breaks, a coach has to say, 'Here's the problem and here's the cause'. It's vital that the cause of any defeat is accurately pinpointed. Your

defeats must be important because they stay somewhere in your mind, especially the ones where you think you could have played better and might have won. I think those ones stay forever.

Q *What were the key factors in the 1991 World Cup success?*
A For starters I think we certainly had those five 'world XV' choices and the five genuine world-class players and the five players who could play without necessarily aspiring to those heights. We had enough players, and the majority of the younger ones didn't fear failure – they had a refreshing exuberance about their play that was infectious. We had enough of them; we probably had a third of the team coming through with those attributes. We'd been together for four years, the majority of the team for even longer, with Alan Jones. Some of them had first come with me back in 1982. By and large we had been together for long enough to understand exactly what was required. Because we had that very good grounding, we had real mental toughness. We believed that what we were doing would ultimately make us successful. We had all the weaponry we needed; we just needed to choose a different weapon if things weren't working. We were very good at that.

Q *How important is the captain?*
A Leadership is important, but it comes from a number of people. Theoretically it might not be necessary to have a sensational captain as long as you have good leadership throughout. In reality, if you do have good leadership then one of those people will be an obvious choice and will

OPPOSITE *Bob Dwyer's focus and passion are graphically captured in these two studies, especially in his address to the Leicester Tigers forward pack (below).*

45

therefore be an outstanding captain. We certainly had one in 1991 — Nick Farr-Jones had that rare talent that enabled him to pinpoint what needed to be done. Coaches can pinpoint the cause of a problem but not necessarily the effect. Nick had the ability to pinpoint little problems off the pitch with people. He made everyone feel comfortable and relaxed, wanted and needed, even if they weren't a first-choice selection. Nick's input on the pitch was obvious, but his capacity off the pitch was equally important to us.

Q *What motivates you and your support team to keep doing it?*
A I think the fact that we can always do something better, the lure or carrot of something outstanding around the next corner. When we see some flashes of brilliance we think we can see it all coming together. We're looking for the perfect game, and every now and again we get a hint that the perfect game is indeed possible. The excitement of being part of something that is very, very good is always attractive, so that motivates you to want to be a part of it. I remember Glen Ella once said to me that if he was playing on the weekend and had been tackled and was out of the play when the team did something terrific and scored a great try, he'd be annoyed for the rest of the week until he could get back and be part of something really great the next week. It's that desire to be part of something great that keeps me motivated.

Q *Have any of the secrets you have learned about winning rugby helped you win at other things in life?*
A Yes, sure. One of the things I've learned is that if you want to be successful you have to concentrate on the *components*

that will enable you to achieve the success. If you concentrate on the components, the success follows as a by-product. That approach has enabled me, in business life, to go through some tough times with a large degree of enthusiasm and optimism because I know a tough time is a period that will let me get things absolutely right. In fact, it also prepares you for the successful opportunity when it comes about. One business I was involved in kicked off during a bad economic period and I've always said that was a very good move, because it forced great lessons upon us in terms of what makes a successful business. It taught us to run a lean machine, to pay great attention to detail. When times became good and work was flowing in, we still had that work ethic. It meant we didn't get fat and sloppy. Rugby certainly taught me that.

Bob Dwyer played 347 senior matches for Randwick, taking over as 1st-grade coach in 1980 and leading the club to seven senior-grade premierships. In his second stint as Wallaby coach he masterminded Australia's 1991 World Cup triumph. After the 1995 World Cup, Dwyer turned his attention to Europe and enjoyed considerable success with Leicester and Bristol. He is now in his second year as coach of the NSW Waratahs.

World Cup results

1987

Quarter-finals

Wales	16	England	3	Ballymore, Brisbane
France	31	Fiji	16	Eden Park, Auckland
Australia	33	Ireland	15	Concord Oval, Sydney
New Zealand	30	Scotland	3	Lancaster Park, Christchurch

Semifinals

France	30	Australia	24	Concord Oval, Sydney
New Zealand	49	Wales	6	Ballymore, Brisbane

3rd v. 4th play-off

Wales	22	Australia	21	Rugby Park, Rotorua

Final

New Zealand	29	France	9	Eden Park, Auckland

1991

Quarter-finals

Australia	19	Ireland	18	Lansdowne Road, Dublin
New Zealand	29	Canada	13	Lille Stadium, France
Scotland	28	Samoa	6	Murrayfield, Edinburgh
England	19	France	10	Parc des Princes, Paris

Semifinals

England	9	Scotland	6	Murrayfield, Edinburgh
Australia	16	New Zealand	6	Lansdowne Road, Dublin

3rd v. 4th play-off

New Zealand	13	Scotland	6	Cardiff Arms Park

Final

Australia	12	England	6	Twickenham, London

1995

Quarter-finals

England	25	Australia	22	Newlands, Cape Town
New Zealand	48	Scotland	30	Loftus Versfeld, Pretoria
France	36	Ireland	12	Kings Park, Durban
South Africa	42	Samoa	14	Ellis Park, Johannesburg

Semifinals

South Africa	19	France	15	Kings Park, Durban
New Zealand	45	England	29	Newlands, Cape Town

3rd v. 4th play-off

France	19	England	9	Loftus Versfeld, Pretoria

Final

South Africa	15	New Zealand	12	Ellis Park, Johannesburg

1999

Quarter-finals

South Africa	44	England	21	Stade de France, Paris
New Zealand	30	Scotland	18	Murrayfield, Scotland
France	47	Argentina	26	Lansdowne Road, Dublin
Australia	24	Wales	9	Millennium Stadium, Cardiff

World Cup results continued

Semifinals

Australia	27	South Africa	21	Twickenham, London
France	43	New Zealand	31	Twickenham, London

3rd v. 4th play-off

South Africa	22	New Zealand	18	Millennium Stadium, Cardiff

Final

Australia	35	France	12	Millennium Stadium, Cardiff

Two Wallaby greats: Simon Poidevin (left foreground) and Nick Farr-Jones (right) played together in the Australian team 1984–91. Their trail-blazing partnership embraced historic Grand Slam, Bledisloe Cup and World Cup triumphs, but this match – the 1987 World Cup semifinal at Concord Oval – was one that got away. France won an epic contest 30–24.

Senior Wallaby forward Owen 'Melon' Finegan soars above his Lions opponents at Stadium Australia in the series-deciding Third Test in 2001. Finegan gives the Wallaby back row a hard edge and is one of the most skilful big men in the game.

It takes two to tango: Wallaby winger Andrew Walker is back-slammed by his Lions counterpart, Jason Robinson, in the gripping Third Test at Stadium Australia in 2001.

George Gregan fires out a pass to a forward runner in the Third Test at Stadium Australia against the Lions. Massive Welsh number 8 Scott Quinnell (left) follows the action.

Line-out hero Justin Harrison embraces Elton Flatley after the final whistle in the Third Test at Stadium Australia against the Lions. Harrison's belated line-out steal helped the Wallabies scrape home in a thrilling climax to the series.

The William Webb Ellis Cup ('Bill') takes centre stage at Millennium Stadium in Wales following Australia's historic 35–12 victory over France in the 1999 World Cup Final.

Wallaby skipper John Eales savours the moment with Australian Rugby managing director John O'Neill following the Tri Nations-clinching win over the All Blacks at Stadium Australia in 2001.

Now is the hour: Eales takes off his boots for the last time in the dressing room after the 1 September game. The champion lock played 86 Tests and led Australia 55 times for 41 Test victories.

During a lap of honour at Stadium Australia following the 2001 Tri Nations win, Eales took time out to greet family and friends.

1 September 2001: the cherished silverware – Bledisloe Cup (left) and Tri Nations trophy – remains in the overcrowded Wallaby trophy cabinet for another year.

That drop goal: Wallaby fly-half Stephen Larkham produced this freakish extra-time 3-pointer at Twickenham in the 1999 World Cup Semifinal against South Africa. The long-range kick launched Australia into the final against France.

Advantage of low body height in a contact situation: hooker Jeremy Paul stems the momentum of his Lions opponent, while prop Nick Stiles prepares to lend support.

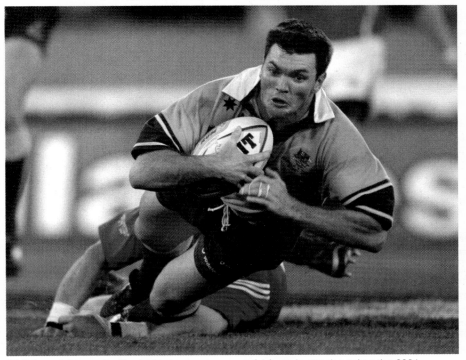

Wallaby outside centre Daniel Herbert was a powerful force in attack against the 2001 Lions. However, Herbie and centre partner Nathan Grey had their hands full in defence against the visitors' lively Irish combination of Rob Henderson and Brian O'Driscoll.

Unstoppable! The Wallaby juggernaut seals the 1999 World Cup win over France. This typical steamroller effort by Owen Finegan saw him plough through four opponents to score Australia's second try as John Eales (left) and David Giffin (centre, on ground) express their jubilation.

Gary Pearse

Outside the square

Finding exceptional new paths to excellence

'Thoughts are the seed of action.'
– Ralph Waldo Emerson

When you are numero uno, others aspire to follow and emulate you. Whether it's the best car, the finest vintage wine or the World Cup-winning Wallabies, competitors will always converge on your position in the marketplace.

To reach that No. 1 spot, any organisation must have an exceptional strategy, an ability to execute decisively and a structure and make-up that sets them apart from the rest. But reaching the summit is only half the battle: staying there is the real test. Competitors will try to copy, mimic and analyse your distinguishing style and strive to move into the same square.

Back in 1997, the Wallabies developed a revolutionary model in order to steal a march on the opposition. Under coach Rod Macqueen, a renowned lateral thinker, they were the first national rugby team to schedule full-time training camps, not only for the preseason period but throughout the domestic Test series.

51

Specialist defence and strength coaches imported from rugby league were another Macqueen innovation. He combined these with specialist dieticians, sports medicine experts, skills coaches and hi-tech video analysis. The Wallabies were clearly one step ahead of their Tri Nation partners and Northern Hemisphere rivals.

Today, all the elite national rugby teams attend similar camp set-ups, eat the same food, and employ the same range of coaching specialists. Some have even taken the next logical step and poached key Wallaby personnel. The former Wallaby backs coach, Tim Lane, was attached to the Springboks, ex-Queensland Reds coach John Connolly has enjoyed considerable success in France, and former NSW mentor Matt Williams is revelling in Ireland with Leinster.

It hasn't taken long for our opponents to make a pretty good fist of squeezing themselves into the same square owned by the Wallabies – the one that launched us to World Cup success and beyond. After a swift appraisal of the current international playing field, it seems clear that under Macqueen's successor, Eddie Jones, the Wallabies will once again need to jump outside that square. The wily Jones must create a new modus operandi that competitors will find difficult to read, counter and mimic – at least in the medium term. But *what* to change? *How much* to change? *Who* to change?

My view is that the answer lies in exploiting the inherent qualities and culture that make Australians so different and unique. A nation's culture is reflected in the way its athletes approach and play their sport. For example, on the rugby pitch French style and flair is reflected in the French players' flamboyant, innovative and passionate commitment. The strong-arm, uncompromising game of the Springboks stems from their Dutch/farming heritage. Their critics have noted the difficulty the Boks are presently experiencing in mimicking the Wallaby style. It's quite foreign to their own culture and psyche.

England coach Clive Woodward and his French rival, Bernard Laporte, are unashamed admirers of the Wallaby way. Both countries have blatantly copied Rod Macqueen's team structures and coaching strategies – so well, in fact, that even the Wallabies were caught on the hop.

OK, where do the Wallabies jump to next? Living in a country of infinite horizons contributes to our expansive game, free of any paranoia as to limits on creativity or execution. Combine this with our inherent 'have a go' attitude and an ingrained reluctance to take a backward step, and I believe we have a natural formula for success.

Eddie Jones knows more about these character traits than most. His rugby-playing days at Matraville High and Randwick have given him a sense of adventure and a passion for uninhibited attack. Wallaby assistant coach Glen Ella reinforces this faith in 'the running game' and will extract every ounce of talent from his back-line players.

However, unless the law-makers see the error of their recent ways, the Wallabies will need to think beyond the use of decoy runners so effectively employed by both the Brumbies and the national team. To my mind this is a case of

> 'Sure I've been dirty on the Test selectors. There were times when I thought I should have been picked and wasn't. But on the credit side, hate is a great motivator.'
>
> Reds coach Mark McBain, speaking during his playing days with the Wallabies

the legislators of the game singling out the Wallabies, but not their competitors. The decoy runner is now being penalised merely for *intent* rather than physical impedance. The International Rugby Board rule-makers will need to address this anomaly quickly or risk the code losing a crucially important strategy in attack.

The breakdown will continue to create concern for both attacking and defending teams. This has been the case from the time Billy Webb Ellis first picked up the ball. But just because a problem is old doesn't mean it will fade away.

Jones and his Wallaby brains trust will need to think outside the square yet again to develop a new style of moving the ball away from these pressure situations. Executed at pace, there is no more awesome sight than watching George Gregan feed a rampant Stephen Larkham with a flat ball at full speed. This initial momentum will provide any number of options to a stable of big, skilful and explosive outside backs.

All this may sound exciting (it's easy to coach from the typewriter) but without a forward pack actually going *forward*, execution of even the simplest moves can be severely compromised. Yet, in many cases, moving too far outside the traditional square for forwards is dangerous. There is no substitute for an aggressive, uncompromising and explosive pack of forwards. The Wallabies should never be content with static play or periods of time without the ball. Defence should create offensive opportunities. There is also never any substitute for tough, confrontational tackling. It disjoints opposition attacks and immediately creates scoring opportunities for the defending team.

I firmly believe that no country in the world can match our

Wallabies when they play their fast, expansive game. When we control the pace of the game – the faster the better! – and live 'in the faces' of our opponents in both attack and defence, then the resultant dynamic is an irresistible rugby power.

This desired framework should come from a belief that such a style is our destiny, and the sure way to victory. Australia has to prepare and execute with 'true believers' on and off the field. Only then will we create that new and even more inaccessible square for our competitors to envy.

Former Wallaby flanker Gary Pearse is an experienced television commentator. He played for Australia between 1975 and 1978 as well as undertaking overseas club stints in Italy and South Africa. He later coached at representative level and is a driving force in the Classic Wallabies movement. Gary is currently a rugby analyst with Seven.

Gary Pearse's rising star stable

Daniel Vickerman (Brumbies) This strapping young lock stands 204 cm and was man of the match in Sydney University's premiership win over Eastwood. Played for South African U21s before deciding to aim for a career with the Wallabies. Possesses outstanding aerial skills and the power and intelligence to achieve his golden goal.

Jone Tawake (Waratahs) Outstanding young back-rower from Sydney University who continues a proud and striking Pacific Island heritage in Australian rugby. Strong and resourceful, he possesses immense ball-playing and running skills and could be a bolter for next year's World Cup squad.

David Croft (Reds) Snapping at the heels of rival open-side flankers George Smith and Phil Waugh, Croft has stepped smoothly and impressively into David Wilson's old number 7 spot in the Reds' line-up, producing canny ball-winning skills at the breakdown. Has plenty of pace and a big heart.

Sam Harris (Waratahs) His rivalry with Steve Kefu is worth following. Under the tutelage of Waratahs back-line coach Gary Ella, Harris has the potential to be a world-class player. Came of age against the Lions last year, impressing with his instinctive ability to create space for supports.

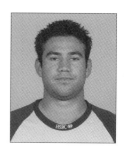

Josh Valentine (Waratahs) Last year's Australian Schools' scrum-half was raised in Singleton but finished his senior schooling at Narrabeen Sports High. Age is no bar and that's why this guy should be fast-tracked to senior representative football. A brilliant pass and exciting vision. Mentor Steve Merrick says he can go all the way.

Sean Hardman (Reds) With long-serving Michael Foley retired, this guy could emerge in a big hurry. A dynamic player with very sound technical skills in the set pieces, he is also a robust defender. All he needs now is game time and more exposure to higher company.

Tim Atkinson (Brumbies) Queensland-raised Tim was the outstanding performer at the 2002 World Rugby Sevens in Brisbane, won by the Aussies. Blistering speed off the mark, a clever stepper and very strong on the tackle, and equally adept at inside centre and scrum-half in the 15-a-side game, Tim is a very exciting youngster.

Van Humphries (Waratahs) Blooded during Super 12, this Moree 'bushie' answered Bob Dwyer's prayers for a tall, athletic line-out forward. Very mobile with an excellent work rate, Van is rated very highly by former All Black captain Wayne Shelford.

Pat Howard

Backs to the fray
The essentials of back-line play

'The world is divided into people who do things – and people who get the credit.'

– Dwight Whitney Morrow

There are few variables in the fundamentals of back-line play. Most rugby people will have slightly differing views on small particulars, but the two issues which confront all back lines and age groups come down to shallow v. deep, and wide v. close.

Before we deal with those scenarios, let's discuss what is *not* up for debate: that hitting the ball while moving is a must, and one of the most often neglected aspects of the back-line game – passing while still moving. These 'first principles' are as true for my brothers and their mates playing schoolboy rugby as they are if you're playing internationals.

If a player stands and delivers the pass it's obvious he's no great threat to the opposition. As a consequence, the player receiving that pass attracts extra defenders, less space, but sometimes more time (although I don't see its benefit). In that situation the big 'wind-up' pass more often than not ends up isolating runners. As always, there are exceptions. At times you may need to manipulate the defence – say, if you want your opposition to drift – but as a general rule it's better to deliver while attacking the defensive line.

Not many players fully understand that the pace at which you hit onto the ball and then pass the ball (while still moving) is not as important as the essential need to just keep moving. A great exponent of this – remembering that I never got to play with Mark Ella – was David Knox. He had the ability to canter to the line and stop opposition sides from drifting, but still create space and time for those outside him. Because David rarely hit the pass at full pace, he had the time to evaluate whether he'd drawn anyone onto him, decide whether to pass, take the hole, or take the half-hole and offload. Even though he sometimes seemed to be almost loitering, it was rare for his involvement not to threaten the defence. None of this is to say that running at full pace is incorrect. I'm just stressing the point that passing drills can be done at half-pace to emphasise accurate passing, and that threatening defences means not stepping to pass.

This leads us naturally to the second principle beyond debate: the quality of handling and passing. For all the planning and the infinity of different moves that go into back-line play, the basic ability to hit the mark under pressure is an absolute necessity. The backs must be able to do this while close to the advantage line, or even sometimes on the line itself. Coupled with that skill is the ability to catch, to catch under pressure, and to catch and pass in one movement.

Those are the fundamentals. Now let's consider the two variables I outlined at the outset. Firstly, depth. Standing deep is only a starting point. Whether you start deep or shallow will largely be dictated by how skilful your inside backs are

at playing 'in the faces' of the opposition. The guiding principle is that the back line should only be as deep as is needed to allow quality passing and handling while still moving forward as you pass. Shallow back-line theories are fundamentally sound, as long as the ball is delivered while the defence is being placed under real pressure. But this approach means it's more difficult (although not impossible) to get the ball wide. Remember that a deep start with a deep finish will result in players not attracting the inside back defenders. This leaves a very good, thick defensive unit for the attacking outside backs.

Width is an even more interesting principle to consider. If you stand close to your back-line comrades you will ensure – or at least encourage – quality handling. For the more talented back lines, standing wide increases the width in back-line defenders, at least in theory. In practice this doesn't always happen. If you can stand wide, move forward as you pass and still deliver accurately, this is obviously the ideal pattern. But don't forget that your support lines and breakdown support lines will become more difficult to sustain. It's essential to remember that it's the ability of your players that will determine the width of your back line – that is, stand only as wide as you can without compromising the basic skills of the team.

Some food for thought. On a 65-metre-wide field, if the distance between the scrum-half and fly-half is 10 metres and you have a scrum 5 metres from the touchline, there is a full 50 metres left outside the fly-half. If the inside and outside centres are then separated by 4 m each, that will leave your back trio – the two wingers and the full-back (and presumably your three most elusive runners) – with more

OPPOSITE *On the charge: after 20 Tests for the Wallabies, back-line general Pat Howard enjoyed four marvellous seasons (1997–2001) with the all-conquering Leicester Tigers before rejoining the ACT Brumbies in 2001.*

than 40 m of width to play in. By contrast, standing 10 m apart (English/All Black style) will leave only 30 m of space out wide, with a consequent increased risk of poor passing.

The French back line against South Africa and Australia last year featured excellent execution with a very wide back line. Their back-line theory is a splendid demonstration of the value of hitting the ball at pace, skilful passing and excellent angle changes. Even though they stand very wide, they have the skills to support that style. The English also stand pretty wide with the fly-half and inside centre not always pressing to the advantage line, which causes opposition defences to drift. For that reason their breaks are primarily made by short passing moves designed to catch out the drift defence, not by moving the ball around their opposition.

Width is ultimately dictated by skills and whether you are trying to go around sides or between them. Depth is only important from the point where you actually deliver your pass, not the depth from which you began. Once again, your team's skills will dictate how close to the opposition a player can catch and pass.

At a more advanced level of the game, there has been a strong tendency (led by Australia) to play multiphase, organised rugby. This has proved extremely successful and teams who have the training time to achieve this level of organisation will find the approach very valuable. I do believe, however, that the practice has been to the detriment of classic 'first-phase' attack. (First-phase rugby is the situation where 16 out of 30 players on a field are confined to a small space – excluding short line-outs. The attacking team knows exactly who they are running at and with what numbers.) Frankly, there's no real reason for its demise. To deal first with the numbers in a scrum situation, normally you will have either seven players versus four, or seven versus five. The difference is that the half-back will be to the left side of the scrum from the attacker's point of view. In later phases you can expect it will take four people to win the ball versus two to slow it down, creating a pattern of 11 attackers, 13 defenders. This simple arithmetic highlights the fact that first phase is still a potent platform from which to attack. Consider, for example, Matthew Burke's try in last year's Test match against England at Twickenham.

In conclusion, the paramount basics of back-line play are:

- passing *for* a player and not *to* him
- not standing still to deliver a pass
- the ability to catch and pass with ease
- inside backs going to the line and delivering with pace to allow the most skilful runners on the outside time and space.

Coaches should carefully assess their personnel and then decide what depth and width are applicable for the team in order to get the best results, in terms of both scores and enjoyment.

Pat Howard played 20 Tests for Australia before departing for Leicester, where he played in three successive premiership-winning sides. In his final season he also acted as back-line coach, was a member of Leicester's European Cup-winning team and was unanimously voted European Player of the Year 2000–01. He then returned to Australia to rejoin the ACT Brumbies. He is a third-generation Wallaby, following in the footsteps of his dad, Jake, and his late grandfather, the legendary three-quarter Cyril Towers.

Pat Howard's back-line brief

Brumbies and Wallaby centre Pat Howard is acknowledged as one of the outstanding thinkers when it comes to the art of modern back-line play. His insights were first nourished at the dinner table by his late grandfather, legendary Wallaby Cyril Towers. The pair used sets of salt and pepper shakers to demonstrate back-line ploys.

Scrum-half   Must have the ability to pass quickly off the ground from either hand. Needs to have strength to deal with the contact of forwards and the pace and fitness to be at every breakdown in the game. Mentally, the scrum-half needs to be authoritative and vocal towards his forwards. A solid kicking game is a bonus but not a necessity.

Fly-half   The decision-maker. Needs to have the ability to pass and kick under pressure. His communication should be primarily with the scrum-half while listening to the inside centre. Due to back-rowers not being allowed to leave the scrum until the ball is out, his defence must also be very good. The fly-half dictates which side of the breakdown to attack.

Inside centre   Primary role is to communicate to the fly-half and offer options. Needs to be the organiser in defence, defending the outside shoulder of his own fly-half while still covering the inside of his own outside centre. Depending on the team strategy he may be a ball player or a penetrating runner – preferably both. A short kicking game is a bonus.

Outside centre   Must be quick and strong with an ability to read the opposition defence patterns (outside centre is often the most difficult place to defend). Ideally the number 13 needs an ability to change angles and utilise the holes created by inside players. These qualities are the hallmarks of most of the world's best outside centres.

OPPOSITE *A great back line must be founded on a powerful and well-organised defence. Note here how the inner players are watching the ball while those further out in the front line check positioning of opponents.*

Blind-side wing   Needs to organise the blind-side defence to trail opposition ball runners and to turn half-breaks into full breaks. Must possess the ability to play as the second full-back. Speed is essential for all of the back three players. Is a second link on second-man plays, so requires good catch/pass skills over long distances.

Open-side wing   Penetrating pace and top-class finishing are essential. Must have an ability to read the degree of notation to help ensure possession is not surrendered. The angles needed at outside centre are more useful in this position due to the increased space available (well, that's the theory).

Full-back   Needs the same attacking qualities as the outside centre – namely, blistering pace and a sure finisher. A quality full-back requires exceptional skills under the high ball. As a decision-maker, he needs to choose between counterattack or utilising a long-kicking game. One-on-one tackling (not defence – there is a difference) must be faultless.

ABOVE *A classic back-line confrontation in the 2001 Bledisloe Cup at Stadium Australia. Wallaby inside centre Nathan Grey (second from left) covers the inside of teammate Dan Herbert (far left). Grey drifts across to tackle Jonah Lomu while Herbert drifts wider to stay on his outside man.*

Part 2
All is revealed

Nature calls?

If international referee Tony Spreadbury needs to raise his voice, take good heed. His is a voice of considerable authority.

A few years back he was officiating in an otherwise uneventful Scottish interdistrict match between Edinburgh and Melrose. Without permission, a Jack Russell hunting dog suddenly scampered onto the field and exhibited every intention of joining in the play. The hapless hound hadn't reckoned on Mr Spreadbury. The ref immediately unleashed a shrill blast from his whistle, gestured violently towards the grandstand and bellowed, 'Off, you! Right now!'

Shortly afterwards, footage of the incident was replayed on the 'What Happened Next?' segment of the popular BBC television quiz show *A Question of Sport*. The picture was frozen just as the dog gazed up at the referee. The best the bemused contestants could come up with as to what happened next was that perhaps the canine had paused to answer a call of nature.

They'd underestimated the authority of Tony Spreadbury. In fact, the dog had been so overawed by the referee's imperious command to take an early shower that it immediately turned and slunk out through the gate – straight into the visitors' change room, where it allegedly left its mark.

PREVIOUS PAGE *A rugby legend, that great Aussie bleeder Chris 'Buddha' Handy, during Australia's heroic win over the All Blacks at the SCG in 1979. Uncompromising and fearless, he regularly spilt blood for his country during his Test career, which included two winning Bledisloe Cup series in 1979 and 1980. He is now an indispensable and always colourful member of the Seven commentary team.*

Wayne Erickson

It takes two to tango

**An international referee tries to give away his
whistle, then explains some finer points of the laws**

The New Zealand v. Scotland Test
at Carisbrook in 1996 was about
30 minutes old. It had been a difficult half-hour for players and
referee alike. The Scots had stuck
tenaciously to their plan to frus-
trate their opponents' rhythm, and
the All Blacks machine, in its first
hit-out of the season, was not yet
firing on all cylinders.

Sean Fitzpatrick, the All Black captain, was acutely
aware of his team's difficulties. One of his coping mecha-
nisms in these circumstances was to take on the tasks of
those around him whom he felt needed his assistance. This
often found him, for example, on the blind side of the ruck
or maul shoring up the back row's defensive effort, or at first
receiver setting up a reliable second phase.

On this occasion he'd obviously decided to extend his gen-
erous services to assist that other great underachiever on
the day – me! Almost from the kick-off, Sean seemed always
to be just behind my left ear. He was telling me about this
knock-on or that forward pass, or 'We don't want that
advantage, Gus' or 'That tackle was a bit high, wasn't it?' He

even changed the All Black scrum call from 'Hit!' to 'Engage!', perhaps because he thought my own 'Engage' call wasn't quite loud enough.

After about half an hour of this nonstop chatter, I was wondering how I might manage to retain the excellent spirit of cooperation but get rid of the bird on my shoulder. Within seconds an opportunity fell out of the sky. The Scottish hooker (who, incidentally, was another less-than-grateful recipient of Fitzpatrick wisdom) threw a dodgy ball into a line-out. Quick as a flash – and well before I'd even considered blowing my whistle for 'not straight' – Fitzy called it. 'Not straight! We'll have the line-out!'

I blew my whistle, because it was indeed not straight, and the All Black skipper confirmed his choice of a line-out. I walked over to the touchline, where Sean was standing holding the ball in readiness. I held my whistle out to him and said, 'No, no. Let me throw it in. You take the whistle for a while. You're obviously keen to have a go at it.'

For about a nanosecond he thought I was serious. Then he smiled, straightened up and said, 'No, it's okay. You're doing all right.' He spent the rest of that afternoon giving advice to all and sundry if he felt they needed it, but thankfully, from that line-out onwards, I wasn't one of them.

In order to simplify rugby's complex set of laws, let's look at three main ball-winning areas through the eyes of the referee.

1. Tackling the big issue

For millions of supporters around the world, rugby's appeal lies in the unpredictability that flows from its multiphased, dynamic structure. But this strength is potentially also its weakness, especially as the complexity of its laws challenges our ability to attract new audiences to the game.

The most difficult part of the game to referee is the tackle. There have been more attempts to fiddle with this phase than any other, and there are many in the rugby community who say that we still don't have it right. Yet it is precisely this difficult quality that gives rugby football such an advantage over so many other games – the tackle is a vibrant, constantly changing part of play in which no two situations are the same. But let's be honest – it *can* be a mess.

Perhaps the best way for the spectator to understand what's going on is to look at the tackle through a referee's eyes (and no jokes, please, about blind referees!). To start from the beginning, a tackle is made and both players are intertwined on the ground. First focus is on the TACKLER.

- Has he released the ball carrier?
- Is his body position preventing the ball carrier from playing the ball?
- Do arriving players jam him in before he can get away, or is he deliberately stopping quick release of the ball?

Next is the BALL CARRIER.

- Has he now been allowed to play the ball?
- Has he played the ball, or is he holding on to it waiting for the cavalry to arrive?

Finally in the tackle phase, we look to the ARRIVING PLAYERS.

- Is there an arriving player on his feet seeking to take the ball from the ball carrier?
- Has he, and has every other arriving player, come from 'the right direction'?

This idea of 'the right direction' is not difficult to understand. Imagine a shot-put circle drawn around the bodies of the players on the ground, and that each player must enter the tackle from the back of the circle which is nearer his own goal line. That's 'the right direction'. (Remember that the tackled player and the tackler do not have to come from the right direction, because they are already in the circle.)

Even when all questions of 'right direction' are settled, the referee has other issues to consider. Have any arriving players fallen to the ground? Were they pushed or pulled, or did they deliberately go to ground to seal off possession or to stop the other team from getting the ball?

The great problem for referees and for spectators trying to understand what's going on is that this all happens so quickly. But if the tackle is analysed by looking at its component parts, a clearer picture may emerge.

It's likely that at some stage you'll disagree with a decision a referee has made at a tackle, and you won't be the only one! Mostly this is because what you've seen in either 'real time' or on slow-motion replay is a different part of the same tackle. The referee may well have not seen that part of play, or has chosen to ignore it because it's not been as important as the part he *has* dealt with. He may have tried to explain this thought process to the players and, with a bit of luck, the television replay will highlight his audible explanation. If referees, helped by informed commentary from the experts behind the microphone, can get this communication exercise right, we will help players and viewers alike to tackle the tackle – rugby's most pressing law issue.

OPPOSITE *Wayne Erickson took up refereeing in the mid-1980s after enjoying a lengthy 1st-grade career at prop for Eastern Suburbs. Here he awards a penalty to the Brumbies in a Super 12 game at the old Bruce Stadium. Wayne is currently a member of the elite 'A' panel of international referees.*

2. 'What the !@%&!# is happening in the front row?'

How many times have we heard commentators ask each other that question? How often do spectators ask it? Nobody should be surprised to know that referees also often find it difficult to answer. A team's scrum success in any given match will depend on the ability of its front row to attain superiority over their opponents. The ball to the number 8 and scrum-half will be cleaner; the force generated by the second and back row will be more efficiently transferred. The best efforts of the opposition will usually be nullified by a dominant front row.

If that clash 'up front' is so important, why hasn't someone sorted out how to identify why it goes wrong? The answer lies in the simple fact that there are six large individuals all locked together in uncompromising physical contact. When the structure falls, who's to say with certainty which one of them caused it to happen? It's likely that in most situations only the guy who genuinely caused the collapse (and the guy who had it done to him) will know for sure. It's unlikely that even their front-row colleagues will have any idea.

The best any referee can do is be better at reading the signs. Consider some of the questions that flash through the ref's mind when he is confronted by a collapsed scrum.

- Were they all straight going into the engagement?
- Are any of them bearing down so that their head and shoulders are too far below their hips?

> 'A player standing up to another may hold one arm only, but may hack him or knock the ball out of his hand if he attempts to kick it or go beyond the line of touch.'
>
> Rugby School law 1845

- Are the props binding on the body of their opponent?
- Is the feet position of each player capable of supporting their body position?
- Who is under pressure, and what is he doing in response?

If these signs aren't clear, the referee shouldn't try to guess who is responsible. That would be unfair. But neither is it fair on players or spectators if an unresolved shambles spoils the whole match, which becomes constantly riddled by reset after reset. Players and their captains have a responsibility to play within the spirit of the game. As a last resort a referee may have to get rid of any boofheads who simply refuse to cooperate.

3. 'These line-outs are a dockyard brawl.'

Sean Connery – who seems to know a thing or three about charming the ladies – once said that there are three things a woman admires in a man: 'Confidence, confidence and confidence'. To continue in that vein, if there are three things a referee admires in a line-out they are 'Gap, gap and gap'.

Here are the first few of the million or so things the referee needs to check at the beginning of a line-out.

- Are the numbers okay?
- Are they all within 15 metres?
- Is there only one half-back?
- Are the rest back 10 metres?
- Is he throwing from the mark?

And that's all before the ball is even thrown in! Once the ball is in, it's fair to say that almost all problems can be traced back to the lack of distance between the teams. Frustration over previous wrongs is the motivation behind some infringements, and this almost always comes about because the gap has been closed down.

The recent ploy of arriving at the line-out just before throw-in, together with the almost constant movement of players changing their positions prior to the ball being thrown, is certainly not helping the problem. While these techniques are all very legal, they have the combined effect of denying the space between the teams that is so vital to a clean contest for the ball.

You can check it out for yourself. Next time there's a problem with the contest for the ball at the line-out in a match you are watching, try to see if there was a closing of the gap prior to throw-in. Or maybe there was just insufficient space in the first place. It may well be that an extra 20 seconds spent by the referee ensuring there is the required gap at each line-out might result in a clean, fair contest for possession.

Having retired from a distinguished career as a player, Wayne Erickson took up refereeing at the age of 27. He played over 100 1st-grade games as a tighthead prop for Eastern Suburbs and UNSW in Sydney and was selected to play for the Sydney representative side in 1983. As a referee, his career has been equally impressive. He has been to two World Cups, officiated in a Lions–Springbok Test and refereed the All Blacks in eight Test matches. Gus, as Wayne is more commonly known, is one of the 'characters' of the international game. He also plays cricket for Briars in the Municipal and Shires Masters competition and has served as a NSWCA umpire.

The laws aren't black and white (or read all over)

Addressing grey areas of the laws is the major challenge facing the game's administrators.

Fifty/fifty decisions can unfairly result in three points against the team deemed to have committed the offence – and may cost them the match. Streamlined, simplified application of the laws will lead to greater consistency and uniformity. That, in turn, will enhance the understanding and enjoyment of the fans. In practice, too many on-field situations are perceived as a lottery by spectators, players and commentators. Subjectivity needs to be eliminated from the referee's decision-making so that the law-makers can achieve the desired 'black and white' model.

In the meantime, the apparent disparity between the written laws and their practical application remains a problem. Here, international referee WAYNE ERICKSON takes some affirmative action on ten every-day match situations that often lead to viewer confusion.

1. Will the referee always penalise players who go to the ground at a tackle?

Players who intentionally fall on other players in an effort either to seal off the ball from their opponents or to stop an opponent from getting up and playing the ball should be penalised. Imagine an aeroplane in flight – referees are looking for arriving players to adopt a 'take-off' rather than a 'landing' body position and attitude when they arrive near players at a tackle.

2. What does the referee do if a tackler won't, or can't, get away from the player he's just tackled?

If the referee is convinced the tackler won't get away even though he has an opportunity, the tackler should be penalised. If he can't get away because of factors beyond his control, the referee should blow the play quickly and set a scrum. It's amazing how many players say that they 'couldn't get away, sir'!

3. Are players allowed to charge in and 'clean out' opponents who are standing over the ball?

Players can 'clean out' opponents by using their arms and shoulders together to drive opponents away from over the ball. They can't shoulder-charge their opponents, nor can they clean out if that occurs more than a metre away from the ball. A positive thing about the clean-out is that as soon as it happens a ruck is formed, and off-side lines mean that space is created.

4. How long is the tackled player allowed to hang on to the ball?

Not long! He must play it as soon as he is tackled. It may be that he can't because the tackler hasn't let him go. If this is the case, the tackler should be penalised because he is ruining any chance of quick ball being delivered. The practice of a player in possession 'buying time' by smothering the ball with his torso and then placing it back through the legs is no longer tolerated unless the process takes place immediately and in the same action.

5. Why are hookers penalised for a crooked throw to the line-out when the other team doesn't jump for the ball anyway?

Line-outs and scrums are all about restarting after a stoppage, and the contest for the ball must be fair. It could be that the reason the other team isn't jumping is that they see no point in contesting if the referee isn't going to insist on a straight throw! Interestingly, we are seeing far more line-outs being contested now that referees are insisting on straighter throws.

6. Shouldn't the referee always come back and award the penalty if no try is scored from advantage?

No, not always. The original and still the main purpose of the advantage law is to reduce the number of stoppages in the game. With this in mind, it makes no sense to give a team an opportunity to capitalise on an opponent's blunder, have them generate either a territorial or a tactical advantage, and then return to the original spot because they didn't score. What a waste of time! Why not just award the penalty in the first place? The answer is that it would be a stoppage and should be avoided if possible.

7. Scrum collapses are dangerous and continually resetting is a waste of time. Shouldn't referees just penalise the offenders?

Probably, but only if the referee truly knows who is the culprit. Try to imagine how difficult it can be to pinpoint the perpetrator from among that interlocking jungle of front-rowers. Referees must strive to understand more about what goes on in the dark recesses of the scrum. (One is tempted to ask why so few forwards ever graduate to blowing the whistle once their scrummaging days are over.) Equally, players have a responsibility to play within the spirit of the game. In the meantime, referees should adopt the attitude, 'Never guess'.

8. Why don't touch judges stop players from getting away with infringements the referee hasn't penalised?

Every referee would like extra assistance sometimes – a few of us need it more often than others! Touch judges have a very specific focus when it comes to general play: they must watch behind and sometimes ahead of the ball, to pick up any foul play. If they were to watch the game in the same way as the referee, serious incidents in back play might be missed. Assistance is nice to get, but not at the expense of the main job.

9. Why can't players use their shoulders when tackling in rugby?

There is nothing wrong with using the shoulders, as long as it is in conjunction with the arms trying to grasp the opponent. A pointed shoulder without arms is a weapon that can do enormous damage.

10. The ball always seems to be trapped forever in a maul. Why don't they get rid of the maul so spectators can see more open play?

The maul does slow the play, but it also draws players into contest in a confined area. This opens up space in other parts of the field. Continually mauling the ball would look like a mobile wrestling match, but a game with no mauls would look like rugby league. The challenge for teams is to mix the options to create space wherever possible.

The maul remains a potent weapon as an attacking option. This particular tackle has become a maul because the ball carrier is on his feet and in contact with a player from either side. France and England use the driving maul very effectively, while New Zealand is expected to utilise the ploy more frequently following the appointment of new coach John Mitchell.

Defence is the most lethal form of attack

A conversation with Wallaby defence guru
John Muggleton

'. . . by all means we can, to defend ourselves.'
    – Thomas Hobbes

Few would argue that the recruitment of John Muggleton was one of the major contributing factors in Rod Macqueen's successful World Cup strategy. A former rugby league international, Muggleton emerged as a pioneering specialist at a time when rugby was still wrestling with the demands of professionalism.

Macqueen quickly recognised that rugby league had a proven track record as a professional code and seized upon league's expertise in the crucial areas of fitness and defence. Steve Nance joined the Wallabies from the Brisbane Broncos, and over a two-year period, chiselled underdeveloped body shapes into granite-hard gladiators. Similarly, Muggleton gave Australian rugby a defensive structure and skills base that proved to be the cornerstone of our 1999 World Cup triumph in Europe.

'My role is to look after all aspects of our defensive formations on the field, whether they be from line-outs, scrums or broken play,' Muggleton explains. 'From that base it is then a matter of putting everything into practice at training – from the required positioning needed in each of those areas as we move forward off the line, to the individual tackling and the various types of tackle we use in given situations. For example, it may be a tackle around the legs to stop the ball, or a higher tackle to try and turn the player over in order to steal the ball, or even a gang tackle (two or three defenders on the ball carrier) to try to stop momentum and drive them backwards to gain the advantage.'

Muggleton's first principle in defence is that the effective tackle must have stopping the ball carrier as its primary aim. 'We are a little different to rugby league in that they try to lock up the ball in the tackle. The downside of that approach is that a lot of tackles are being missed because of the strength of the player in possession. We would rather stop that player and still give him the chance to offload because our defence formations should, in theory, be strong enough to handle any contingency.' In other words, the Wallaby approach is to keep it simple and avoid the complication of trying to come up with a hard-and-fast mode of tackling that might not be as effective.

'The other feature of our defence is that we have a set line with set responsibilities,' Muggleton says. 'We never have players coming out of that line and working individually. If we're in an overlap situation, we'll stay in the line and let the line work from the inside to cover us rather than going up and trying to defend against a whole lot of players. If one defensive player goes out of the line it automatically makes it harder for the others to cover.'

Are there exceptions to this rule, though? What about in

Defence is the most lethal form of attack

the Second Test against the Lions at Colonial Stadium when Joe Roff came up out of the line to secure that wonderful intercept try? 'Joe came up off the line but he didn't try to specifically take an intercept. As it turned out, Jonny Wilkinson tried to throw the ball over Joe's head. In that case Joe was presented with the intercept. If you can pick off a nice long pass like that or hit the man as he receives the ball, that's okay because you're attacking the ball and it's a more stable situation. But overall, if you play the odds, you'll come out with a better result if you hold the defensive line.'

So what inner-sanctum tips can John pass on to the army of players outside professional ranks? From grassroots to club level, emerging players are always hungry for improvement. 'Most young players miss the tackle because they put themselves in a position where they can't *make* the tackle – in other words, they move across field first. What we try to do is focus on the hips of the opponent. We move up on his inside hip so if he sidesteps we're still in a position to tackle him because we're still going front-on. If he keeps running it's then just a matter of adjusting our angle. However, if a player goes for the outside hip of the ball carrier, the defender's body is immediately turned and out of play if the opponent sidesteps. Another important reason to focus on the hips for younger players is because it's the prime target area. It's the point of contact for your shoulder drive, so it makes more sense to watch that inside hip and drive into it for the start of the tackle.'

When tennis players prepare to volley, they take a quick split-step as their opponent makes contact with the ball. This lets them make a fast reaction to get into the right position. Does the rugby tackler adopt a similar strategy with his feet to prepare for the ball carrier? 'Generally the rule is that you need to get one foot into the opponent's space. We don't have our feet together at all. We adopt what we call a split stance in the tackle – one foot in close to the opponent, the other foot back to drive in after the shoulder impact.

'To illustrate, if a player in possession is moving to my right, I try to get a foot right in between his feet, or close enough to the imaginary line between his feet. That cuts down his space and lets me drive in that area. It allows me to absorb any bump and then counter it. A simple exercise in understanding this technique is to push someone in the chest who has their feet together. They would have to take a backward step to maintain balance. It's a different story, though, if they have one foot forward and one back.'

Positioning of the head is also an important aspect of tackling technique. Is it simply a matter of tucking your head in behind the backside of the oncoming opponent? Muggleton explains: 'The head must be straight. It's technically good to hit up and through. That applies to kids and Test players alike. In other words, the tackling motion is replicating how a front-rower would pack into a scrum. One foot forward, nice straight back and then drive through to the other side of the player with a good line of force. By taking that one more step you then effect a good aggressive tackle rather than just a soft contact. Coincidentally, when you line up correctly on the inside hip it automatically puts your chin in the right position. By being half a body off your opponent, you're ideally placed to tuck your head in behind. In a scrum, the front-rowers don't pack head to head – they pack half a body to the side. The same technique applies to tackling.'

OPPOSITE *The 'Tongan Torpedo', Willie Ofahengaue, was renowned as a punishing defender. His massive thighs enabled him to fully exploit the John Muggleton dictum of driving hard through the tackle.*

So John Muggleton's summary for head position is as follows: chin on your chest (which hunches your shoulders) and a nice straight back and head position (which keeps your face out of harm's way). Don't hold your head up because that arches your back, which puts you in a bad position.

And what about a good simple training drill for kids that can be done easily at home? 'Well, this may not meet with universal approval, but I used to put my shoulder pads on and use the telegraph pole out the front of our house. I'd step back as if I was packing into a scrum and then just lean into it. I also tried the same technique on Mum, with the proviso that she stepped back on contact so she didn't get hurt. She survived okay.

'Another exercise with a partner is to work in a 10-metre-square area with each of you starting on opposite sides. The aim is to take it in turns to get over each other's goal line using the correct tackling technique, but instead of tackling you use a two-handed push because that still puts you in good position for a match situation. The defender should be half a body inside and with feet in good position. You step down and push through on the opponent's hip, driving off your foot.'

John Muggleton has been the Wallabies' defence coach since 1998, after moving from rugby league to rugby union in 1996. A former rugby league international, he has played an influential behind-the-scenes role in all Australia's international successes over the past four seasons.

Three golden rules in defence

A well-organised defence relies on successful execution by individuals. Here is John Muggleton's fundamental brief for the tackler. This simple advice is applicable at all levels of the game.

1. Know who you have to tackle.
2. Catch that person.
3. Effect the tackle with strong drive.

The first two rules are the hardest to follow when you're in a defensive line. If an opponent is running with the ball, someone has to nominate him. Whoever carries the ball must be nominated as their man by someone in the defensive line.

Australia has relied on one-on-one defence in the past, whereas a team such as England would rather cram it up and get closer together, thus allowing two players to make the first tackle. Because the game is changing so quickly we are constantly evaluating our approach, but it's safe to say that the 'three golden rules' will never change.

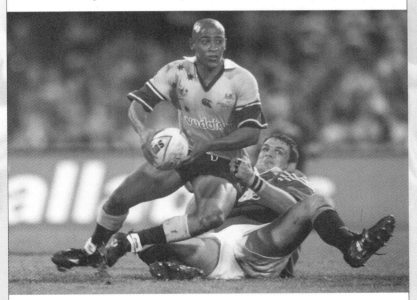

Sometimes a defender must stray from the textbook to ensure an effective tackle is made. Here Wallaby scrum-half George Gregan receives such treatment from Lions centre Rob Henderson at the Gabba in the 2001 series. Because of George's power and low centre of gravity, he presents a difficult target for would-be defenders.

John Mackay

Behind the front line

**The manager's postscript to a winning
World Cup campaign**

'Forewarned, forearmed; to be prepared is half the victory.'
— Miguel de Cervantes

No pain, no gain – it may be a cliche, but the most satisfying aspect of my time with the Wallabies was the fact that it was a very tough start. Sometimes you have to go through the hard times in order to appreciate the good times, and we certainly did that.

Beginning with Greg Smith in 1997, they were extremely difficult times for all concerned. We couldn't take a trick. We had a plague of injuries and things kept going wrong. After our 61–22 flogging by South Africa in Pretoria, Greg lost his job as national coach. Shortly afterwards it was revealed he had a life-threatening brain tumour.

With the arrival of Rod Macqueen I had a battle to hold on to my own job. Rod had clear ideas about the future of the Wallabies, and I didn't figure in those plans. Nevertheless, I was supported by ARU managing director John O'Neill as well as the players, so in the end it was a matter of just starting all over again.

We really struggled in Argentina and the tour proved to be a watershed because several of the players in that squad took no further part in the World Cup campaign. Rod learned a lot in 1997, just as Eddie Jones did on last year's European tour. There's no doubt in my mind that you need those tough tours to bring you back to earth. Any successful outfit must first do the hard yards.

The core of our World Cup team was probably forged on the 1996 tour of Europe. We had a 13-match program and I had the role of Gear Steward, which was a terrific learning experience. A lot of the guys really kicked on during that trip. Talented young players such as Stephen Larkham, Ben Tune, Andrew Blades, Richard Harry and David Giffin were all relative newcomers who went on to play in the World Cup final. We'd all been through the difficult times together, so it was especially satisfying to succeed.

The key to our success in the 1999 World Cup was planning and preparation. Just as we'd established the base-camp concept at Caloundra in 1998, our first objective was to provide a similar set-up for our three-week stay in Dublin. John O'Neill initiated contact with Tony O'Reilly, who owned the Portmarnock Hotel and Golf Links on the outskirts of Dublin, and Rod made a quick inspection at the end of the 1998 tour. We met on his return and decided I would go over to Ireland in March 1999 to establish our Cup base.

I went through the whole accommodation layout, set up a gymnasium at the Portmarnock Leisure Club and organised training fields. The hotel even purpose-built a field especially for us. Six months out from the World Cup we already knew pretty well which rooms individual players would have. During my trip I took the opportunity to visit the other hotels and training venues we would be using during the Cup campaign, as well as organising gyms and pools. The whole exercise was most beneficial as we were able to formalise our entire travel schedule.

Rugby World Cup administrators weren't exactly over the moon about our preparations. Indeed, we had great difficulty convincing them that such detailed levels of planning were necessary, but at the end of the day we were so organised they simply couldn't knock us back – especially as it didn't cost them a penny extra. When it came to the official World Cup Managers' Tour of accommodation, facilities and venues two months later, I was dotting the i's and crossing the t's while many of my fellow managers were starting from scratch. As a result, Rod and I were quietly confident that we had the best preparation. Our critics suggested we were based too far out of the city, but few of the team would agree. On match days we were given a police motorcycle escort, so we never stopped once between the hotel and Lansdowne Road. (We also made sure the police motor- cyclists were always wearing green and gold scarves!)

A tour manager's job isn't confined to booking hotel rooms and coach transport. Our match against Ireland was successful in terms of the result but a disaster as regards the judiciary. Dan Herbert was cited for a dangerous tackle on Kevin Maggs, while Toutai Kefu was also summoned after a violent incident with Trevor Brennan. The hearings took place in London and in each case we were able to present video coverage that the judiciary hadn't previously seen. In Kefu's case the footage showed that Brennan had actually initiated the incident on the ground. Toutai received a two-match suspension, which ruled him out of the match

Temporary respite during the heat of battle: former Wallaby manager John Mackay (left) played a key organisational role in the last World Cup campaign. Medico Dr John Best (right) was also a highly valued member of an outstanding support team.

against the US and the quarter-final; Herbert was exonerated. Rod was pretty disappointed, but privately we were reasonably pleased with the result.

From a logistical viewpoint, the whole World Cup exercise was organised down to the finest detail. To give just one example, all the 'shadow' players back in Australia had been measured and fitted for their full range of gear – 60-odd items each to take as team uniform, if required. As it turned out, two players were called across – Glenn Panoho and Rod Moore. Both had already been booked on flights before I rang them with the good news. It was then simply a matter of calling into ARU headquarters on their way to the airport to pick up their three bags of gear.

In Wales for the climax of the tour we stayed at the Cardiff Bay Hotel, which was quite fortuitous because its facilities were excellent. It hadn't been our scheduled accommodation for the final; although we'd stayed there for the quarter-final against Wales, the Rugby World Cup officials had booked us into the Park Royal Hotel in the centre of town and the All Blacks had been booked into the Cardiff Bay. I argued with officials that we deserved first choice of hotels as we were already in the final. However, at the time we set out by bus from London for Cardiff, we were still staying at the Park Royal. A phone call came when we were an hour out of Cardiff to inform us that RWC had finally agreed to the change. (The All Blacks, incidentally, didn't have a problem with our proposal.)

There was another hiccup on the day of the final when we left the hotel – two cars had parked across the driveway and the team bus couldn't get out. Thankfully, Chris 'Buddha' Handy was on board and he and several of the 'dirties' (non-playing reserves) physically lifted one of the offending vehicles out of our way. Old front-rowers still have their uses!

After the euphoria of our victory, I found the post-final dinner at the Cardiff Convention Centre disappointing. It seemed to be dominated by officials patting themselves on the back. The traditional exchange of gifts with the opposing team manager, Jo Maso, actually took place at the French table after the official proceedings had concluded. If I'm not mistaken, even our winning captain, John Eales, wasn't called on to say a few words.

Thanks to Rod Kafer's handiwork, the side moved on to Brannigan's nightclub to celebrate with family and friends. Because we had an early start next morning I elected to head back to the hotel, the William Webb Ellis Cup firmly tucked under my arm. Some time after midnight I had a call from Jason Little saying he was coming up to my room for a beer. In tow were his wife, as well as Tim and Mandy Gavin and Peter and Jo Shipway. The door of my room was ajar due to the careful placement of a large, steel-padded box. We'd all enjoyed a few celebratory drinks before Tim demanded, 'OK, Macca, where's Bill?'

I replied, 'He's over there', pointing to the doorstopper. The priceless trophy had been stepped over by my guests and even sat upon by an unknowing Tim Gavin. 'Bill' was taken out of the box for the mandatory photos and I finally got to bed at about 3.30, only to resurface on the team bus at 6.45 a.m. – in 'Number Ones', of course. (As you might expect after such a big night, a lot of the guys just made the bus having never changed out of their 'Number One' uniforms.)

I dealt with a trio of different national coaches during my

time as Wallaby manager and can confirm that all three, directly and indirectly, had input into our World Cup success. Greg Smith was a very good, innovative football coach. There are still things being used by the Australian team that he initiated back in 1996–97, for example, much of the 'up the middle of the field' play, the pick-and-drive and the setting-up of mini-mauls. However, it proved to be a big step for Greg to go from being English Master at Randwick Boys High to travelling the world with the Wallabies. Some of the media criticism got a bit personal and he found coping with that flak a major adjustment. In hindsight he probably could have consulted a bit more with a wider group of people.

Rod Macqueen developed Greg's football ideas even further by working different channels up the field. He also used his business background to telling effect. He's the type of person who has a long-term vision and then makes sure it's turned into reality by getting the best people involved, such as Steve Nance and John Muggleton. Rod worked well with John O'Neill, who in turn had the foresight to recruit Jeff Miller, whom I thought played a very big role during the World Cup period. Nance copped some criticism late last year but my response is simply to tell people to look at the scoreboard. He made hard training seem okay. When you have 30 players and 12 staff, training isn't going to suit everyone. You do your best for the group because the team always comes first over the individual. Everyone has to be treated equally.

As for Eddie Jones, I have no doubt he is the best-prepared coach ever to come into the position, a direct result of professional rugby. At the same time, Australian rugby is not overendowed with elite coaches at the moment, which is why the ARU is trying to bring others up to speed as quickly as possible.

To my mind, what Eddie needs is people constantly challenging him – because, as Greg Smith found out, it's very hard to do it all by yourself. Like Rod Macqueen, Eddie has experienced his back-to-earth Wallaby tour and now appreciates how hard it really is at the top. Unlike Super 12 matches, when you play a Test match you're playing for your life – not for a bonus point or a second chance the following week. In a Test series, everything's on the table every time you take the field.

From a purely personal standpoint, to be part of the Wallaby team, travelling around the world playing rugby, being an ambassador for your country – it really doesn't get any better.

John Mackay was Wallaby manager from 1997 to 2001, the most successful era in Australian rugby history. He stepped down after the historic series win over the Lions and is now CEO of Waratah Rugby.

Super 12 – the teams

Super 12 begins each year in late February and continues until the end of May. The tournament started in 1996 and features the leading provincial squads from Australia, New Zealand and South Africa. A feature of the tournament is the incentive of bonus points. Teams can gain an extra point by scoring at least four tries in one game and/or losing by seven points or less.

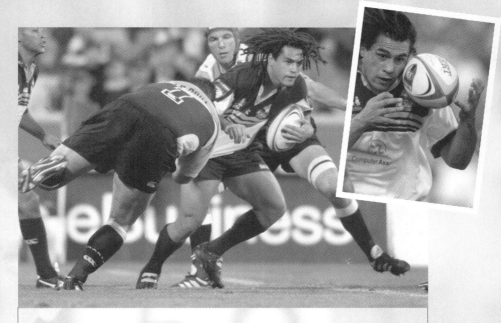

Australia

ACT Brumbies – based in Canberra; winners in 2001.

QLD Reds – Brisbane; 3rd in 1996 and 1999.

NSW Waratahs – Sydney; best finish: 3rd in 2002.

New Zealand

Blues – based in Auckland; winners in 1996 and 1997.

Chiefs – the Waikato; best finish: 6th in 1996, 1999 and 2001.

Crusaders – Christchurch; winners in 1998, 1999 and 2000.

Highlanders – Dunedin; best finish: runner-up 1999.

Hurricanes – Wellington; best finish: 3rd in 1997.

South Africa

Bulls – based in Pretoria; best finish: 4th in 1996 (as North Transvaal).

Cats – Johannesburg; best finish: 3rd in 2000.

Sharks – Durban; best finish: runner-up in 1996 and 2001.

Stormers – Cape Town; best finish: 4th in 1999.

Matt Gray

Women also rule

The rise and rise of female rugby

'Women's rugby has battled perception problems in some sections of the rugby community. Critics say the sport is not a game for women, but I think those numbers are dwindling. People are being converted when they see what our female athletes can do.'

— Bob Hitchcock, Wallaroos coach 1995–98

How presumptuous of those rugby establishment diehards to assume that 'the game played in heaven' is an exclusive male domain. Women's rugby has recently enjoyed a world-wide explosion and is now recognised as one of the fastest-growing international sports.

In Australia, women's rugby dates from the Second World War, when the game was played in small pockets throughout country New South Wales. At the end of the war, as the men returned from abroad, the female game dwindled and eventually nodded off into a 50-year slumber. Women's rugby was played on a minor scale in colleges and universities but it wasn't until the 1990s that the game developed its current remarkable popularity.

Joan Forno, president of Australia Women's Rugby, explains how the modern game was resurrected. 'Touch football became quite popular with women. From that interest a Newcastle fellow named Wal Fitzgerald came up with the idea in the early nineties of having a long weekend in June and inviting some of the girls who were playing touch to take part in 15s. It was a direct response to several complaints about a lack of women's rugby teams. Initially six teams took part and the matches were quite good despite the players' lack of technique. They were very good at running, but their tackling wasn't particularly great and their scrummaging was terrible.

'From that point women suddenly wanted to play rugby and the message grew rapidly. There were teams springing up all over the country. The following June long-weekend competition had 12 teams participating, including two sides from New Zealand. The game really took off from there.'

Club and state sides quickly emerged and more regular competitions developed. In 1993, at the invitation of the New Zealanders, Australia formed a national women's side for the first time. Across the Tasman women had been playing rugby for more than 15 years, so the Australians faced a tough initiation. That first game against the Kiwis proved to be as hard as expected and the Australians were defeated handsomely. Despite the drubbing, a touring party was formed the next year for a three-week campaign in New Zealand. Since that visit, annual scheduled games have been organised between the Silver Ferns and the Australians.

The establishment of regular international competition meant choosing a name for the national team. Perhaps in recognition of their Wallaby rugby brothers, the women chose the name 'Wallaroos', after a marsupial of the same family as the wallaby and kangaroo. Although there are many different types of wallaroos, they are typically much smaller than a kangaroo but slightly bigger than a wallaby. They have bare muzzles and are known for their relatively large ears.

It is not widely known that, at the same time, the Australian women's hockey team was going through the process of picking a name. Amazingly, they too chose 'Wallaroos' but the matter was eventually resolved when the hockey team yielded. They went on to become the Hockeyroos, a name they have successfully used on the way to winning two consecutive Olympic gold medals.

While more and more women were playing rugby in Australia by the mid-1990s, the organisation and infrastructure left a lot to be desired. In 1995 Bob Hitchcock was appointed as national coach in the women's game. He brought a rich background in coaching at both under-age and senior level. Bob had coached the ACT senior side, the Australian President's XV and the Australian Under 21s and was also the inaugural coach of the Emerging Wallabies. He proved to be the ideal man for the job. Recalling those early days in women's rugby, he says, 'When I came in at the national level in the mid-1990s I saw the need to have a national championship as there was a mixture of state sides and club sides and things like that. In those early days the skill level wasn't high. The enthusiasm has always been there, but there were only small numbers playing.

'Over the years we've seen a dramatic change in the appreciation of the game. I think women certainly know more about rugby these days. They are far more athletic in their application and are starting to understand what's required to be at the elite end of the sport. Numbers are still not what we'd like, but that's an issue the Australian Rugby Union is tackling in earnest. One of the difficulties is that women's rugby is not a traditional game and therefore has no stocks of resources to draw upon, mums and dads and people who can help out to administer the game – many of the girls who are playing also have to be involved in the administration side. There are also problems with some sections of the rugby community who say it's not a game for women, but I think those numbers are dwindling and people are being converted when they see what our athletes can do.'

Women's rugby in Australia saw a real breakthrough with the establishment of national championships in the mid-1990s. Hitchcock describes this development as a landmark in the women's game. 'I think there was a fairly significant advance when we went to a state-level national championship. This changed the structure from a mixture of state and clubs to a regular state system every year. It was implemented by the ARU, recognising that if we were going to play regular

> ## A command performance
>
> Meaghan Roach, captain of Newcastle High back in 1996, was one of four classical ballet dancers who played in the school's state champion female rugby team. Commenting on an early-season training collision with fellow dancer and school vice-captain Alexandra McGarvie, she recalls, 'We both went in for a tackle and clashed heads. Alex lost her four front teeth and I finished up with a big scar on my forehead. But that's football, isn't it?'

matches at the international level we were going to have to implement the right preparation.

'The national championships were moved around to the various capitals, national squads were chosen and we traditionally played New Zealand. Another opportunity emerged to play the USA when they came "down under". The contested scrummaging had to be addressed, and it was important that the best people were on display.'

By 1998 women's rugby in Australian was well established and the Wallaroos were ready for their first big test, the World Cup. The progress made in only the previous few years in Australia had been achieved many years earlier in other countries. Australia was the youngest rugby-playing country at the 1998 World Cup (won by New Zealand) and aside from playing regular games with New Zealand, they hadn't played on the international rugby circuit. Hitchcock, who coached the Wallaroos at that first World Cup, reflects on the strength of the women's game internationally.

'It has long been strong in England and the other Home Countries. England is especially organised. They receive a lot of money through their new sporting subsidy structure and picked up former Wallaby full-back and AIS coach Geoff Richards, and ex-NSW development officer Rob Drinkwater. They have the financial backing and the depth of players and that's why they will always be very difficult to beat.

'The game is strong in the other Home Countries as well because they compete in a regular six-nations tournament involving England, Ireland, Wales, Scotland, Spain and France. So they get the opportunity to play each other regularly and obviously the cost factor is not so high and they have a bigger player base. Women's rugby has also been very

OPPOSITE *The Wallaroos met their match in 2001 against England. Here Australian full-back Bronwyn Laidlaw is about to get an unwanted taste of the T.G. Millner turf in Sydney during the 19–41 loss in the First Test.*

strong in the US college system – there are more female players in America than male participants in Australia. Sixteen nations take part in the World Cup. Canada and the States are both former world champions. Then there is New Zealand, which has won World Cups and except for one loss in 2001 has rarely been beaten. The game isn't just played in the traditional rugby countries. Women play in the Netherlands, Sweden, Germany, Russia and Kazakhstan. When we last played Kazakhstan they were a very tall and physically big side yet still very athletic as a lot of them are in the armed services.'

Someone must have forgotten to tell the Wallaroos exactly how hard the task of playing these more experienced nations should have been. Wins against Ireland, France and Spain enabled our team to finish fifth in their first World Cup after taking out the Plate Final by defeating Scotland. The women played some brilliant rugby and finished well above many people's expectations.

The positive effect back home following the 1998 World Cup was tremendous, with more and more women taking up the game. Joan Forno explains that the big area of recent growth has been in the school system. 'We're hoping that the aftermath of the 2002 World Cup in Spain will increase awareness of the game. We certainly saw major growth in the sport after the 1998 World Cup. The really startling expansion has taken place in the schools. Each year secondary schools compete in the Dick Shaw Shield, held annually in Sydney. In its first year there were about 75 teams. The next year over 150 entered and that trend has continued. The game is also taking off in rural Australia. The Hunter region has a schools competition involving over 20 teams.'

With this growth in numbers there has understandably been a significant improvement in the skill levels of the women. They have also developed their own style of play, which involves a lot of ball movement and an entertaining brand of running rugby without anywhere near the level of kicking found in the men's game. Commensurate with the on-field improvement, the game has earned heightened levels of appreciation and respect from the general rugby community. Hitchcock assesses the skill levels in the game and the reaction of sceptics after they've seen the quality of women's play. 'Firstly, the most important thing is that the girls are far more athletic now than they were five or six years ago – they have to be. The second part of it is that they are starting to understand what the game is about and the skill level is reflected in that. The third reason the skills are improving is that the girls really work hard at them. Because they're new to the game they listen a lot more. This contrasts with guys, many of whom have been playing since the under 8s. It's a new sport for the girls and they've adapted to it extremely well.

'They don't shy away from the physical nature of rugby but they do play it quite differently. They like to pass and run the ball and hence their ball-retention skills have improved. We're getting much more running rugby than we had before. In the early days it was marked by scrums; it was basically "scrum, scrum, scrum". But the skill level has improved and the game is now far more exciting.

'I think the girls have demonstrated to the sceptics that they know how to catch and pass and tackle. They have shown that they understand the strategic areas of ball retention and ball usage. They're playing their own brand of football, but it has less kicking in it and a bit more ball movement. It will get even better as their ball-retention skills improve.'

The stronghold of the women's game has always been New South Wales, which is where the majority of players and clubs are situated. Queensland also has a strong and skilful group of players, while the ACT has been very competitive. The non-traditional rugby states have always managed to put teams on the field, but with varying results. The team that has shown the most improvement recently is the Combined Services side. Victoria, Western Australia and South Australia have also improved recently and the Northern Territory was one of the inaugural national champions.

Women's rugby numbers are still low and, like many other Australian sports at present, the enthusiasts are facing a constant battle for finances. Not being able to attract paying gates is a major factor, and they must compete with a plethora of other minor sports for the sponsorship dollar. Breaking the common misconception that rugby isn't a game for women is half the battle. It's hard enough to convince many mothers that rugby is a safe game for their sons, let alone their daughters.

Women and men play and enjoy the game for exactly the same reasons. The sense of team spirit and camaraderie that marks male rugby also exists in the women's game, and slowly a tradition is building. It's also one of the few physical contact sports available to females. Joan Forno has firm views on the 'danger factor' for women and explains that the women's game is played in a far more 'placid' way than the men's version. 'Women's rugby is basically only ten years old in Australia and, like men's rugby (which has been around for over 100 years), some parents still think it's dangerous for children to play. I always say it's a kinder, gentler form of rugby that women play on the pitch.

'I always remember Mark Ella's words after a Test match we played against New Zealand. He said the girls were very technically correct in their game; they didn't try to outsmart the referee, there were no elbows coming up from the side or any dirty tactics. They played it in the spirit of wanting to win, but not at any cost.

'The reason women play the sport is because they see how much the men enjoy it. You ask any girl why she plays and she'll say it's for the fun of being out there with a group of girls. It's the camaraderie they derive from it.'

So what does the future hold for the women's game? The ARU managing director, John O'Neill, believes the game will develop strongly, with the key objective being to build the player base in the junior ranks and at club level. 'Women's rugby has enormous potential, and this is recognised with the Wallaroos taking part in their second World Cup campaign in Spain in 2002. The future of women's rugby lies with grass-roots development. We need to lift the player base, which remains small. The ARU now employs full-time staff with responsibility for women's rugby, so we're confident we can move forward with an action plan to lift participation among women. Girls compete in knockout carnivals, but that's not translating into participation as adults. That's the challenge for us in the future.'

When legendary wit Dr Samuel Johnson first saw a woman preaching, he remarked, 'It is like a dog walking on its hinder legs. It is not done well, but you are surprised to find it done at all.' Women's rugby has already come a long way from that stage. If growth rates can be sustained at the same levels as the first ten years, the female game has a rosy future.

Matt Gray is an associate rugby producer with the Seven Network, a rugby researcher and a statistician.

Did you know?

William Gilbert manufactured the first official Rugby School football in 1851. A distinctive oval shape, the ball was actually an inflated pig's bladder and was easily distinguished from its equivalent in the round-ball code. Needless to say, that original shape and the Gilbert name are still going strong

It's a woman's world

That discarded rugby marketing slogan 'It's gonna get you!' has particular significance for NSW Women's Rugby president Amanda Lingwood.

The former Hawkesbury Agricultural College student caught the rugby bug while acting as strapper and trainer for the college's 1st XV. 'I just got sick of being on the sidelines,' she reveals. There's no question that the spirit of William Webb Ellis is firmly embedded in some ancient branch of Amanda's family tree. During the Second World War, her grandmother and five sisters founded the West Tamworth Women's Rugby Team to help raise the funds that eventually built the Tamworth Base Hospital. An eye-catching lot they were, too, posing for their first team photo (below) in rugby strip – supplemented by matching shower caps and even some high-heeled shoes.

Richard Graham

Sevens heaven

The magic of seven-a-side rugby

*'Back to thy punishment, False fugitive, and to
thy speed add wings.'*

— John Milton

An Australian sports journalist once compared the newly created international Sevens circuit to that of a travelling circus. Introduced by the Scottish in 1883 when one team failed to turn up, the game of Sevens has gone from strength to strength. It launched the magnificent careers of Wallaby captain George Gregan and his teammates Joe Roff and Ben Tune. Across the Tasman, the abbreviated game triggered the emergence of such superstars as Christian Cullen and Jonah Lomu.

Sevens is not, and never will be, a substitute for the 15-a-side game. Both have their own identity. However, the famous Hong Kong Sevens tournament can certainly take credit for revitalising many of the skills of the longer game. Renowned for its quality rugby, larrikinism and carnival atmosphere, the annual three-day Honkers tournament began in 1976 in a city more famous for its skyline than its rugby. Its subsequent success has given Sevens a genuine global prominence in the 21st century. Twenty-six years after the first tournament, Sevens rugby has achieved incredible success, including three World Cups, unprecedented acceptance and a rapidly developing global support base. As a result, the shortened game is now a massive marketing tool for nations that don't include rugby among their top sports. Most 15-a-side international matches between developing countries don't even rate a mention in their local papers. But put a team on the international circuit against such stars as Roff, Gregan and Tune and suddenly the media becomes interested.

It may have taken the International Rugby Board a little longer to realise what everyone else already knew, but finally in 1999 they launched the World Series of Sevens, to be contested over 12 tournaments. The World Series incorporates the established tournaments of Hong Kong, Dubai, Argentina and Uruguay with new locations such as Australia, New Zealand, Malaysia, China, South Africa, England and Wales.

Life on the Sevens circuit is a demanding and full-time profession. While a number of the players are college students or casually employed, it can be hard to maintain a normal lifestyle during the season. For example, over a six-month period during the 2000–01 season, the Australian side was either in camp training, travelling, living overseas or playing for at least 140 days. While that may sound more arduous than enjoyable, please don't get the wrong idea. Australian Sevens players experience more in a season than most would in a lifetime. The tours have filled my passport twice over, provided me with the opportunity to visit exotic and not-so-exotic destinations, and introduced me to friends in every corner of the globe.

In recent years Australia has used the Sevens circuit as a development phase for identifying talent and blooding players on the international stage. The return for the Australian Rugby Union is that, one day, these players might play Super 12 or even for the Wallabies. Coaches can assess the ability of players to handle the intense pressure experienced in front of 40 000 people on a regular basis. Moments of sheer brilliance or acts of madness can make or break a player in this environment. Bear in mind that not every good Sevens exponent makes a great 15-a-side player, and vice versa. Possibly the two biggest stars of the game, Eric Rush and Waisale Serevi, have never achieved success in 'real' rugby.

Because of a crossover with Super 12 and the Northern Hemisphere season, the World Series of Sevens rarely fields household names. The New Zealanders use international stars such as Jonah Lomu and Christian Cullen whenever possible, the French and Argentinian sides field Test players sparingly, and Fijian stars such as Canterbury winger Maraika Vunibaka can no longer play whenever and wherever they wish.

I have now played in about 30 international Sevens tournaments and I've had my fair share of ups and downs, laughter and despair – and amassed a large number of frequent flyer points with various airlines. During that time three tournaments stand out above all others: Hong Kong, Argentina and the 1998 Commonwealth Games in Malaysia. Each has its own unique culture, atmosphere and memories.

Trying to convey the drama and guaranteed theatre of an

international Sevens tournament to the uninitiated can be a difficult exercise. Short grab tackles, blinding skills, loping strides – all at frenetic pace and providing value far beyond the price of admission. As a regular member of the Australian squad I already have scores of stand-out memories to savour forever. For starters, I got engaged to be married in Hong Kong!

For the players, Hong Kong is the ultimate: three days of football, a state-of-the-art stadium, 40 000 wild fans, the 'pie man' and a 24/7 social life. As an Australian in Hong Kong, another piece of history makes it special too. Since the early 1980s, whenever an Australian side enters the playing arena, the crowd boos in unison. *Everyone* is against you.

Argentina is enjoyable for many different reasons. The Australian team lives in Mar Del Plata, a coastal town that trebles in size during the summer break. The people are completely uninhibited and show their passion all the time. It's a poor country, which allows us the opportunity to give the people small gifts of things they could never normally afford. The unique culture of South America means that people eat dinner around 10 or 11 p.m. – and quite a few of our games are still going at 1 or 2 a.m.! If you've ever seen a South American soccer game you'll understand when I say the support from the fans is unlike anything you can witness in Australia. Guards with machine guns and a moat surrounding the field protect the players from dancing, fire-cracker-wielding, adrenaline-charged supporters.

The Commonwealth Games added a whole new dimension to rugby. Team sports weren't part of the Games until 1998, when Sevens paved the way for our sport to gain more exposure on the international stage, along with cricket and

2002 EDITION

The Official Sports Drink of the Wallabies

POWERĀDE

Wallabies®

WALLABY GOLD RUSH

THIRST QUENCHER

POWERED BY 'POWERĀDE'®

Fly Half

Full Back

Lock

Blindside Flyer

Inside Centre

Wing

Prop

Hooker

Flanker

Ford Australia – Official Sponsor of the Wallabies

Wallabies

www.ford.com.au

We have ignition

netball. We not only had the chance to win a medal but also to meet superstars such as Steve and Mark Waugh, Viv Richards, Kieren Perkins, Ato Boldon and Frankie Fredericks. Never before had we mixed with other team sports or associated ourselves with individual athletes. Marching with 400 Australian athletes in front of a crowd of 100 000 is an experience I'll never forget.

Richard Graham has been Australia's Sevens captain for three years. In 2001 he played full-back for Australia A against the touring Lions at Gosford. He is also a member of the Queensland Super 12 squad.

Did you know?

Former US president Bill Clinton was introduced to rugby as a Rhodes scholar at Oxford, where he was described as a 'handy and enthusiastic second-rower'. After returning home to Arkansas, the future president dutifully turned out for Little Rock Rugby Club.

Richard Graham's Sevens strategy

The early style of Sevens rugby was simple: impersonate the principles of XVs, that is, pick big men and outmuscle the rest. It wasn't until the late 1980s that Sevens rugby changed – when Campese, Serevi and the Ella twins began to weave their wizardry.

Today, Sevens bears little resemblance to its early predecessors. Maximum fitness levels, great agility, pure speed and mercurial handling skills are all essential parts of the abbreviated game. While the general principle – 'Keep the ball for longer than the opposition and you'll probably win' – is still true, defence has now become the all-important aspect. A structured defensive line that can continually pressure the opposition often leads to turnovers and easy tries. It is this structure that has seen a vast improvement by the lesser nations such as Korea and Croatia.

All-time seven-a-side superstars
1. **Waisale Serevi** (Fiji)
2. **David Campese** (Australia)
3. **Eric Rush** (New Zealand)

Thrills and spills in Hong Kong, the home of Sevens rugby. Seven-a-side superstar Eric Rush (top) celebrates yet anoher trophy success in 1994. Kiwi captain Rush forged a magnificent partnership with coach Gordon Tietjens (behind), ensuring NZ's domination of the World Sevens circuit over recent years.

Yes, but what does it all mean?

Wayne Erickson explains some of the things you might hear from the referee during a match telecast.

Advantage   A knock-on, offside, high tackle or some other turnover infringement occurs. The referee can then let the other team try to gain 'advantage' from the possession they've been handed. Signalled by holding one arm horizontally and pointing towards the team receiving the advantage.

Hindmost foot, or 'last feet'   The law that establishes the offside line when both sides are engaged. An imaginary line drawn across the field through the last feet of the last player in the ruck/maul/scrum is the offside line for all other players.

Maul   When a ball carrier is held in a standing tackle and one of his teammates binds onto him and the tackler, a maul is formed. Essentially, the players involved are on their feet and the ball is in possession off the ground. Other players usually join in, and if the ball doesn't come out, the scrum feed goes to the team that *didn't* have possession when the maul was initially formed.

Offside   Any player in front of a teammate who has the ball, or who last played the ball, is offside and might be penalised if he interferes with play.

Ruck   A ruck occurs after a tackle when at least one player from each team, on his feet, makes contact over the ball. In the case of a ruck, the ball is usually on the ground or in the process of being released or played by the tackled player, who must do so immediately. Players using their hands to secure the ball must stop when the ruck is formed, or they might be penalised for 'hands in the ruck'.

Binding, or 'stay bound'   Players in a scrum/ruck/maul have to bind with at least one whole arm around the body of another player, and they can't drive into the side of the ruck/maul.

Professional foul   In effect, this is a deliberate infringement usually committed to deny the other team quick, valuable possession, and should normally result in a 'sin-bin' and occasionally a penalty try.

Gap   At the line-out, the referee tries to ensure that opponents stay at least 1 metre away from each other *until the ball is thrown in*. Most problems at line-out occur when the gap is illegally closed by players from the team not throwing the ball in.

Collapsing   In open play, players try to bring the ball carrier to the ground, but when a structure such as a ruck/maul/scrum has been formed, it is dangerous to attempt to collapse it or bring it to the ground. Collapsing is a penalty offence and can also result in a 'sin-bin'.

A Tri Nations clash with the Springboks is always extremely physical. Here Wallaby number 8 Toutai Kefu is greeted by a South African 'headshrinker'. Tackles must be effected below the level of the shoulders, so clearly this one should have been penalised as both high and dangerous.

Murray Deaker

Rugby and the media

Calling a spade a shovel, from across the ditch

'With regard to modern journalists, they always apologise to one in private for what they have written against one in public.'

– Oscar Wilde

The media's role is to inform the public about what is happening in the world of rugby in an interesting and entertaining way. If it is not entertaining, the viewer won't watch, the listener will tune out and the reader will turn to another article in the newspaper or magazine. The end result is that the information is not given to the public and rugby suffers.

Professional rugby could not survive without the media. At the same time, a large proportion of the sporting journalists assigned to cover rugby matches depend on the game for their living. You would think that such a level of mutual dependence might foster understanding, cordiality, directness and honesty. Rarely is that the case and, sadly, the opposite is too often true.

With the advent of professionalism, the situation has worsened rather than improved. The players are now surrounded by management teams of ever-increasing size. Most

Rugby and the media

of these team officials seem anxious to prove that there really is a need for their particular position – not only to exist, but also to be given more resources, power, money and people. Already we are seeing rugby unions with two media liaison officers. The day is not long away when we will have an assistant media officer to the assistant media officer! They are on the gravy train and there is no way they're going to get off.

In the old days a journo would work on building up relationships with the players or the coach. Prior to the World Cup of 1991 it was easy to get hold of players like Sean Fitzpatrick, Buck Shelford, Grant Fox or Alan Whetton: you simply picked up the phone and rang them. If they didn't want to speak they told you, but usually you'd get your quote immediately.

That was before the days of the media liaison officer. Presumably such a position was created to help bring the media and the players together. Nothing could be further from the truth. The MLO is paid by the rugby union and the old proverb, 'Whoever pays the piper calls the tune', certainly applies. When a coach, team or player is doing badly, the MLO becomes the MPO – Media Prevention Officer. If the journalist has written or said something critical about that team, it's likely that the only person 'on limits' to the writer will be the MPO. No one enjoys criticism, but despite all the management teams of advisers, the modern rugby player is more 'precious' than his predecessor. He would argue that he has more to lose – money, that is.

Which brings us to the real issue facing today's journalist. The public in New Zealand is aware that most All Blacks earn ten times the national average wage. Consequently, their expectations of the players have changed. Before professionalism, if a goal kicker missed a penalty it was dismissed as 'bad luck'. Now it's more likely to be greeted with, 'These jokers are paid big money and should get over a kick a primary school kid would make.' With the big money have come higher public expectations, sharper analysis and less tolerance. The journalist is faced with the dilemma of whether he is reporting on a game or a business.

Most rugby fans want to preserve the ethos and culture of the game – the 'playing for the jersey', 'giving your guts' every time you run onto the paddock. As well, they cling to the local, provincial and national rivalries. For them it is still a game. But for many administrators it is now more a business, with the bottom line dominating their actions. They may profess to be doing their best for 'the good of the game' but increasingly they talk about franchises, salary caps and sponsorship – not rucks, mauls, tackles and line-outs. I've even heard some of the marketing gurus around the NZRFU refer to the game as 'the product'.

There are further complicating factors. Most of the journalists covering rugby are used to covering the game but totally inept at reporting business. Secondly, the most powerful component of the media, television, is responsible (through payment of broadcasting rights fees) for keeping that business going. The potential for conflict of interest and management pressure on editorial independence is obvious. Television reporters have always received preferential treatment over other media members; it may only be a short time before their bosses start telling them what they can and can't report in the interests of 'growing the product'. When that happens, television will really control the game.

Before television, radio and newspaper reporters were much more powerful. Sir Terry McLean, the doyen of New Zealand print journalists, often tells the story of travelling for miles on a bus in the country passing dozens of letter-boxes with *Herald* delivery signs on them. It reminded him that the farmers whose papers were delivered into those boxes relied on him each Monday to describe in the newspaper what had happened in Saturday's game. Today there would be little point in him writing a descriptive piece because all of those farmers would have watched the game on television from the comfort of their own couch.

It's equally unlikely that we will ever see another radio commentator assume the importance of Winston McCarthy. No matter how vivid, emotional, informative and exciting his broadcasts were, they simply couldn't have competed with television. Those of us working predominantly in radio like to kid ourselves that we can beat TV to the stories, but the reality is that most fans form their views from what they see and hear on television. Radio talkback largely follows television. Most callers base their knowledge of the game on what they saw or heard on the box.

Television is all-powerful. If a player spits while on it, doesn't sing the national anthem when the camera pans onto him, stutters during the post-match interview, looks too grumpy, or shows too much emotion after scoring a try, he is just as liable to be ripped to pieces by talkback callers as if he missed a penalty right in front to win the World Cup. That 'big eye' sees everything and turns couch potatoes who have never been to a game (let alone played it) into world authorities.

Despite that, the stars should still always be the players.

Not the coaches, not the selectors, not the managers – the players. In more than a decade of attending rugby press conferences I have never seen a player present himself with real 'star quality'. Perhaps that is because players are usually accompanied to press conferences by coaches and selectors. The coach takes centre stage and the player has the bit role.

We in the media have contributed to the development of this 'cult of the coach' by directing most of our questions to the coach. Rugby will have found a new level when a press conference is held after a Test match featuring only the captain and his deputy. You can bet your size 11 boots, studs and all, that the team that does that will have won the game, because most of the important decisions will have been made on the field, not off it.

Some years ago the NRL introduced a player induction program that included detailed training in media skills and public presentation. Unquestionably it has resulted in an improved standard of performance in all branches of the media by many league players. Some rugby union players have also benefited from similar training. Others are naturals. Todd Blackadder handled the media as well as any other rugby player I've seen. His performances were honest, direct, straight and concise and natural (yet measured) and led not only to increased personal support for Todd but also growing support for his Canterbury and Crusader teams.

Perhaps the best illustration of the way an effective media policy can assist a team's performance came at the 1991 World Cup. The All Blacks were favourites to retain the title they'd won in 1987 but their perceived arrogance, combined with their inability to handle the media, eventually meant they antagonised the public. The Wallabies were open and

OPPOSITE *John Eales and Matthew Burke share a laugh with the media (above), and a small army of British photographers capture the moment following Australia's 2001 series win over the Lions.*

available to all, winning media approval and consequently becoming the darlings of the public. By the time the two teams ran on to play their semifinal at Lansdowne Road in Dublin, the Wallabies had won over the crowd to such an extent that they may as well have been playing at the Sydney Football Stadium. An effective media policy had given them a 'home' advantage.

Surprisingly, I have generally found Australian rugby teams more cooperative to deal with than the New Zealand sides – surprising because there is no real benefit for the Wallabies in making themselves available to a New Zealand radio and television broadcaster. The Brumbies, for example, have been a dream to deal with. I once arranged to interview five of them in Hamilton for my television show. When I arrived at their hotel they were ready and waiting and just 40 minutes later I was back on the road to Auckland with five separate interviews in the can.

The most media-savvy New Zealand rugby team I've dealt with were the All Blacks of 1996 and 1997. This was orchestrated by coach John Hart and administered by media liaison officer Jane Dent. A lot of criticism has been directed at John for the All Black losses in 1998 and 1999, but no one should ever doubt his ability to deal with the media in his first two years as coach. People may have forgotten the interviews, articles and photos they were able to enjoy as a result of Hart's open dealing with the media at that time.

Rugby is so dominant in New Zealand that officialdom can afford to treat the media, and indeed the public, with arrogance. In Australia, where union fights league, Rules and soccer for coverage, the attitude is entirely different. Perhaps one spin-off from the growth of individual sports in

New Zealand and the decline in numbers playing the game will be an improvement in the relationship between rugby and the media. They should go together like bacon and eggs. Sadly, there are times they're more like chalk and cheese.

Murray Deaker is acknowledged as the voice of New Zealand sport. The popular, often outspoken radio talkback host has won numerous awards, including NZ Sports Broadcaster of the Year. He hosts his own weekly national TV sports show and is the author of the bestselling book The Man in the Glass.

Did you know?

Legendary horror-movie actor Boris Karloff was a passionate rugby man. Details of his playing career are sketchy, but it is known that at one stage he was secretary of the Southern Californian RU.

The Bledisloe Cup

The Bledisloe Cup has symbolised rugby supremacy between Australia and New Zealand since Lord Bledisloe, Governor-General of New Zealand, donated the trophy in 1931. The huge solid-silver cup has since become one of the most recognisable and sought-after trophies in trans-Tasman sports.

The initial Bledisloe Cup game was held on Australia's tour of New Zealand in 1931, when the All Blacks triumphed 20–13 in Auckland. The Wallabies captured the Cup for the first time in a two-match series in 1934. They won the first game in front of 40 000 spectators in Sydney and then drew the second Test. Trevor Allan's Wallabies again won the Cup on their historic 1949 tour of New Zealand, but the big trophy then eluded the Australians for an incredible 30 years. It wasn't until 1979 that they again drank from the mug.

Part of the unique appeal of the Cup is that it has had no fixed format. Bledisloe competitions have varied from one to three Tests, sometimes with a three- or four-year gap between series. However, in 1982 both countries agreed that at least one Bledisloe Cup Test would be held annually. In 1996 Tri Nations matches were incorporated within the Bledisloe Cup (or perhaps it is the other way around!).

Up to 2002 the Cup had been contested on 43 occasions. New Zealand had won or retained the Cup 32 times and Australia just 11. A total of 97 Bledisloe Tests had been played, with New Zealand winning 65, Australia winning 28, and four nail-biting draws.

Prior to 1979 New Zealand had a stranglehold on the Cup, winning 19 of the first 21 contests, but since then the competition has been much more even, with Australia on nine victories against New Zealand's 13. Many see the 1978 series in New Zealand as a turning point in Australia's Bledisloe Cup fortunes. After losing the first two Tests in Wellington and Christchurch, they faced another series whitewash. Confounding their critics, the Wallabies then pulled off a famous triumph in Auckland, downing the All Blacks 30–16. That remarkable game is best remembered for the incredible tally of four tries scored by Greg Cornelsen.

The Bledisloe Cup returns to Australian soil after a lengthy absence. Paul McLean (left) and skipper Mark Loane carry the old trophy on a lap of honour at the SCG in 1979. Victorious coach Dave Brockhoff (centre background) joined the on-field celebrations after the famous win.

Bledisloe Cup results since 1979

Year	Winner	Score	Venue	Cup holder
1979	Australia	12–6	Sydney	**Australia**
1980	Australia	13–9	Sydney	
1980	New Zealand	12–9	Brisbane	
1980	Australia	26–10	Sydney	**Australia**
1982	New Zealand	23–16	Christchurch	
1982	Australia	19–16	Wellington	
1982	New Zealand	33–18	Auckland	**New Zealand**
1983	New Zealand	18–8	Sydney	**New Zealand**
1984	Australia	16–9	Sydney	
1984	New Zealand	19–15	Brisbane	
1984	New Zealand	25–24	Sydney	**New Zealand**
1985	New Zealand	10–9	Auckland	**New Zealand**
1986	Australia	13–12	Wellington	
1986	New Zealand	13–12	Dunedin	
1986	Australia	22–9	Auckland	**Australia**
1987	New Zealand	30–16	Sydney	**New Zealand**
1988	New Zealand	32–7	Sydney	
1988	Drawn	19–19	Brisbane	
1988	New Zealand	30–9	Sydney	**New Zealand**
1989	New Zealand	24–12	Auckland	**New Zealand**
1990	New Zealand	21–6	Christchurch	
1990	New Zealand	27–17	Auckland	
1990	Australia	21–9	Wellington	**New Zealand**
1991	Australia	21–12	Sydney	
1991	New Zealand	6–3	Auckland	**New Zealand**
1992	Australia	16–15	Sydney	
1992	Australia	19–17	Brisbane	
1992	New Zealand	26–23	Sydney	**Australia**
1993	New Zealand	25–10	Dunedin	**New Zealand**
1994	Australia	20–16	Sydney	**Australia**

BUNDY.® PROUDLY SUPPORTING THE WALLABIES

Bundaberg Rum encourages responsible alcohol consumption

Bundaberg RUM ™

RUGBY SERIES

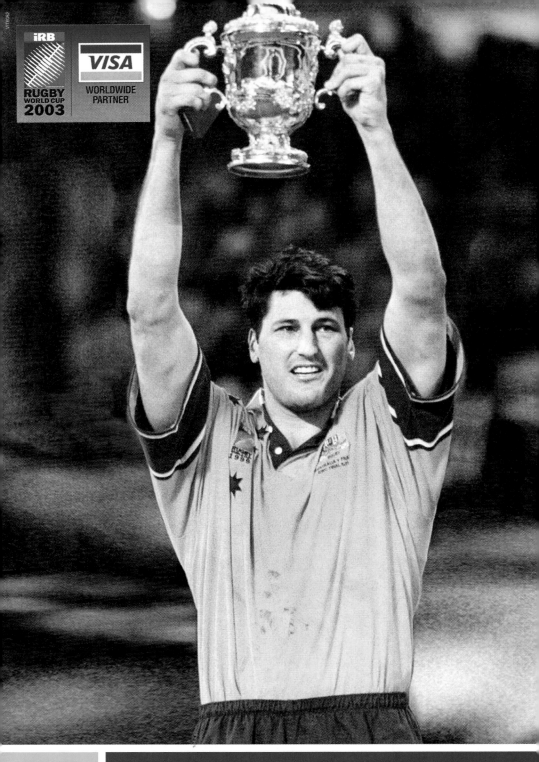

1995	New Zealand	28–16	Auckland	
1995	New Zealand	34–23	Sydney	**New Zealand**
1996	New Zealand	43–6	Wellington	
1996	New Zealand	32–25	Brisbane	**New Zealand**
1997	New Zealand	30–13	Christchurch	
1997	New Zealand	33–18	Melbourne	
1997	New Zealand	36–24	Dunedin	**New Zealand**
1998	Australia	24–16	Melbourne	
1998	Australia	27–23	Christchurch	
1998	Australia	19–14	Sydney	**Australia**
1999	New Zealand	34–15	Auckland	
1999	Australia	28–7	Sydney	**Australia**
2000	New Zealand	39–35	Sydney	
2000	Australia	24–23	Wellington	**Australia**
2001	Australia	23–15	Dunedin	
2001	Australia	29–26	Sydney	**Australia**

Never too rusty

There comes a time when even club loyalty has to go out the window.

In 1996 Gordon's 6th grade were a prop short for their game against Manly. So, in a truly sporting gesture, Manly's player-coach Russell 'Rusty' Mackie (below) swapped his beloved red-and-blue jumper for the Gordon strip and packed down with the Highlanders. To make matters worse, Russell then proceeded to score a try against his own team and help Gordon to a 23–0 lead.

Now that really was a bit rich, especially when Mackie had played 26 straight seasons and around 700 club games for the Seasiders.

But the story has a happy ending. Manly stormed home to snatch a dramatic 24–23 win, and the club management still had the good grace to reaffirm Rusty's shaky tenure on the 6th-grade coaching position.

The following season, our hero was acting as touch judge in a social game when a player was tackled over the touch-line, smashing Rusty's knee almost beyond recognition. A builder by trade, he was forced to be off work for 12 months but had not taken out loss-of-earnings insurance. Club members rallied and a benefit night helped ease Rusty's considerable pain.

Rugby is special.

Part 3
Tools of the trade

PREVIOUS PAGE *The original ABC outside-broadcast 'Pye' van was built in England and shipped to Australia for the 1956 Olympics in Melbourne. It was also used to transmit the first pictures of a rugby match in Australia.*

A strange and superstitious lot

Early last century, the wearing of hats and caps by players during matches was acceptable practice. P.V.J. MacNamara of Pirates (and, later, Eastern Suburbs) always wore an old brown hat on his head and a handkerchief scarf around his neck. The fact that this made him look more like the local 'Rabbitoh' than a rugby player seems not to have bothered either him or the crowd.

Jimmy Duncan, the famous All Black captain of that era, was another to sport distinctive headgear on the field. He always wore a woollen cap to cover his bald pate. Imagine the roar from the SCG Hill the day a NSW player snatched it from his carefully protected dome in a tackle. Such indignities were rare, however, despite the fervour and zeal of Duncan's on-field commitment.

Many sportsmen are superstitious. Form can be such an elusive quality that players fear changing *anything*, no matter how trivial, lest it break the thread of optimum performance. Luck, too, plays its part in sporting success. So it's hardly surprising that even today many of our top rugby players maintain their idiosyncratic and quirky habits.

- Former Wallaby **Damian Smith** had a strict superstition of always wearing the same lucky pair of black underpants when he played.  Somehow Damian forgot to pack them in his bag for the World Cup in South Africa in 1995 and was forced to play the first few games in a pair of less-than-satisfactory knickers. The original lucky undies were held so dear by him that he arranged for his dad, Baden, to personally transport them to the Republic when he came over as part of a supporters' tour. After a remarkable eight years of action, the favourite black undies finally died a natural death in 1998. Damian now wears lucky black swimmers instead.

- For six years **Dan Herbert** always sat next to John Eales on the Wallaby bus on the way to games. Now that Eales has retired Dan's superstition has been broken, but his odd habits haven't ended. He makes sure he always runs out after the player who wears the number 13 jersey. Last year, for example, he found himself following in the footsteps of Nathan Grey – all the way from Melbourne to Madrid.

- ACT Brumbies and Wallabies utility back **Graeme Bond** has had a horrendous run of injuries throughout his career. These have included shoulder reconstructions, repeated knee damage, broken hands, hamstring strains and a crippling back injury. As the majority of these disasters were suffered while wearing the number 13 jersey, Graeme now avoids that number at all costs. Last season he kept the commentators and spectators guessing by swapping numbers with Nathan Grey.

- Former Queensland Reds back-rower **Sam Scott-Young** employed a quirky practice that was more cunning than superstitious. His ploy to impress Reds coach John Connolly at the beginning of each season always seemed to have the desired effect. Half an hour before the first session of the year was due to start, Sam would turn up at the old gym at Ballymore and do as many sets of bicep/tricep curls as he could. He would then put on the tightest singlet he could find and go out to the start of the session and stand right next to Connolly to make sure the coach got a good look at his guns. Never twigging to the con, 'Knuckles' was suitably impressed, no doubt presuming that Sammy had done a huge amount of work in the off-season!

- Another borderline superstition was **David Campese**'s habit of always running out last for the Wallabies. On the one occasion he elected to break that ritual, there were near-disastrous results. For his 100th Test (against Italy) Campo was given the honour of leading the side onto the field; the Wallabies came very close to a shock defeat that afternoon. Although Campo insists he isn't superstitious, he always liked to sit at the front of the bus and invariably wore the number 11 jumper – even when not playing on the left wing.

- All Black centre **Joe Stanley** observed a strange and rather distasteful ritual before every game. His preparation always included a bilious expectoration down the dressing-shed latrine. Apparently it released the tension for him.

- Another former All Black, full-back **Alan Hewson**, often raised team-mates' eyebrows when he played in women's pantyhose. 'Hewie' insists he was no cross-dresser – it was merely his way of combating those fierce Antarctic winds off Cook Strait.

- NSW Waratah prop and crowd favourite **Matt Dunning** always sits on the left-hand side of the bus in the window seat four rows back. This territory is normally reserved for the backs, but as yet none has been brave enough to suggest Matt shift down the back and join the other front-rowers.

Gordon Bray

Talk is precious

The art of television commentary

'Drawing on my fine command of language, I said nothing.'
— Robert Benchley

How many times have you watched a sporting telecast and thought to yourself, 'I wish those bloody commentators would give us a *break*!'?

Of course, such pleading usually falls on deaf ears (after all, we commentators are the ones being paid to do the talking), but all sensible commentators know that their efforts can sometimes generate more irritation than illumination. What that knowledge does is to underline and remind us that we should strive for the ideal balance between talk and silence. That's what enhances the sports viewing experience – and sustains viewer enjoyment. Overstep the parameters either way and the audience is likely to take drastic action. Turning the volume down is the obvious option, but disgruntled viewers have also been known to resort to hurling the closest heavy object in the general direction of their television screen. No commentator likes to be the cause of such mayhem.

The art of television commentary is a delicate balancing act. Viewers don't need to be bombarded with detailed and colourful descriptions of events they can plainly see unfolding before their eyes. To give one clear-cut example, in its tennis telecasts Seven Sport discourages commentators from

138

talking at all during a rally – the picture speaks for itself. Instead, commentary and analysis are interjected at the end of each point, and sometimes not at all.

To take that notion a little further, consider the following remarks made after the same point by different experts:

- Expert A: 'That is an absolutely brilliant overhead smash!'
- Expert B: 'He worked away down the backhand side with excellent depth. Ultimately his opponent came up with the short lob. Easy put-away.'

Which comment added more value to the passage of play just witnessed by the viewer? Expert A offered us little more than an obvious, one-dimensional comment, while Expert B took their tactical observation to a higher level.

Regrettably, in everyday practice one-dimensional comments proliferate during television sports broadcasting. With the odd exception – notably Richie Benaud – we commentators can be regularly found guilty on the charge of 'stating the bleeding obvious'. You will never hear Benaud describing a loose delivery simply as being 'driven through the covers' or 'played wide of mid-on'. More likely, Australia's former skipper of 40 years ago might say, 'Look at that – the sheer beauty of sound footwork', or, 'Straight from the coaching manual, that'.

Next time you listen to a football commentary, take a few moments to evaluate the technique of the different callers. Even allowing for the wide variety of personal styles, you're likely to discover at least one common denominator: in fast-moving passages of high excitement action, most football commentators automatically slip into a radio style in which each component of the unfolding play is described in short-hand and every player involved is named. This helps to generate greater excitement as the movement reaches its climax. In these situations I prefer to adopt a more clipped style of commentary, identifying players only by surname as each receives the ball. Where possible, I also strive to introduce the element of anticipation: 'If he gets the bounce, he scores!' is a very effective way of raising viewer excitement levels before the event actually takes place. A predictive comment like that, followed by a pause to embrace the crowd reaction, can be far more effective than simply saying, *post facto*, 'Burke gets the bounce and he's over for a great Australian try'.

It would be presumptuous to suggest that there is one right, or wrong, way to commentate football on television in Australia. With somewhat characteristic perversity, the AFL has traditionally favoured a radio-style call and that technique often emerges in contemporary telecasts of the code. At the other end of the commentary spectrum, one should never underestimate the dramatic effect of pausation. As Rolf Harris is fond of saying, a little pause goes a long way.

Of all the games of rugby I've called on TV, the one people seem to remember most vividly is the ABC live broadcast of the World Cup quarter-final at Lansdowne Road, Dublin, back in 1991. Nursing a narrow lead inside the last few minutes, the Wallabies looked set to progress to the semis. But suddenly we seemed doomed when Gordon Hamilton streaked over for a dramatic late Irish try. Lansdowne Road erupted.

At that precise moment I gestured to fellow commentators Chris Handy and Gary Pearse to hold back any commentary. For a full 29 seconds we just watched our television monitor

OPPOSITE *Behind the microphone with Wallaby champions from different eras. Mark Ella (above left) commentated for the ABC after his retirement in 1984, while Tim Horan (below right) was Player of the Tournament at the 1999 World Cup.*

in stunned silence as the Irish fans streamed onto the field. The stadium was awash with a human sea of pure Irish joy. Those graphic pictures provided their own narrative and interpretation. Any remarks from the commentators would have been superfluous – and simply overwhelmed by the unbridled hysteria of the patriotic local fans.

A decade later we three commentators are still praised for what some consider a defining moment in our broadcasting careers. Yet we'd said absolutely nothing! My two partners – who had instantly turned a whiter shade of pale – were both frozen in a state of shock. (For the record, the Wallabies rallied magnificently to score a converted try in the dying seconds of the match and snatch a heart-stopping victory. It would be the turning point of Australia's triumphant 1991 World Cup campaign.)

'Remember, Gordon, silence is golden', as legendary Welsh commentator Cliff Morgan always reminded me on my regular Wallaby sojourns to Britain. Morgan was a magnificent wordsmith behind the microphone. His call of the unforgettable try by Gareth Edwards in the Barbarians v. All Blacks clash in 1973 is firmly etched into rugby folklore. In the second minute of that epic encounter at the old Cardiff Arms Park, Welshman Phil Bennett elected to run the ball from in-goal. Two prodigious sidesteps ensued and a daring counterattack was launched. Morgan was suddenly in his element. 'What a sidestep!' he exulted. The spectacular running and support play that followed drew from him a simple, controlled reaction for the BBC telecast: 'Brilliant!' Excitement enriched Cliff's voice, as did the emotional warmth that comes from a genuine appreciation of the skills on display. In short, it was a classic piece of understated television commentary that splendidly complemented one of the greatest tries of all time.

Ten years later I caught up with Morgan in the back seat of a London cab. With tape recorder rolling, I asked him to recall the extraordinary Baa-Baas match. Budding commentators would do well to bottle the following pearls of wisdom about the craft – and the label might read: 'Secrets of Successful Commentary'.

'Yes, it was understatement', Cliff explained. 'The point is, I went into the commentary box that day without a program, but I'd been living with the Lions on tour the previous year and knew everybody. I wasn't a brilliant commentator, but I knew their backsides and the backs of their heads. I didn't have to have a program or a number on the back, so I could indulge myself in what I am so arrogantly good at doing – talking.'

By now he was in full flow. 'I was commentating on the game as if I was talking to someone in a pub over a pint of beer. I just said what I saw. I think in television there are too many commentators who state the obvious: "The ball is being passed, and it goes to so-and-so". You must build expectation. You say I called it well; I called it well because I knew the boys. That's one of the joys of being part of rugby – I got to know so many smashing people in the world.'

If there's a general rule about commentary, it's this: if you have nothing to say, don't say something just for the sake of it. During outside broadcasts of sporting events, television producers occasionally get unsettled if no words are flowing from the commentary booth. On rare occasions the call of 'Cue the commentator!' has even come through on my headset in response to a period of silence. In fact, in those cases I have always been deliberately allowing some breathing space in the coverage.

That's why a good television commentary will always rely heavily on teamwork. A skilled director will let his team know the details of a stand-out shot *before* he puts it to air. This gives the commentators precious seconds to gather their thoughts. For example, if the director is ready to show us a big close-up of Stephen Larkham standing by, the smoothest effect will be achieved if the commentator starts talking about Larkham a second or two before the waiting camera shot is taken. Thus, a comment such as, 'I wonder if Stephen Larkham will contemplate a drop goal?' just before his image is transmitted allows viewers to make their own judgement as soon as the shot is taken. Good teamwork between the TV crew and the commentators adds special value to a telecast.

Because the laws of rugby can be very confusing, rugby commentary also lends itself to an interpretive style of delivery. In most broadcasts viewers can now hear the referee's running comments to the players quite clearly. This affords a wonderful opportunity to help explain the rulings. For example, a call of 'Coming in on the side of the tackle' by the referee gives the commentator room to point out that players can only enter the fray from the right direction behind the tackle.

However, the use of the referee's microphone in telecasts is currently a point of contention. Some producers like to put the ref's dialogue to air at full volume, which effectively means that the man-in-the-middle becomes an extra com-mentator. To my mind, this is an experience most of us would prefer to be spared. Whatever happened to the premise that an enjoyable game of rugby depends on an unobtrusive referee? Playing his comments to air non-stop effectively turns the ref into a major player.

The larger danger is that the referee can become bigger than the match itself. My preferred option is a compromise that features referee comments only after penalty decisions and during reports and cautions. If the ref's mike is kept at low level on most other occasions, the viewer won't be exposed to the constant chatter that may be necessary for the firm control of a match but is extremely irritating for anyone other than the players. Otherwise, those handy heavy objects we talked about earlier might be hurled at the TV set again.

In summary, good commentators don't state the obvious, don't talk over each other, don't speak unless they have something to say and don't make false predictions. Good commentators do their homework, know the laws of the game, allow a telecast to 'breathe', are passionate about what they are doing and, above all, have fun doing it.

It's been said that television commentary is like the effect of lobbing a pebble into a millpond. The ripples are far-reaching and the viewer has ample time to evaluate their impact. Nothing irritates or enrages quite so much as inappropriate or ill-considered prattling. If a commentator has added to viewer's enjoyment by complementing the 'live' vision rather than simply describing it, he or she is well on the way to appeasing the long-suffering audience.

And, at the risk of stating the bleeding obvious, you can't hope to please everyone every time. You might not manage to satisfy even one person every time. But you can keep trying. Happy rugby viewing – and listening – on Seven.

Favourite rugby web sites

Australian Rugby Union official web site www.rugby.com.au
An encyclopedia of information for Australian rugby fans. Some of the sections: up-to-date news stories; schedule and ticket information for upcoming games and tournaments; information on the Wallabies, Sevens, women's rugby, under-age teams, coaching and refereeing.

News Limited sports site www.sport.news.com.au
Follow links to the rugby section for a thorough news service for rugby fans in Australia and abroad. The site is continually updated with articles from the News Limited chain of newspapers as well as other worldwide services. When a story is broken, this is a good site to check out.

Planet Rugby www.planet-rugby.com
An excellent site providing information on competitions and players from all over the world. The site is continually updated with news from competitions such as the European Cup, Six Nations, Tri Nations and just about any major international game. Also contains an archive section with tremendous information on players and games of the past.

Rugby Heaven www.rugbyheaven.com.au
Provides thorough news coverage of rugby in Australia and abroad. Includes up-to-date news articles on Super 12, Tri Nations, Six Nations and other international competitions. Also contains relevant information on rugby schedules and rules, and links to other web sites.

Scrum Rugby www.scrum.com
Primarily focused on the Northern Hemisphere, but has an excellent section on women's rugby. The 'Dictionary' pages are highly recommended for curious newcomers.

Stuff NZ www.stuff.co.nz

Official site of Independent Newspapers Ltd. Has a comprehensive rugby section that provides a balanced Kiwi perspective and includes reports from NZ national newspapers and press agencies.

Tarik's SANZAR Guide www.tarik.com.au/rugby/rugby.html

A dream web site for statistically minded rugby fans. ET the Statsman provides a wide range of fascinating stats on the Super 12, Tri Nations and World Cup tournaments. Included in this thorough service is a weekly update that previews upcoming games for the week.

ACT Brumbies official site www.brumbies.com.au

Provides Brumbies fans with comprehensive information on their team. Includes news, match profiles, player profiles, coach's comments, photos, season schedules, ticket information and live scores.

NSW Waratahs official site www.nsw.rugby.com.au

Comprehensive source for rugby fans, players and officials in NSW. Includes news, profiles and schedules of the Waratahs as well as information on club rugby and refereeing, and links to other sites.

Queensland Reds official site www.qru.com.au

Enter the Reds Zone to find the latest news on the Reds, up-to-date scores from the Super 12, player information, photo galleries, ticketing information, details for coaches and referees, and interactive sections.

Rugby World Cup official sites

Visit www.irb.org or www.worldcup.rugby.com.au for up-to-the-minute World Cup information from the IRB and host nation Australia.

Bill McGowan

Three cameras, one scrum, no critics

The formative years of televised rugby

*'When I did my first television show, five million sets were sold
next day. Those who couldn't sell theirs threw them away.'*
— Bob Hope

When television was first introduced to Australia in 1956 it was
estimated that in Sydney 75 per
cent of the sporting public had
never seen a game of rugby union.
All this was about to change.

In the mid-fifties the entrenched
propaganda machine of rugby
league was so successful that most
football fans were like the children in *The King and I* who
refused to believe that Siam wasn't the biggest and most
important country in the whole wide world. One of the
easiest ways to win money was to bet a rugby league fan in
the local pub that when both the Kangaroos and the Wallabies
toured England in the same year, the Wallabies would draw a
bigger crowd when they played England. Likewise, it was
nearly impossible to convince league followers that union

was the major game in New Zealand – they always believed that any NZ league side would easily beat the All Blacks.

Back home, although the NSW Greater Public Schools always thrashed the Combined High Schools at rugby, the CHS players who transferred to rugby league became 'great' players but the GPS players who went on to play club and representative rugby union were generally regarded as far inferior footballers.

Not surprisingly, in this climate there was no such thing as paying a rights fee to cover any sport on television. All a TV network had to do was seek permission from the relevant ruling body if it wanted to telecast their sport. Forty-five years ago the administrators of rugby league felt television coverage of their competition would harm gate takings. But their 'elitist' rivals had no such worries (perhaps because the regular weekend crowds for the 15-man game were so small!). Whatever the rationale, the first telecast of a Sydney club rugby union match was presented 'live' on Saturday 6 April 1957 from Chatswood Oval. The fixture was between Gordon and Manly.

Arthur Wyndham, the ABC producer for that historic broadcast, fondly recalls those early trailblazing days. 'We were starting from scratch. Not one of the crew had ever been involved in a football telecast before, so it was a learning curve for all of us. In order to get the picture back to the studio, the signal was beamed by microwave dish. That meant you needed to establish "line of sight" contact with the Gore Hill tower. So, whenever we did a telecast of a Randwick game from Coogee Oval, we had to put an extra relay dish on top of a block of flats at Taylor Square.

'Excluding the commentators, we had just 11 staff for that

first rugby telecast. There were three cameramen, a floor manager, a producer and his assistant, plus five audio and technical people crammed into what was called "the Pye van" – I suppose we called it that because that was the brand name on the side of the truck. We had two cameras on a raised platform with turret lenses, and one fixed camera at ground level with a huge 40-inch lens. This meant that when a scrum was put down in front of that camera we were able to get a remarkable look at what was going on in the heaving mass of bodies.'

The first rugby coverage was a far cry from the massive team of 120 outside-broadcast staff who worked on Seven's most recent Bledisloe Cup telecast. Today's coverage uses 18 cameras and at least eight videotape machines – yet what goes on between opposing front rows is still largely Secret Men's Business.

The original ABC commentators were Dick Healey and Cyril Towers, and a promising young broadcaster named Norman May called the reserve-grade matches with Mick Cremin. Healey, who also doubled as the ABC's Sports Supervisor for NSW, informed Towers that as the players were all amateurs he was not to criticise individuals. Cyril – always a forthright character – had been a fine footballer in his day and was now a wonderful analyst of teams and their tactics. He listened dutifully to Healey's instructions and didn't criticise a single player – for at least a fortnight!

Reacting sourly to the raa-raa's TV debut, one cynical rugby league scribe cheekily predicted that when a player had to leave the field injured, he would now no doubt be 'carried off by half of his teammates in order to get their faces on television'.

Norman 'Nugget' May's lasting memory of that first reserve-grade match was that Manly won 3–0, with the try scorer's main claim to fame being that he was having an affair with Norman's girlfriend's mother. Sydney club rugby was a pretty small world in the 1950s. And in true ABC style, there was to be a bureaucratic backlash after that historic first telecast. May received an indignant call from Healey's secretary to present himself immediately to the supervisor in his William Street office. 'Listen, May. Why on earth are you claiming six miles for vehicle allowance to Chatswood Oval when I've only ever claimed five miles?' Nugget's intuitive reply hardly endeared him to his boss. 'Well, that's OK for *you*, Mr Healey, but at least I actually own a car.'

The ABC didn't hold a monopoly on the code in those pioneering days. Channels Seven and Nine also telecast early club rugby games, sharing facilities and pictures. Harold Tolhurst called the action for Seven and Ted Harris, later to become head of Ampol, was Nine's first rugby commentator.

To complement the ground-breaking telecasts, the ABC linked their outside broadcast coverage through a studio-based program called *Sportsview*, compered by the polished but irreverent Bob 'Rocket' Moore. Progressive football scores and race results were superimposed over the 'live' pictures during breaks in play. Like any prudent host of a live TV show, Moore had a repertoire of fall-back positions to cover technical disasters or moments when the rugby became impossibly tedious due to inclement weather. His trusty stand-by device was to prattle away amiably about sporting trivia. Moore could always call on a handy supply of instant material because the Saturday ABC TV staff never failed to solve every clue in the sports crossword from that morning's edition of the now-defunct Sydney tabloid newspaper, the *Sun*. Rocket cleverly reasoned that a lot of his viewers would have been shopping in the morning and come home with the paper and a few bottles of beer. By three o'clock, many would be in a pickle and unable to finish the crossword, so they'd ring up the ABC sports department for help. *Sportsview* soon became the authoritative weekend source for sporting facts and figures.

One memorable call came in on a damp Saturday afternoon just before half-time in the 'Match of the Day' telecast. The fellow on the other end of the line said he was ringing from a pub and had a lot of money riding on an answer in the *Sun* crossword. 'Who won the 1950 rugby union premiership?' he pleaded. A quick look at the record book revealed that the answer was Manly. The caller then shouted out for all to hear: 'I *knew* it was Randwick!', and promptly hung up. Another way to win a bet.

Back at the rugby, Norman May remembers a panic-stricken moment after Sydney University won a grand final in the early 1960s. He'd just begun interviewing the University captain on the sideline after the match when a dozen joyful students leapt over the fence, hoisted the skipper onto their shoulders and carted him away in triumph. End of interview. Even the indefatigable May was momentarily stuck for words.

Nugget was also involved in a football first when film of a recently played overseas Test between Australia and France arrived (at considerable cost) with no commentary. Somehow the commentator's pearls of wisdom hadn't been

OPPOSITE *Gordon Bray (above right) learns from the ABC's legendary Norman May, one of the pioneer rugby commentators in Australia. Technology has come a long way since the late 1950s. Computerised stats and state-of-the-art commentary suites are now the norm.*

recorded, just the crowd sound effects. 'What do we do?' came the cry from management. Norman just shrugged and offered to call the game 'off the monitor' as the precious film of the Test was being played to air.

'You won't be able to nominate all the players,' came the reply. 'Then they won't get a mention,' insisted the legendary commentator. Norman got his way and did his usual magnificent job. The final effect was so convincing that next day in the pub he was asked if he'd overcome his jet lag.

Dick Healey entered the NSW Parliament in the mid-1960s to begin a less-than-distinguished career in politics. It was a move that would eventually give Australia its best-loved sports commentator. Norman May took over as the ABC's main football caller and became the 'Voice of Rugby' for the next two decades. Nugget also soon established himself as a remarkable all-rounder, describing everything from surf carnivals and cricket to the Olympics. One of his most memorable rugby asides occurred when a craggy Randwick front-rower arrived very tardily to a ruck. 'He was so late to that ruck he was nearly posthumous,' declaimed Norman in his best ABC voice.

Ron Davies was another colourful commentator, who called matches whenever May was away on assignment. He produced two unintentionally hilarious one-liners within 60 seconds during a club rugby telecast. As the match wound down, Ronnie earnestly informed viewers, 'We are in the dying moments of injury time', followed by '. . . and yes, the referee looks at his watch – and blows it up!'

Back in those black-and-white days of rugby telecasting there was no TV service to regional Australia. In NSW, the diehard union fans of Wollongong and Newcastle built special 10-metre-high antennas on their roofs to receive the Saturday telecast from Sydney.

Not that the coverage was always worth the effort. On one occasion, at T.G. Millner Field, two of the ABC's three cameras broke down. All that remained was a single elevated camera with a zoom lens. The cameraman carefully followed the play, always conscious of providing the viewer with an accurate perspective. The following Monday, a senior ABC executive rang the sports department and remarked that the rugby outside broadcast was the best football telecast he'd ever seen. All with one brave camera.

Perhaps – in the current high-tech world of multiple viewpoints, flashy graphics and endless slow-motion replays – there's a message there for today's television directors.

Bill McGowan is a researcher and statistician for Seven's rugby coverage. His behind-the-scenes career at the ABC included coordinating and collating the results services for a host of programs, including Sportsview *and* Sportsnight. *But his greatest strength was always his uncredited role as the tireless 'eyes and ears' for the ABC's team of first-class sports commentators.*

Matt Gray

The numbers game

The role of a rugby statistician

'There are three kinds of lies – lies, damned lies and statistics.'
– Mark Twain

Despite Twain's famous rebuttal of the numbers game, the goal of a rugby statistician is certainly not to tell lies. It's to provide the armchair viewer with an extra insight into the 'how and why' of the game as it is being played out before their eyes.

Television has an almost inexhaustible capacity to add value to sporting coverage via the magic of computer-driven facts and figures. These enhance every stage of the telecast: the pre-game discussion and team introductions, during play, at half-time and during major stoppages and, finally, in the post-match analysis. With so many different statistics now being monitored during a game, there is literally no breathing space in the commentary box. Consider this typical scenario during a game.

1. It's the 60th minute of the Second Test in Melbourne between Australia and the Lions, with the Wallabies on the attack. They are desperate to square the series, but still have plenty of work to do as they are leading by just a converted try. The score is 21–14. Next . . .
2. David Giffin wins a line-out and the ball goes to Nathan Grey. He crunches through Neil Back's attempted tackle

but is then felled by three swarming Lions defenders. The ball is recycled, but still the Wallabies can't get through. They work into the Lions' quarter before big Owen Finegan runs over the top of Irishman Rob Henderson and, with his left arm stretched, throws a miracle pass to Matt Burke, who dives over in the corner.

3. The Wallabies celebrate, Australian fans everywhere around the country are on their feet and commentator Gordon Bray emphatically calls the try.

4. In the other corner of the commentary box, the poor statistician is in a state of controlled frenzy. From the time Giffin won the line-out until Burke crashed over, just 29 seconds elapsed. Yet during that brief half-minute, 20 different statistics were recorded. They included:

   - Giffin's line-out win
   - 4 Australian ruck and maul wins
   - 5 scrum-half passes from George Gregan
   - 1 fly-half pass from Stephen Larkham
   - 5 Lions successful tackles
   - 1 Lions missed tackle
   - a 22-metre raid for Australia and, of course,
   - Burke's try.

5. Once all this has been entered into the computer, a note is quickly passed to the commentators to let them know that if Burke successfully converts his own try he will tie the record held by Alan Hewson and Don Clarke for the highest number of points (18) scored by a single player in a Test against the Lions. Phew!

It's obvious that only a tiny part of this work could have been achieved by the old pen-and-paper method. Not only would it be impossible to write down the information quickly enough, but modern sports television coverage also demands instant access to the statistics so that updated figures can be immediately relayed to viewers.

Three cheers for the awesome data-processing power of computers! To streamline the statistician's role, a specially designed rugby keyboard is used to enter all the relevant data. It looks nothing like the familiar 'QWERTY' arrangement we inherited 20 years ago from the manual typewriter. Along the left- and right-hand sides of the keyboard, each player on each team is listed from 1 to 22 (starting team plus the seven reserves), with a separate gold key for each player. In the middle of the keyboard all the vital statistics are listed, such as the phase (ruck/maul/tackle) counter, tackles made, tackles missed, fly-half pass/kick/run, scrum-half pass/kick/run, line-out win, scrum win, handling error, kicking error, possession, territory, kicks in general play, penalties, sin-bin, as well as all the scoring options.

Here's how it works. When George Gregan makes a tackle, the keyboard operator presses the '9' gold key followed by the 'tackle' key. Typically there will be two operators working during the game, with one purely there to punch in the stats while the other watches the game and calls out what is happening – at least in statistical terms! All the numbers are then neatly summarised and instantly updated on a screen that sits in front of the commentators. At the end of each half, the computer produces a scorecard that tabulates the complete stats for the game.

The customised display monitor for the commentators is organised so numbers underlining key tactical aspects of the match fall naturally under their eyes. They have instant access to such indicators as the number of phases of play at any point of time, 'line-outs lost on own throw' and 'restart possession regained', i.e., ball regained from a kick-off.

In live telecasts nothing ever goes absolutely according to plan and there's the odd hairy moment. A senior commentator with a penchant for drinking tea during his call has been known to spill the entire contents of his thermos all over our stats sheets. And there's not much room left for the statisticians when we try to squeeze into a tiny commentary box alongside two well-nourished ex-Wallaby front-rowers (Messrs Chris 'Buddha' Handy and Richard Harry).

Even state-of-the-art equipment can fail, as it did during the high-rating telecast of the First Test against the Lions in Brisbane. Our computer chose that occasion to go on a wildcat strike. Amid the ensuing chaos in the outside-broadcast van, the incorrect score was shown several times on screen. I'm told that those responsible have been shot.

Despite all these pitfalls, whenever and wherever the Wallabies are playing there is simply no other place to be come kick-off time – perched high in the commentary box, enjoying the best seat in the house and getting paid for the pleasure. The number-cruncher's task may be demanding, but it's also hugely rewarding.

Matt Gray is the Seven Network's rugby statistician. He was a dashing number 8 in Eastwood's premiership-winning 1st-grade Colts XV in 1993, but now misguidedly spends his leisure time playing Aussie Rules for Pennant Hills' 1st-grade side.

Matthew Burke's record Test haul

Waratah skipper Matt Burke has been a prolific point-scorer in Test matches. He became Australia's front-line goalkicker when Michael Lynagh retired in 1995. Ten years in the Wallaby jumper have seen him amass a remarkable list of milestones at international level.

Most points in a calendar year
189 6 tries, 27 conversions, 35 penalty goals, in 11 Tests in 1996 (This is a world record. Neil Jenkins held the previous record of 181.)

Most points by an Australian in a Test series on tour
74 1996 – 4 matches (1t, 9c, 17pg) in Europe

Most points by an Australian in a Test
39 v. Canada, 1996, Brisbane (Ballymore) – 3t, 9c, 2pg

Most penalty goals by an Australian in a Test
8 v. South Africa, 1999, London (Twickenham) – World Cup Semifinal

Most conversions by an Australian in a Test
10 v. Spain, 2001, Madrid

Most Tests at full-back for Australia
50 Roger Gould held the previous record of 25. (Also played 6 Tests on wing, 2 at outside-centre.)

Most points by any player in a World Cup Final
25 v. France, 1999, Cardiff (Millennium Stadium) – 2c, 7pg

Most points by any player in a Test against the British and Irish Lions
25 2001, Melbourne (Colonial Stadium) – 1t, 1c, 6pg

Most penalty goals by any player in a Test against the Lions
6 2001, Melbourne (Colonial Stadium) – equals record held by Don Clarke (NZ) set in 1959

Most points by an Australian in a Test series against the Lions
44 2001 – in 3 Tests (1t, 3c, 11pg)

Most points by any player against New Zealand in Tests
147 Scored in 12 Tests

Most points by an Australian in a Test against New Zealand
24 1998, Melbourne (MCG) – 2t, 1c, 4pg

Most penalty goals by an Australian in a Test against New Zealand
7 1999, Sydney (Stadium Australia)

Most penalty goals by an Australian in a Test against South Africa
8 1999, London (Twickenham), World Cup Semifinal

Most points by an Australian in a Test against Scotland
25 1998, Sydney (Sydney Football Stadium) – 1t, 4c, 4pg

Most points by an Australian in a Test against England
22 1998, Brisbane (Suncorp Stadium) – 1t, 4c, 3pg

Most points by an Australian in a Test against France
25 1999, Cardiff (Millennium Stadium), World Cup Final – 2c, 7pg

Most penalty goals by an Australian in a Test against Wales
7 2001, Cardiff (Millennium Stadium)

Most points by an Australian in a Barbarians game
24 1996 – 2t, 4c, 2pg

Scored all the team's points in a Test
24 points v. New Zealand, 1998, Melbourne (MCG) – 2t, 1c, 4pg
21 points v. Wales, 2001, Cardiff (Millennium Stadium) – 7pg
19 points v. England, 2000, London (Twickenham) – 1t, 1c, 4pg
18 points v. France, 2000, Paris (Stade de France) – 6pg

Letter to the editor

Mr Editor, I write these few loose notes because I want to see our team (Australia) improve. We have the finest material, which, properly used, should be unbeatable. I do not wish to belittle England. I do not know what her 1922–23 was like, but I am prepared to believe its improvement has kept pace with the times. I sincerely hope it has. But if I have seemed to criticize England harshly, remember her team had three essential rules, which have stood the test of time. (1) To the forwards, 'Be always on the ball.' (2) To the backs, 'Run straight.' (3) To both, 'Tackle low.' Neglect of these rules was fatal to any player's chance of retaining his position.

Did you, Sir, notice last Saturday a Maori went for Raymond high, and was handed off? He made a second attempt and Raymond pushed him off and sent him flying into touch. The crowd rightly cheered Raymond, and a man near me said, 'It was a plucky tackle.' As a matter of fact it was a rotten tackle and he could have got Raymond the first time if he went for his knees.

Now, the other side of the picture. Did you see Crossman? Every one of his tackles was low, and he got his man every time. He ran as straight as a gun barrel and never lost his head. His pass to Elliot, cool and well thought out, when hemmed in on the line was in my opinion one of the best things in the match.

One last thought, Mr Editor. Rugby is essentially a team game. You will, I know, admit that as long as a try is scored or a goal is kicked, it is immaterial who does it. Don't you think the weekly list you publish of the numbers of tries gained by individuals rather encourages selfish play?

An old rugby player.
Sydney Mail 1931

Paddy MacDonald

The thrill of the chase

Collecting rugby memorabilia

'This snug little chamber is cramm'd in all nooks
With worthless old knicknacks and silly old books'
— William Makepeace Thackeray

Monetary value may be important, but if truth be known, collectors are brushed with a splash of eccentricity. How else could we possibly justify all those unproductive hours spent in the cause of collecting memorabilia?

Rugby union, with its long history and unique traditions and folklore, has spawned a lucrative collectable industry. To those of us infected with the memorabilia bug, this joyous pastime is an inexhaustible labour of love. We collect everything, from limited-edition prints to stamps, books, programs, figurines, autographs, jerseys, footballs and – dare I say it – hip flasks (yes, there is even something there for we expatriate Celts who like to sample a wee dram on match day).

The thrill of the chase is most of the fun. I once concluded a mutually satisfying deal with a gentleman in Newcastle who had a full set of original Qantas posters. He'd advertised in the *Sydney Morning Herald*. Having purchased the lot,

163

I then sought his permission to use them as I chose. 'Thank you for asking, Paddy,' he replied. 'These are a family heirloom but the time is right to let them go. Use them as you wish.' Honour among collectors is an unwritten law.

Where to look for hidden treasures? Antique and knick-knack stores are very good places to start. Newspaper advertising notices under 'Antiques and Collectables' should be constantly monitored, as should magazines and the collector and antique annuals put out by Carters and Millers. The Internet also provides a vast array of opportunities through rugby web sites. Swapping memorabilia with fellow collectors will produce many satisfying results, and then there's the endless round of weekend garage sales.

If I'm travelling overseas I always make a point of visiting antique stores, print stores and bookshops. The easiest way to locate these is via the Yellow Pages of each city. For me, there is no more exhilarating adventure than uncovering an old piece in a faraway land. Recently a colleague was thrilled to find a leather football from the early 1900s in the Paris antique quarter.

Whenever I go to a rugby match I always buy the program. If I can't make it to a game, I'll ask a friend to pick up a program for me. Match programs not only provide a wonderful source of memories down the years but, if you manage to assemble a full set, also result in an asset with increasing monetary value. Some of the older ones can be worth hundreds of dollars. For example, a copy of the match program from the Barbarians clash with the All Blacks at Cardiff Arms Park in 1973 is a rare and valuable piece. In this case, the fact that the game is still revered as perhaps rugby's greatest-ever showcase makes the publication all the more special. Some overseas programs feature distinctive artwork on the cover. My favourites often come from far-flung rugby outposts such as Romania and Czechoslovakia. Their comparative rugby remoteness makes them more intrinsically attractive and unusual. One memorabilia-mad friend has a full set of match programs from all four World Cups. The value of such a collection translates to what someone is prepared to pay, but there's no doubt that my friend has established, at the very least, a sound hedge against inflation.

The economic law of supply and demand governs not only the price of collectables, but their availability. I vividly recall a Bank of Ireland poster heralding Munster's upcoming match against the Wallabies. It was freely available before the fixture, but do you think I could get my hands on one the day *after* Munster's famous victory? Here was a case of supply and demand in its purest form.

Publications such as *Rugby World* and *Rugby Monthly* in the UK carry quite extensive classified advertising sections devoted to memorabilia. A colleague of mine visited the premises of one of the advertisers, in Neath, Wales. It was a tiny terrace house and every room was stacked to the ceiling with programs, books and other merchandise. The prized item of this Welsh collector was a large portrait of the 1924 NZ All Blacks, 'The Invincibles'. Alongside each player was their original autograph. The collector was a triathlete who travelled the world attending competitions, and the income he generated from trading rugby memorabilia supported this other passion.

The various national rugby bodies around the world will happily provide an up-to-date list of merchandise available for purchase. For example, check out the ARU's excellent web site (www.rugby.com.au). And a recent visit to the Irish Rugby Union offices in Dublin proved a rewarding exercise. Despite having the devil of a time trying to follow the receptionist's directions to headquarters, the chase produced an unexpected windfall for me when a kindly fellow generously parted with his back copies of Irish international programs over the last two decades.

Rugby songs on cassette, record and CD are yet another corner of the collecting world. The Welsh and Max Boyce enjoy international renown for their richness of voice, but there are many less well-known musicians who have been inspired by the 15-man game. Swiss composer Arthur Honegger (1892–1955) devoted a full movement to rugby in his *Symphonie No. 1*, making it clear that his aim was to express, in the language of music, 'the attacks and counters of the game, the rhythm and colour of a match at Colombes stadium'.

Limited-edition prints continue to enjoy popularity. Prints of George Gregan's Bledisloe Cup-saving tackle on Jeff Wilson back in 1994 at the Sydney Football Stadium seem to pop up all over the place. However, you're unlikely to find a copy at NZRFU headquarters – that moment was no laughing matter for our Kiwi cousins. One of the most stunning recent limited-edition pieces I have encountered is the 1999 World Cup commemorative print of the Wallabies, with accompanying action photographs. Individually signed portraits of each squad member celebrate a cherished triumph in our sporting heritage. This is available for purchase on Seven's web site, www.sportswatch.com.au.

Stamp collectors are well catered for when it comes to rugby. Australia Post released a marvellous collection in 1999

Certain items of memorabilia, especially old programs such as the two shown here, are prized items for rugby collectors. Here you can also see a Sydney Mail from 1921 and an early fixture, designed to be folded into three and stowed in one's wallet or pocket.

to celebrate our rugby centenary. More recently, a limited-edition set featuring the great John Eales proved very popular. Most rugby-playing countries have produced stamps celebrating their involvement in the sport. When you consider that there are more than 100 nations participating in the game, the scope for rugby stamp collectors is bountiful.

Autographs are another grand source of value. George Bernard Shaw was a great authority on autographs, mainly because everyone wanted his personal signature. He once wrote to an admirer, 'Don't waste your time in collecting other people's autographs, my boy. Devote it to making your *own* autograph worth collecting.' To another correspondent he suggested, 'Your business in life is to make your signature valuable, even if it is only at the bottom of a cheque.' And a little girl once wrote to Shaw asking if she could name her new pet pig after him. 'I have no objection,' he responded graciously, 'but I suggest that you ask the pig first.'

Sir Donald Bradman's signature has long been the most sought-after in Australian sport. My personal approach to him was simply to express my heartfelt best wishes in his declining years and enclose a lottery ticket for good luck. I was thrilled when he wrote back under his signature. That is one of the added pleasures of collecting autographs – you can actually write to famous people.

Size has never been a barrier in my pursuit of old relics. I once decorated a prominent Eastern Suburbs hotel with traditional Irish memorabilia. Yes, that Munster v. Wallabies print was there, and so too were a full-scale horsedrawn carriage and an authentic postbox. Those latter items were spotted in Ireland and shipped out by container!

Leading sport memorabilia dealer Tony Burgess has the

best range of collectables, in my experience. Based in Sydney at 531 South Dowling Street, Surry Hills, his shop celebrates our magnificent sporting past and provides a fascinating festival of nostalgia. His rarest rugby item is a photo panorama of Australia's First Test against the All Blacks at the SCG in 1903. This original photograph was taken by a celebrated American photographer who was visiting Australia to demonstrate his wide-angle skills. Tony has match programs and signed postcards from the first Wallabies tour in 1908, priced between $300 and $3000. A full set of original photographs of that tour is available for the hefty sum of $12 000. Maybe you fancy a pre-World War I *Australian Rugby Annual*? That item will set you back a minimum of $750. Tony says that programs are by far the biggest collectables. His rarest are those from Australia's first-ever Test Match, in 1899 against the British team, and the 1903 Test against New Zealand.

In summary, the clear message for both amateur and professional collectors is that gathering memorabilia is a full-time obsession. Whether you are travelling on business or for pleasure, make the effort to visit curiosity shops and antique centres. Allocate a little extra time to pursue your passion. To be sure, there is nothing quite like the thrill of the chase – and the pleasure of a subsequent prize capture.

Paddy Macdonald is a lifetime collector. Following a career in television with the ABC he now devotes his talents to Paddy Macdonald Enterprises, specialising in 'Creative Concepts – Props – Memorabilia'. Phone him on (02) 9436 1737, or fax (02) 9437 1737.

169

Memorabilia sources

Collectables Trader
Bimonthly magazine available at newsagents and bookstores.

The Collector's Sports Books
Proprietor: Mark Burgess
PO Box 198, Earlwood 2206
Phone (02) 9558 1829

David Kirby Sportsworld
PO Box 61, Mount Eliza 3930
Phone/fax (03) 9787 2124
Web site: sportsworld.alphalink.com.au
Rugby-related postage stamps.

www.sportswatch.com.au
Seven's web-site shop. Limited-edition prints (*Champions of the World, Eales: The Kick, The Golden Decade* etc.).

Josef Lebovic Gallery
34 Paddington Street (corner Cascade Street), Paddington 2021
Phone (02) 9332 1840; fax (02) 9331 7431
Web site: www.joseflebovicgallery.com
Prints and photographs.

Lancaster's Toowoomba Antique Centre
Proprietors: Graham Lancaster and Gary Lancaster
3 Railway Street, Toowoomba 4350
Phone (07) 4632 1830; fax (07) 4613 1111
Web site: www.lancastersantiques.com

Legends Genuine Memorabilia
15 Hordern Place, Camperdown 2050
Phone (02) 9565 1431; fax (02) 9565 1982
Web site: www.lgm.com.au
High-quality limited editions, including *Golden Decade of Australian Rugby*.

Melbourne Sports Books
Proprietor: Santo Caruso
80 Flinders Street, Melbourne 3000
Phone (03) 9662 1085; fax (03) 9662 1282
Web site: www.melsportsbooks.com.au

Rugby Relics
Proprietor: Dai Richards
61 Leonard Street, Neath, Glamorgan, UK SA11 3HW
Phone 01639 646 725; fax 01639 638 142
Web site: www.rugbyrelics.com
Programs, books, magazines, ties etc.

Sports Memorabilia
Proprietor: Tony Burgess
531 South Dowling Street, Surry Hills 2010
Phone (02) 9361 3244; mobile 0414 977 519

Tony Ward's Printique Gallery
82 Queen Street, Woollahra 2025
Phone (02) 9363 1422; fax (02) 9363 1049
Decorative antique prints.

Tri Nations

As its name suggests, the Tri Nations is a triangular tournament that pits the three Southern Hemisphere rugby giants – Australia, New Zealand and South Africa – against each other on a home-and-away basis each year. The tournament has built up a tradition of tough, entertaining rugby over its first six years and massive crowds have turned out to watch these traditional national rivals do battle.

Each country receives four points for a win; a bonus point can be gained for scoring four or more tries in a match, or for losing by seven points or less. The team that finishes the 'round-robin' play in first position is declared the winner; there are no play-offs.

The Tri Nations was first contested in 1996, when the New Zealand All Blacks were crowned inaugural champions. The Kiwis continued their early dominance of the tournament the following year when they again went through the competition undefeated. Yet, remarkably, New Zealand didn't win a single game in 1998. South Africa claimed the title that year as the climax of a red-hot form streak that saw them win 17 consecutive Tests.

New Zealand bounced back to win the 1999 tournament, leaving Australia winless after four years of trying. The drought finally broke in 2000, when an injury-time Stirling Mortlock penalty goal in Durban secured the Wallabies their first Tri Nations crown. Similar dramatics were played out in 2001, when Australia again clinched the title during injury time of the final game. Toutai Kefu muscled over to score the last-minute try that downed the All Blacks before a packed Stadium Australia in Sydney.

Titans of Tri Nations: Australian outside centre Daniel Herbert (opposite) and his All Black counterpart Tana Umaga (above).

Tri Nations results

Date	Teams	Score	Venue
6 July 1996	New Zealand v. Australia	43–6	Athletic Park, Wellington
13 July 1996	Australia v. South Africa	21–16	Sydney Football Stadium
20 July 1996	New Zealand v. South Africa	15–11	Jade Stadium, Christchurch
27 July 1996	Australia v. New Zealand	25–32	Lang Park, Brisbane
3 August 1996	South Africa v. Australia	25–19	Free State Stadium, Bloemfontein
10 August 1996	South Africa v. New Zealand	18–29	Newlands, Cape Town
19 July 1997	South Africa v. New Zealand	32–35	Ellis Park, Johannesburg
26 July 1997	Australia v. New Zealand	18–33	Melbourne Cricket Ground
2 August 1997	Australia v. South Africa	32–20	Lang Park, Brisbane
9 August 1997	New Zealand v. South Africa	55–35	Eden Park, Auckland
16 August 1997	New Zealand v. Australia	36–24	Carisbrook, Dunedin
23 August 1997	South Africa v. Australia	61–22	Loftus Versfeld, Pretoria
11 July 1998	Australia v. New Zealand	24–16	Melbourne Cricket Ground
18 July 1998	Australia v. South Africa	13–14	Subiaco Oval, Perth
25 July 1998	New Zealand v. South Africa	3–13	Athletic Park, Wellington

1 August 1998	New Zealand v. Australia	23–27	Jade Stadium, Christchurch
15 August 1998	South Africa v. New Zealand	24–23	King's Park, Durban
22 August 1998	South Africa v. Australia	29–15	Ellis Park, Johannesburg
10 July 1999	New Zealand v. South Africa	28–0	Carisbrook, Dunedin
17 July 1999	Australia v. South Africa	32–6	Lang Park, Brisbane
24 July 1999	New Zealand v. Australia	34–15	Eden Park, Auckland
7 August 1999	South Africa v. New Zealand	18–34	Loftus Versfeld, Pretoria
14 August 1999	South Africa v. Australia	10–9	Newlands, Cape Town
28 August 1999	Australia v. New Zealand	28–7	Stadium Australia, Sydney
15 July 2000	Australia v. New Zealand	35–39	Stadium Australia, Sydney
22 July 2000	New Zealand v. South Africa	25–12	Jade Stadium, Christchurch
29 July 2000	Australia v. South Africa	26–6	Stadium Australia, Sydney
5 August 2000	New Zealand v. Australia	23–24	Westpac Trust Stadium, Wellington
19 August 2000	South Africa v. New Zealand	46–40	Ellis Park, Johannesburg
26 August 2000	South Africa v. Australia	18–19	King's Park, Durban

Tri Nations results continued

Date	Teams	Score	Venue
21 July 2001	South Africa v. New Zealand	3–12	Newlands, Cape Town
28 July 2001	South Africa v. Australia	20–15	Loftus Versfeld, Pretoria
11 August 2001	New Zealand v. Australia	15–23	Carisbrook, Dunedin
18 August 2001	Australia v. South Africa	14–14	Subiaco Oval, Perth
25 August 2001	New Zealand v. South Africa	26–15	Eden Park, Auckland
1 September 2001	Australia v. New Zealand	29–26	Stadium Australia, Sydney

The Great Escape: Wallaby number 8 Toutai Kefu about to touch down for the match-winning try in the 2001 Tri Nations decider against New Zealand at Stadium Australia.

Wallaby fly-half Stephen Larkham soars above NZ scrum-half Byron Kelleher in the 2001 Bledisloe Cup clash in Sydney, while former All Black skipper Taine Randell looks on.

Strath Gordon

Rugby incorporated

Tracking the journey to professionalism

'A business that makes nothing but money
is a poor kind of business.'
— Henry Ford

In the time before the revolution — the professional revolution — the Australian Rugby Union was pretty confident about its place in life. At the end of 1994, when only the faintest far-off rumblings of the professional tumult could be heard, the Union had recorded healthy incomes and good results for the national team, the Wallabies. There had been the famous 'Gregan tackle' Test against the All Blacks at a sell-out Sydney Football Stadium, which had produced excellent television ratings, particularly on the east coast. The code had embraced innovation with the introduction of a national junior pathway. The Reds had emerged victorious in the Super 10 competition.

But there were other aspects to consider. In 1994 the ARU reported an annual turnover of just over $5 million, but most of that money disappeared in the cost of administering the game and running Test matches. Australian rugby was managed by a small, dedicated administrative team; a raft

Hall of fame: maestro Wallaby winger David Campese played 101 Tests for his country. From humble beginnings in working-class Queanbeyan, he rose to the highest echelons of international rugby and will be remembered as one of the greatest attacking talents the game has seen.

Coach Alan Jones's meticulous preparation and passion for the Wallaby cause left an indelible mark on Australian rugby.

Waratah coach Bob Dwyer imparts his wisdom to squad members at the New South Wales State Academy of Sport on Sydney's northern peninsula. The NSW team reached the Super 12 semifinals for the first time in 2002.

New Wallaby coach Eddie Jones (left) will guide Australia to the 2003 World Cup. Here Chris Whitaker takes instructions at the Wallabies' winter camp in Coffs Harbour.

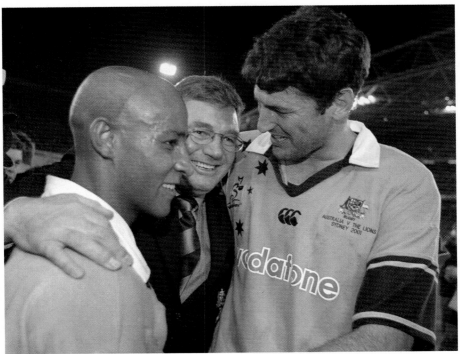

Rod Macqueen, flanked by his captain and vice-captain, bows out as Wallaby coach in the best possible manner at Stadium Australia. Macqueen's remarkable four-year reign finished with the historic series win over the British and Irish Lions in 2001.

Arch-rivals in Super 12: Crusaders and All Black winger Caleb Ralph scores against the Queensland Reds. He also scored four tries against the Waratahs in 2002.

Waratah lock Van Humphries had an excellent rookie season in Super 12 2002. Here he pulls down a two-handed line-out catch against the Highlanders at Aussie Stadium as dreadlocked flanker Des Tuiavii prepares to rip.

Champion fly-half Mark Ella's unique ability centred around running, passing and support skills complemented by uncanny on-field vision. Ella now coaches the Avoca Sharks on the NSW central coast.

Frantic action at the Hong Kong Sevens. Since its inception in 1976, Hong Kong has become the Sevens capital of the world. Officials have always encouraged rugby minnows to take part against the major powers.

From Thailand to Tunisia, Kenya to Korea, the annual Sevens gathering has become an international sporting showpiece – a magnificent cross-fertilisation of rugby cultures and styles with a special accent on fun and camaraderie.

After falling at the final hurdle in 2000, the ACT Brumbies cracked their first Super 12 crown the following year. Here Joe Roff holds the coveted trophy aloft, enthusiastically supported by Peter Ryan (foreground) and Jeremy Paul. The Brumbies downed the Sharks from Natal in the final 36–6.

of 17 committees and a small group of honorary officers carried responsibility for everything from marketing to the match program – and even for coaching the Wallabies.

How quickly times changed after that! Within 12 months, the Union had exhausted its finances in an unsuccessful defence of the World Cup. At the same time, it was facing a mass defection of almost all its leading players to a pirate professional rugby 'circus'. The real upheaval had finally begun and the game would be changed forever.

Flash forward to the end of 2001 and the world looked very different. Turnover had reached $57 million and rugby Tests had outrated league's 'State of Origin' nationally on television. A staff of 80 now worked from the ARU's North Sydney headquarters as they prepared to host the 2003 Rugby World Cup. The committee system had gone and an eight-person board carried the governance responsibility for the corporatised Australian Rugby Union Ltd. The number of people attending Test matches had doubled since 1994, with sell-out games played in Sydney, Brisbane, Melbourne and Perth and crowds of 100 000 or more attending Test matches. Australia were World and Tri Nations champions and, for the first time, the ACT Brumbies had won the Super 12 competition. Through the Tri Nations and Super 12, Australia had forged stronger links with South Africa and New Zealand. The ARU's player payment bill topped $15 million, with some of the game's most elite players now earning hundreds of thousands of dollars. There were almost 100 full-time professional rugby players in Australia.

How did all this happen in such a short space of time? Like most revolutions, it began in chaos. The ARU woke to the dawn of professionalism with empty pockets. In the first year of professional rugby, the imperative for the administration was to generate enough cash to run a professional game and clear debts associated with that transition. Professionalism in rugby was something most rugby people felt was inevitable, even desirable, but the consequences were tough for some to accept. Could the essentially Corinthian values and ethos of the game survive the quest to provide rugby union with the solid financial footing it so badly needed? The transition to professionalism necessitated a search for new, innovative ways to finance the game's growth. The key was to ensure that Australian rugby's greatest brand – the Wallabies – would stay at, or near, the top of the world game.

In Australia, rugby remains dwarfed by the strength and size of the older professional codes, AFL and rugby league. In participation terms, soccer outstrips them all. But it's where rugby is heading that counts. In late 1995 the ARU joined in a ten-year broadcasting deal with News Limited. That agreement remains the single biggest source of income for the Australian, New Zealand and South African rugby bodies. The deal also rescued the game's governing bodies from the besieging rebel World Rugby Corporation and provided the financial clout for the Unions to embark on two new professional competitions, the Tri Nations and the Super 12.

The News Limited contract put rugby on prime-time television. The Seven Network now telecasts Test matches 'live' across the country and Fox Sports also screens virtually all Super 12 matches live. Each year the national figure tuning into rugby has grown. More than three million Australians watched the 2001 Bledisloe Cup match played in Sydney.

After broadcasting, sponsorship has become the second-largest source of revenue for the ARU. More than $12 million pours into the ARU coffers each year from sponsors such as Vodafone, Bundaberg Rum, Canterbury and Qantas. These companies and the ARU's other supporting sponsors actively promote their sponsorship of rugby.

Gate revenue was once the financial cornerstone. While it no longer holds that mantle, it remains a significant contributor. In 2001 the sell-out Tests in Brisbane, Perth, Melbourne and Sydney generated $11.3 million in ticket sales.

Meanwhile, the Wallabies have emerged as Australia's national winter team, commanding a special place in the Australian sporting landscape. To complement this development the ARU set about promoting a 'Wear gold' or 'Gold rush' campaign. This has proved successful not only in the traditional rugby markets of Sydney and Brisbane, but also in the new centres such as Melbourne and Perth. Can an Adelaide International be far around the corner?

Sydney remains Australia's single biggest rugby market. Despite some reservations about the willingness of fans to abandon their cars and catch trains, Test matches at Stadium Australia have already carved their place in history. A world-record rugby crowd of 109 874 attended the 2000 Bledisloe Cup at the former Olympic Stadium and at least two Tests will now be played at the venue each year.

The 1997 decision to take the Bledisloe Cup clash with New Zealand to Melbourne caused some disquiet in the traditional rugby heartland. However, the gate revenue from the 92 000 fans who attended pushed the ARU over the line and into the black for the first time in two years. It also made an impact on the Melbourne sporting market and opened the door for future opportunities in that city. The 2001 clash between the Wallabies and the touring Lions at

Melbourne's Colonial Stadium set a new ground attendance record and captured the city's imagination.

There has been similar success in Perth. Both Melbourne and Perth made very strong franchise cases for a fourth Australian Super 12 team, but expanding the Super 12 competition has proved a difficult task that will require the agreement of all three partners in the joint venture between South Africa, New Zealand and Australia (SANZAR).

Most ARU advertising is aimed at selling match tickets, so the challenge has been to distinguish rugby from the other football codes. The game's unpredictability and tactical nature have been the focus of recent campaigns, carrying the theme, 'Rugby. Anything Can Happen', which Steve Larkham's 1999 World Cup drop goal epitomised. While the game's complexity may be a barrier for those unfamiliar with it, it is also the key to unlocking a new audience.

Whenever a Test is played in Australia, thousands sit down on match night at corporate functions as part of the ARU's corporate hospitality program. ARU licensees have developed products in an extraordinary array of categories – from ties, soft toys and sports drinks to videos, electronic games and sportswear. These activities alone generate more than $3 million in revenue annually.

However, this emphasis on revenue generation has not always sat comfortably with a rugby community used to getting on with life in the traditional 'rugby way'. Multimillion-dollar surpluses can engender suspicion when the great majority of clubs continue to rely on their own limited resources and the energy of volunteers. The bulk of the ARU's income is channelled directly to the state or member unions who use those funds to run their own programs, including the critical coaching and development components. The Super 12 and Australian Rugby Shield competitions are fully funded by the ARU, as are the U19, U21, Sevens and women's programs and various national championships. The regular Schools tours to Europe are also fully funded by the ARU.

Recent innovations include the creation of an on-line rugby community on the Internet. Given the title 'Rugby-Net', it links all rugby clubs in Australia and provides a free web site for every Australian club and the latest practical information for club volunteers. Another innovation is the 'Try Rugby' program, which gives kids and their parents an opportunity to taste the rugby experience. The ultimate aim is that if the kids enjoy the fun and skills, they'll join a rugby club. There's no pressure and it's hoped the scheme will prove popular in areas where rugby has not normally been a dominant sport.

These initiatives, research into safe practices, developing promotional campaigns and practical support for the volunteers are all part of the ARU's brief. Despite the professional revolution of the past few years and the corporatisation of the sport, the Union remains a 'not for profit' organisation that distributes its earnings back into the game, not into the pockets of private individuals.

Strath Gordon, an ex Sydney grade player, is the ARU's Senior Manager – Media and Communications. Formerly a sports reporter and producer with the Seven Network, he was senior producer of Seven Nightly News between 1992 and 1997. His career has also embraced state and federal politics, in the role of press secretary.

State of the Union

Idle curiosity once prompted me to ask Mark Ella, 'What was the hardest game you ever played?'

'Easy!' he replied. 'My first interstate clash with Queensland in Sydney. Mark Loane and Tony Shaw kept coming at me for the whole game.'

Now that was real intensity. There seems to be a special brand of fervour the Reds bottle and save up for their annual battles against the Blues. To be fair, the Waratahs have themselves generated plenty of self-styled 'passion' of late, but for a Queenslander to pull on that red jumper against the arch-enemy is apparently a unique experience.

Centre three-quarter Richard Tombs, later a NSW representative, can claim the rare distinction of having played for both sides. His first State of the Union match was for Queensland in 1988 at Waratah Stadium. Wily coach Bob Templeton chose the fanatical Queensland patriot Peter Grigg to be Tombs' roommate.

It was a day Tombs remembers only too well. 'On the morning of the game Griggy was so fired up I thought he was going to start warming up on me! It was all aimed at "Those #?@!%&! Cockroaches" and any other name he could come up with. I was mentally exhausted by the time I ran out onto the field.'

But it was all to no avail. As the afternoon unfolded, the Waratahs bolted home 37–15. Perhaps super-psyched Griggy had played his clash before the kick-off. Ian Williams, the opposing winger, ran in four tries. Not bad for a mere cockroach.

Gordon Bray

Chris Handy
Fun, fun, fun
The doctrine of rugby, according to Buddha

'Ballet, opera and sheer bloody murder.'
– actor Richard Burton, on the front row

Whenever anyone asks me what my proudest moments in rugby are, I immediately think of two events 21 years apart. Both times I was overwhelmed as a rookie: first, for my Test debut as a Wallaby in 1978, and second, for a special privilege afforded me at the 1999 World Cup final.

I never really imagined I'd get the phone call I received during the 1999 World Cup tournament to give the now-traditional address by an old Wallaby to the Australian side. For a commentator to be asked made it even more unexpected. It wasn't as if I had to say something before a match against Romania; it was trying to find the right words for the mood before the World Cup final itself in Cardiff. Those four days and nights leading up to the final were like the countdown to my first Test against the All Blacks. There's nothing else like it. I lay awake, this time thinking of how I could possibly put all of what I feel about the Wallaby jumper into a few words.

The tour group I was leading at the time got the sneak

preview – I just had to spill my guts at the front of the bus as the coach drove into Cardiff, with all its colour, banners and people, on the day of the final. It almost seemed as if I crowd-surfed to the team hotel. So many people were there in the streets, so many noisy Australians in green-and-gold anything. At the team meeting, I spoke to the players about how they were representing every former Wallaby's dreams and hopes. Most of those great players they would never have met, but all would be galvanised by today's Wallaby performance as they watched it on a TV somewhere. 'What-ever happens – win, lose or draw – today will change your life forever,' I remember saying.

When I presented the Wallaby jumper to John Eales after my speech I added something extra: a bottle of 1991 Grange Hermitage (I don't suppose it would be me without a drink involved somewhere!). For me, the Wallabies winning the World Cup in 1991 was the greatest thrill I'd had as a commentator and spectator. Secretly I'd never believed the Wallabies would ever be able to achieve such heights, but they're like the vineyard from which Grange comes, the best of the best – and the bottle of Grange represented that. 'Enjoy at the right moment,' I thought. By the time Jason Little and Rod Macqueen had spoken and the inspiration of Herb Elliott, our troops in East Timor and the bravery of Australians at Villers-Bretonneux in World War I had been evoked, you couldn't help but be pumped.

However, even on World Cup final day there can be unexpected hurdles. So many people were in Cardiff, with so many vehicles jamming the streets, that the team bus couldn't get out of the hotel car park because two cars were blocking the way. No problem. Rod, members of the team

Chris 'Buddha' Handy, high on rugby and pumped for the 1999 World Cup campaign, addresses the team before the Cup Final in Cardiff at the invitation of Wallaby management, before presenting the captain's jersey to John Eales.

management, the 'dirty dirties' and yours truly got out and manhandled the cars onto the footpath to give the bus a clear run at the history the players were about to make at Millennium Stadium.

In my day as a player, in the '70s and early '80s, there was always the chance to smell the roses. On the Wallaby tour of NZ in 1978 it might have been going shooting, golfing or jet-boating, visiting the famous horse studs at Cambridge or even skiing. (Can you imagine a Wallaby team on tour today being given R&R on the slopes of Mt Hutt? Break a leg? Sure!) The biggest problem with my one and only attempt at skiing wasn't even on the mountain. I put on the skis and suddenly found myself going backwards, out of control, through the car park. I only stopped when I banged into some rubber tyres and gave myself minor whiplash.

We finished that 1978 Wallaby tour without the late Daryl Haberecht, our coach. He'd suffered a heart attack and was laid up in Wanganui Hospital while the Third Test at Eden Park unfolded. The players made a pact to win, both for Daryl and ourselves. It was time to draw that proverbial line in the sand. The Wallabies hadn't beaten the All Blacks for 20 years. I was 28, nervous as a kitten, and in need of some comforting milk to get to sleep that week (plus half a bottle of Kahlua, just to keep my eyes from watering). Our 19-year-old debutant at fly-half, Tony Melrose, was doing it cool and easy. Team manager Ross Turnbull delivered the rev-up for the forwards and identified the giant All Black lock, Andy Haden, as our nemesis. It was my first Test and I was nominated to take him out. Ross didn't mention anything about the stepladder I might be needing.

We hit the paddock running and the frenetic try-scoring

meant Andy and I were rarely thrust head to head. Every time I did come across him I tried to belt him, stand on him or push him out of the way. It was just one of those days when everyone marked up hard on the opposition. At the end of it all, we'd racked up the highest-ever Australian score against the All Blacks (30–16). What a way to end the tour!

Rugby has always been my other family. Touring was like living in boarding school because there was always that 'rope ladder' to slip down to get away for some fun. The commentary team has now become my next family.

There are those people who will say I've never grown up. At my 50th birthday, someone said they'd known me as a child, a teenager and an adult – often on the same day. I'm still that same kid who gets as emotional about a big match, a big Test, as when I played. There's still that same exuberance in pre- and post-match celebrations. Partly, that's because of the hard times. There was a period in the dark days of the early '70s in Australian rugby when a lap of honour was contemplated just for winning the toss.

When I started in commentary in the early '80s it meant I was able to tour again. Now we take a whole busload of people away as a tour group and it's like reliving those happy, fun-filled days with Queensland and Australia. While the Wallabies are butting their heads against brick walls on the field, their mums and dads are touring like the days of old. The Gregans, the

> 'In my first five years of amateur Test rugby I made a lot of new friends. In the second five years of professional rugby I made a lot of money and no new friends.'
> Dan Crowley, former Queensland Reds and Wallaby prop

Littles, the Kafers, the Heaths, the Bowmans, the Cordingleys, Ealesie's parents, and many more – they've all been away.

This has all been made possible by my role in commentary. Over the years my distinct role has evolved as the 'sideline eye'. It's the best seat in the house – I can say exactly what I want and get paid for it. I'd do it for nothing, of course, but no one asked me to do it for nothing. As for my personal style, well, you'd like to think there's still room for a smile and a sense of fun even in today's tough professional environment. In New Zealand, rugby fans either know or introduce me as 'that fat, biased, Aussie, "go-you-good-thing" commentator bastard'. I have no problem with that. As long as I'm calling Wallaby victories over the All Blacks, I know who's having the most fun.

The Australian players know that wherever I go, the old wrestling suit goes with me. It doesn't fit quite as well as it used to when I first got it, on the 1978 tour, but it's always there under the jacket and tie, on sidelines around the world. For one brief moment it's revealed – when I'm standing for the singing of the national anthem, there's an almost unwritten contract that I've somehow got to reveal it. If there's any eye contact with Daniel Herbert or John Eales, I have to show, with a little spread of the shirt and buttons, that the old wrestling suit is still on. It's the 'fun suit' – a reassurance that, hey, there'll be some fun tonight.

In truth, it's that sense of fun that underlies everything in rugby for me. The people involved with the Maroubra Sea Lice, the Kuttabul Camelboks, the Jindabyne Bushpigs, the old Baa Baas-style games in Darwin, or a froth-blowing weekend at the Hong Kong Sevens – they're all as passionate about the game as anyone at the higher levels. As a commentator, I try as best I can to give the public some feeling for this spirit of rugby. The football itself is great, but it's the old clubhouse after the match, the drinking, the laughing, the singing and all the stories that are so essential to the fabric of our game.

That 1991 vintage bottle of Grange Hermitage came out a short while after the World Cup final in 1999. It wasn't sipped from fine wine glasses – Australia's best wine was splashed around into paper cups in a victorious rugby dressing room. And it's probably never tasted better.

Chris Handy began his television commentary role with the ABC in the mid-1980s following a successful playing career with Brothers, Queensland and Australia. After working for four seasons with the Ten Network (1992–95), he became a mainstay of the Seven commentary team. Chris enjoys the distinction of beating the All Blacks in three straight Test matches in successive years, at a time when Australian wins over the Kiwis were thin on the ground.

Part 4

Reminiscence and reflection

A memento from the birthplace.

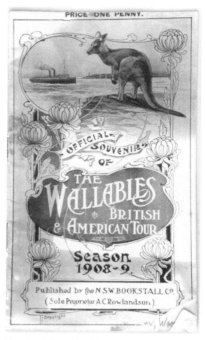

Handbook from the Wallabies' first overseas tour.

Program from the 1927 game won by NSW 5–3.

Program from a game attended by 50 000 fans, won by the home team 10–8.

Spiro Zavos

In the beginning . . .

The arrival of rugby in Australia

'But the voice of a schoolboy rallies the ranks:
"Play up! play up! and play the game!"'
— Sir Henry Newbolt

The ancient Greeks had a game called *episkyros* that had many similarities to modern rugby. Therefore, rather than the dubious claims that William Webb Ellis was the inventor of rugby, one of my ancestors should get the guernsey.

Most societies in history, especially if they liked to embark on wars, played forms of football. The Romans, borrowing, as usual, from the Greeks, called their game *harpastum*. English soldiers in medieval times liked to celebrate their victories by kicking the heads of their slain opponents around the battlefield. Edward II banned football in London in 1314; perhaps he thought his head might one day be booted around some field.

The connection between rugby and warfare remains strong to this day. The terminology of rugby reflects its battle-ground origins: we talk about 'bombs'; players make 'torpedo' kicks (less frequently these days with the AFL drop punt); attacks are mounted along the 'flanks' of the opposing side;

195

In the beginning: the inaugural Test match between Australia and the All Blacks in 1903 at the SCG. Australia had played its first Test match at the ground four years earlier against the British team.

It was New Zealand's first full-scale international match. The tourists won 22–3 before a splendid crowd of 30 000.

NZ skipper Dave Gallagher (right) charges upfield.

'offensive defence' is espoused as the best way to disrupt the other team 'launching' its attacks with the ball; and half-backs 'snipe' around the blind-side.

The first report of a football match in Australia, appropriately enough, involved the military. On 25 July 1839 the *Sydney Monitor* reported: 'The soldiers of Sydney barracks amused themselves with a game called football'. Wherever the British military went in the 19th century, it took football as part of its baggage. In South America, soccer – which came to be called 'association football' in the 1860s – took hold as the main winter game, but in the English-speaking colonies of Australia, South Africa and New Zealand, it was rugby that took root.

Why did a game invented by the chinless wonders of the most famous English public schools become accepted by egalitarian colonials over the working-class game of soccer? My guess is that being identified with the British army and navy did not help soccer. Soccer players, even in the 20th century, were known as 'homies'. This identification of soccer with those who played with England, rather than Australia, prejudiced nationalistic young men against the game. The rough, tough nature of life in colonial Australia, too, meant that a body-contact sport where courage was continually tested and where the elements of warfare were obvious had an immediate appeal.

Finally, there is the cult aspect to rugby. Dr Arnold, the headmaster at Rugby School who encouraged the playing of the Rugby Rules game on the Big Field (to exhaust the students, more than for any other reason), was a believer in 'muscular Christianity'. Rugby School boys were taught they had a mission to go out into the world and save it from

197

lazy depravity. An energetic game like rugby, with its ethic of teamwork, fair play and fitness, was an ideal weapon to take to all corners of the empire to encourage conversion to the principles of muscular Christianity.

Between 1840 and the 1860s the rules of a number of famous public schools, including Rugby, Eton and Charterhouse, were codified into two types of football: soccer and rugby. Rugby kept hacking and running with the ball. Hacking was abolished in 1877 but in its earliest days the newly codified rugby game was a terrifying activity. In 1903, when Australia played the first rugby Test against New Zealand at the Sydney Cricket Ground, Law 47 read: 'No hacking or hacking over, or tripping up shall be allowed under any circumstances. No one wearing projecting nails, iron plates or gutta percha [a type of rubber] on any parts of his boots or shoes will be allowed to play in a match'.

Leo Fanning, a rugby writer of the time, suggested that the sport was more a field of broken bones than of broken dreams. The *Bulletin* called the game 'the undertaker's friend'. And in 1864, a year before the first rugby club in Australia was formed by students at Sydney University, Eldred Harmer, MP, introduced a bill into the NSW Parliament which had as its object a total ban on playing the game. Rugby matches, Harmer told his fellow MPs, were nothing more than 'vicious displays of brutish fist-fighting'. No doubt other members, many with links to Sydney University, defended the game, insisting that the tough play was merely 'youthful exuberance'.

In 1862 the first and most essential technological advance in rugby equipment was invented: the indiarubber bladder. The original pigskin bladders had been so disgusting to blow up that the boys at Rugby School left the task to Mr Gilbert, a nearby bootmaker. The bladders also lost their shape and disintegrated quite quickly with the relentless kicking they received. The invention of an indiarubber bladder solved all these problems. The rubber could be shaped into a perfect sphere for soccer balls, or into an egg shape for rugby. Properly blown up and encased in tough leather, the bladder produced a ball that resisted the elements and multitudinous kicks almost indefinitely.

The sequence of development that followed the production of a reliable ball is, in my view, no accident. Not long after the indiarubber bladder came the first codified laws of rugby, which were followed, in turn, by the establishment of a club at Sydney University specifically for the purpose of playing rugby and spreading the rugby ethic. That was in 1863 or 1864 (the records are not precise). On 21 August 1865 the *Sydney Morning Herald* ran the first of what have now become tens of thousands of reports about rugby matches and rugby matters. It ran: 'Football. A match was commenced on Saturday afternoon, on the University ground, between players of the University and the Sydney Club. After an exciting struggle, which lasted about an hour and a half, during which no goal was obtained, the match was drawn, owing to a misunderstanding regarding the rules.'

The misunderstanding may have had less to do with the rules of rugby than to *which* football rules should be played. Football played in the state of Victoria, which became Australian Rules, codified its rules in 1864. Between 1864 and the mid-1880s a 'football war' was fought out along the eastern seaboard of Australia as to which form – Australian Rules or rugby – would prevail. There was never a doubt in parochial, provincial, protectionist Victoria, where Australian Rules football won out, but, after an intense struggle, rugby prevailed in NSW and Queensland.

Philip Sheridan, an Irishman who loved Gaelic football, became the dominant official in the Sydney Cricket Ground Trust between 1880 and 1910. Sheridan was determined to make Australian Rules (Gaelic football without sticks) the main winter sport of Sydney. He brought the South Melbourne team to the ground to play a series of matches and at the after-match dinner the prediction was made that rugby would 'disappear' from Sydney grounds. That forecast failed for several reasons. People in NSW were not of a mind to desert, for an import from the detested state of Victoria, a game they'd introduced to Australia. More importantly, the officials involved with the Victorian game were too close-fisted with their money and narrow-minded in their expectations to sponsor interstate tours. Remarkably, a proposed tour to Sydney by Australian Rules players from Queensland in 1882 became a *rugby* tour and resulted in the first Queensland–NSW clashes. Canny NSW rugby officials sponsored the tour – stipulating that only rugby was to be played.

Yet in 1882 the main winter game in Brisbane was still Australian Rules; 19 Aussie Rules matches were played, in contrast to just three rugby fixtures. Not surprisingly, 12 of those first Queensland tourists to NSW in 1882 were Australian Rules players. They were soon indoctrinated into the joys of rugby tours and converted to the game. 'All assembled,' the *Queenslander* reported, 'and the sparkling fluid was handed around'. NSW won the match either 26–4 or 28–4, depending upon what scoring system was used (or how much amber fluid was consumed by the scorers).

The lure of tours – back to Queensland by NSW players, to New Zealand by NSW and Queensland players, and to Australia by British and New Zealand teams – became the main recruiting agent for rugby players. During the tough Depression years of the 1890s the players found the tours a source of pleasure and joy. A team of Sydney players, for instance, 'narked' some Auckland officials, according to the *Bulletin* in 1894, when they made their farewells at One-hunga wharf. 'Several ladies,' it was reported, 'friends of the executive officers of the Auckland union, were at the wharf, having gone out specially to say farewell to the gentleman of the team. But there were also in their four-wheelers a bevy of notorious *nymphes de pavé*, who were more than affectionately farewelled by certain of the departing guests. These women were first cheered as the lines were cast off, and then cheers were given for the Auckland boys, who had no option but to be silent after such an insult to the respectable women present.'

The Greeks had another word for the behaviour of the NSW players off the field. And it wasn't *episkyros.*

Spiro Zavos is one of Australia's leading rugby writers, having been the rugby columnist for the Sydney Morning Herald *for more than 20 years. He is currently writing his sixth book on the code and is also the author of a controversial, bestselling biography of former New Zealand prime minister Sir Robert Muldoon.*

Spiro Zavos' ten memorable moments

1 1882: The first interstate match between NSW and Queensland is played.

2 1899: The first team endorsed by the Rugby Football Union (the England union) plays Australia and loses the first Test at the Sydney Cricket Ground.

3 1903: The first Test between Australia and New Zealand is played at the SCG.

4 1907–8: Dally Messenger defects to the new code of rugby league and Joynton Smith buys the 1908 Wallabies to play a series of matches against the rugby-league Kangaroos.

5 1908: The Wallabies, representing Australasia, win the gold medal for rugby at the London Olympic Games.

6 1929: Queensland rugby union is reinstated and, playing as the first Australian side since 1914, the combined NSW and Queensland players win all three Tests against the All Blacks.

7 1937: NSW defeats the Springboks ('the greatest team to leave New Zealand') in the finest exhibition of wet-weather rugby the game has seen.

8 1984: Alan Jones's Wallabies win the Grand Slam of Tests against England, Ireland, Wales and Scotland, with Mark Ella creating a record by scoring in each Test.

9 1991: The Wallabies, coached by Bob Dwyer and sparked by the genius of David Campese, become the first team to win the Rugby World Cup away from home.

10 1999: The Wallabies, coached by Rod Macqueen, with John Eales towering in the forwards and Tim Horan playing majestically in the backs, become the first team to win two Rugby World Cups.

Wallaby pioneers – who was our greatest forward?

In 1935, the Sydney Mail *newspaper attempted the onerous task of evaluating the merits of Australia's best forwards in history. The editor's verdict on the best back was clear-cut, with the legendary H.H. 'Dally' Messenger getting the nod on the strength of his instinctive genius. But the question of who had been our stand-out forward provided an incredible array of candidates – and a surprise result. The author of this extract from the* Sydney Mail *feature wrote under the nom-de-plume of 'Light Blue'.*

. . . In this exercise the champion forwards of the different years and countries will be conjured into being to pass swiftly across the moving-picture screen of memory so that they may be appropriately measured according to the quality of their play.

What a wonderful film! Fancy seeing again such renowned players as the Warbricks, Tom Ellison, Jack Taiaroa, the top-rank forwards of the Maori Native team of 1889. Imagine seeing once more those hectic struggles between Fred Henlen (NSW) and W. ('Offside') McKenzie (NZ), giant wing forwards, or peeping into the past and watching Dave Gallagher, that famous All Black leader, heading his cohorts down the field in those devastating charges, or picturing those Wallaby stars the Burge brothers – Peter and A.B. ('Son') – joining forces with 'Paddy' McCue, Syd Middleton, Norman Row and 'Tom' Richards in their sorties into enemy territory. There go 'Jumbo' Frazer and his smaller brother 'Zoong', the auburn-haired, and two of a later decade's second-row forwards, W.W. ('Billy') Hill and Harold Judd, wearing the royal blue jersey of the Newtowns.

Ah, here is a fine forward pack; one which made history at the front in the Great War, and, in the back lines, at sport – the famous AIF team whose forwards displayed form here and abroad which entitles them to rank with the best vanguard yet seen in Australia. Look at their adventurous leader, W.T. ('Billy') Watson, who played through a Test against New Zealand covered with boils, the after-effects of 'mustard gas' used by the Germans. No wonder he won the Military Cross on active service. Two of the finest exponents of breakaway play are in his pack – big chaps, too – 'Babe' See and 'Blue' Thompson. Few are better than these two, who proved false the words of the football song that 'breakaways don't shove at all'. They push every ounce of their power, and yet do not neglect to shield the clever little half-back 'Rat' Flanagan or tackle the opposition half or five-eighths as they endeavour to launch hostile attacks. What a splendid combination in these army forwards. Verily the proverbial blanket will cover them at almost any instant of the game, so well do they keep together. Britishers, Springboks or All Blacks cannot terrify this big, capable, virile organisation comprising 'Bill' Cody, 'Viv' Dunn, 'Johnny' Bond, George Horsey and the others already mentioned.

Wallaby pioneers – who was our greatest forward?

Manly football enthusiasts will be delighted to see old favourites appear on the screen in 'Ted' Thorn, that inspiring forward leader who so often led the Villagers and New South Wales to victory, and Bob Loudon, the phenomenal scoring forward whose uncanny instinct for tries made him an asset to any pack.

Mention of breakaways sends Wylie Breckenridge (now Hon. Treasurer of the Union) careering across the screen to demonstrate his wonderfully effective defensive methods. Another flank forward, Ivor Jones, the Welshman of the 1930 British team, will not be kept out of action. He insists upon re-enacting his desperate solo effort (which Cyril Towers so decisively and dramatically finished) to snatch victory from Tom Lawton's Australian team of that season. Old-timers in P.M. ('Paddy') Carew also appear on the screen to show that the forwards of other days are just as good as those of the present era.

Who is this huge chap handling and running like a crack centre-threequarter? Surely it is the Waratah champion Jack Ford, who carried his 15-stone weight so speedily. Yes, and here is a splendid quartet wearing the 'Silver Fern', the New Zealand rugby trademark: 'Morrie' Brownlie, 'Jock' Richardson, 'Ron' Stewart and 'Cliff' Porter, known to Australian players as the 'Galloping Clydesdales'. Huge chaps, these champions of the 1924 invincible All Blacks, but none of them the equal of two predecessors, A.H. ('Boiler') Francis (1907) and C.E. ('Broncho') Seeling (1905–07), probably the greatest of the many great personalities from New Zealand, that home of rugby forwards. But what of 'Ranji' Wilson (1910–14), and Archie McMinn (1907), the chap who kicked the ball with that curious wobble which made his high punts so hard to catch. It's tough enough having to take the ball in the face of a horde of black-jerseyed devils – but a spinning ball as well as – pouf!

Here are some more racing across the screen – T.S.R. ('Ironsides') Davis and W.H. ('Wild Bill') Cerutti – two of the greatest front-row forwards since the war, fit to rank with men like 'Jimmy' Clarken, 'Bull' Hammond, 'Jum' Carson and other stars.

There goes Cecil Murmin, that fine line-out champion, and in the background another high marker, Charlie Fox, the Waratahs' vice-captain – great forwards these in the fullest sense of the word.

Who are these in the tricolour jersey of Eastern Suburbs? None other than Harold George, Fred Thompson, C. ('Doss') Wallach – all lying in Gallipoli graves – Harald Baker and 'Ted' Fahey, the five of whom, from the one club, at the one time, played first for the State and then for Australia against the All Blacks just before the war bugles called them to the 'larger playing fields'.

The moving film goes swiftly on as we see F.M. Stout, J.W. Jarman, of the 1899 British team, A.F. Harding, the famous Welsh champion, and D.R. Bedell-Sivright, the Scottish champion, both of the 1904 team and among the greatest of visiting British forwards.

Ah, here are a couple of Springboks of the 1921 team, J.W. Van Rooyen – christened 'The Tiger' in New Zealand because of his amazing strength and devil – and W.H. ('Boy') Morkel, one of the famous sporting South African family. Two outstanding men are these hefty athletic members of a heavy pack.

Frank Burge dashes past the vision, the greatest of the trio

New Zealand v. New South Wales——The Rival Teams.

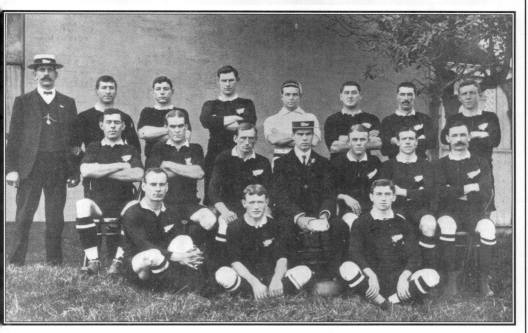

The New Zealand (top) and NSW teams that met in Sydney on 13 July 1907. In the Waratahs line-up, Sydney University flanker Jim Hughes (back row, third from left) was regarded as one of our greatest forwards.

of brothers who helped to make the League game so popular. So, too, does Aub. Hodgson, voted by African critics as the star forward of the 1933 Wallabies, who so bravely held their own in South Africa in contests against a world-renowned Springbok pack.

The film still records its story, for we see a bunch of big chaps clad in the blue and gold of 'Varsity. Yes, there's Howard Bullock, who played for 'Varsity, New South Wales, Australia, Oxford and England, and with him are Leo Reynolds, 'Jim' Hughes, John Hughes, 'Paddy' Moran and Norman Johnson. What a galaxy of stars in this strip of the film. Can you see them? Bullock has secured the ball on the line-out, wheeled around and passed it on to that splendidly built athlete 'Jim' Hughes, who gives his hips to the would-be tackler and off he goes on a glorious sprint down-field worthy of a three-quarter's classic effort.

The film has ended, the lights go up, and off we go musing over these moving snapshots of the great ones, past and present. Thereupon, after mature reflection and much weighting of the many pros and cons, I make bold to declare Jim Hughes, now Dr James Hughes, a Macquarie Street specialist, the greatest forward I have seen on Sydney's football grounds.

One of the secrets of his greatness was his early training as a five-eighth at St Ignatius College, where he led a strong fifteen and played so ably – not as forward – but as a clever back. I can see him yet at the Riverview Oval sailing speedily and unswervingly for the goal line brushing off sterling defenders with ease by using his powerful hips. He was a class back, possessing a super-abundance of football sense and brains, which enabled him, when he went on to the Sydney University, to take his place as breakaway forward

Wallaby pioneers – who was our greatest forward?

in the vanguard and to adapt himself readily to the many new requirements of this position.

His name (with many others) is emblazoned on the honour boards of his old school as a champion athlete. He was school captain – a successful performer on the athletic track. At cricket, in a grade match, he knocked up an amazing double-century for Paddington at the Sydney Cricket Ground, but it will be his football triumphs as a forward genius for 'Varsity, New South Wales and Australia that will be most remembered for many years to come.

New Zealanders Francis and Seeling were outstandingly great, but in my opinion Jim Hughes, a champion athlete and sportsman, was greater still in all-round skill as a Rugby Union forward – one of the supreme tests in sport.

According to Jack Pollard's Australian Rugby, *Jim Hughes was a stand-out in one of Sydney University's greatest packs. He made his state and Australian debut in 1907 playing the two Sydney Tests against the All Blacks, missing the Brisbane Test due to a cost-saving measure. In 1908 he was rated the best forward in the country after topping the Sydney try-scoring list, but thereafter he decided to concentrate on his medical studies.*

A country connection

Orange full-back Larry Dwyer has the unique distinction of captaining the Wallabies in their first victory over the All Blacks on New Zealand soil (16–5).

The celebrated event took place back in 1913 at Lancaster Park and remains the only time in 100 Tests between the two countries that the opposing skippers both played at full-back.

Three years earlier, Dwyer had also starred in our first win over New Zealand in Australia, but he only managed that feat after overcoming considerable hardships. His employers, a penny-pinching legal firm in Orange, demanded that Larry work back on the Friday night to compensate them for the time he'd be taking off to play rugby for his country. As a consequence, he just managed to catch the midnight mail train to Sydney and then walked from Central Station to the SCG. Thirty thousand fans saw Australia lose the first Test 0–6, but two days later the Wallabies exacted their historic revenge, triumphing 11–0.

No doubt the extra recovery time made all the difference to Larry, who was acclaimed the 'man of the match'.

Simon Poidevin

Scaling Mount Everest

Australian rugby takes a quantum leap in the mid-1980s under ebullient Wallaby coach Alan Jones

In 1984, the Grand Slam sweep of the four Home Unions – England, Ireland, Scotland and Wales – created euphoric reaction around Australia. Two years later, there was another first: a three-Test series win against the All Blacks on New Zealand soil. In partnership with his on-field general, Andrew Slack, coach Alan Jones lifted the Walla-bies to a new dimension of self-belief and high-level con-sistency.

At the heart of both campaigns was Simon Poidevin, now a commentator for the Seven Network. 'Poido' assuredly ranks with the greatest players to pull on the coveted gold jumper. He eventually retired in 1991, bowing out a winner at the highest possible echelon: an unbeaten season with the NSW Waratahs, an eighth 1st-grade premiership with Randwick and then, to top the bill, World Cup glory at Twickenham on 2 November and Yardley Player of the Year, covering all four football codes.

211

In this extract from his book For Love Not Money, *as told to Jim Webster, Simon takes us into the Wallaby inner sanctum to relive those two glorious milestones of the mid-1980s.*

The emotion came quickly. We'd only just trooped off Murrayfield into our dressing room on that sullen, overcast afternoon. In between tugging off their sodden jerseys and the rest of their gear the Wallabies were shouting, pumping each other's hands, slapping backs, ripping the tops off Fosters cans and smiling for all they were worth. Jonesy was stomping around in his Wellington boots in the darkly lit room, quoting from Shakespeare or Churchill or somebody else to the Aussie media boys who'd followed us in.

We'd just comprehensively whipped Scotland, thus enabling us to successfully complete the 1984 Grand Slam of the British Isles; the only Australian team in history to do it, and among the precious few international rugby sides ever to defeat England, Ireland, Wales and Scotland on the same tour. Hence the unbridled jubilation.

It's extremely difficult at times like that to fully appreciate what you've done. A bit like winning a gold medal at the Olympics I guess. The full realisation doesn't sink in for weeks, even months afterwards. In the meantime, though, we were really doing our utmost to savour the immediate and overwhelming feeling of success, achievement and pride in what we'd done.

It wasn't simply having won the Grand Slam, but also the manner in which we'd done it. We scored exactly a century of points in the four Test victories, the most ever by a touring team in Britain. Our 12 tries was also a record. The 37–12 hiding of Scotland that afternoon was Australia's highest Test score against a major rugby nation and also the biggest winning margin. Michael Lynagh's 21 points against the Scots equalled the record number of points for an Australian against an International Rugby Board country, and his total of 42 points for the Test series was also a record. Finally, Mark Ella's tries in each of the Tests was also the first such feat ever performed by anyone in a touring team. In the end, there were hardly any records left to be broken.

While all this sank in, some of the boys continued to sit there elated and exhausted, but most stripped off, jumped under the piping-hot showers and began singing 'I Still Call Australia Home' at the tops of their voices, horribly off-key. And our Argentinean prop Enrique ('Topo') Rodriguez was declaring to all and sundry in his very best English: 'Un-bee-lievable, mate; bloody un-bee-lievable . . .'

While there were all these outward signs of emotion, and almost of hysteria, inwardly I wasn't feeling that way at all. Deep down I was numb. I'd been around a fair while and had suffered more than my share of Test defeats. So I was more in a state of disbelief. I just couldn't conceive that we'd finally achieved what we'd set out to do those many weeks before. All those training sessions . . . Jonesy yelling and driving us on, often in the bitter cold and wet, those countless rucks and mauls, repeating the same moves over and over again, and so many scrums and line-outs that you'd nod off to sleep thinking about them and wake up the same way.

An enormous responsibility had also been blown away, the horrible fear of losing that last international and being denied the Grand Slam – something which haunted each and every one of us as the wins accumulated – had at last gone forever. Earlier that day in his talk to the team, Jonesy

had used the analogy that Martina Navratilova had only just lost her first major tennis event after winning umpteen matches on the trot. He likened the Wallabies to her. Did we similarly want to falter after coming so very, very far? We'd beaten England, Ireland and Wales. Only the Scots to go. Were we going to let the Scots stop us now at the most crucial moment of all?

In his most erudite and stirring way, Jonesy had put that question to us and laid the challenge firmly at our feet. Now in this packed and noisy dressing room, as the Murrayfield grandstands emptied the last of their 65 000 spectators, it was finally over. And thankfully we hadn't let down ourselves or Jonesy.

After things finally settled down, we all dressed and boarded the bus for the ride back to the North British Hotel where our first duty was to dump our bags and head for the traditional happy hour which the Wallabies always have after each tour game: a time when the players and team officials get together behind closed doors for a natter about the game, maybe have a song or two and sometimes a bit of skylarking. Generally it's light-hearted (just how light-hearted being determined by the score that afternoon) and we were obviously all looking forward to this particular happy hour.

I arrived at the team room and spotted our big second-rower Steve ('Swill') Williams. Swill was just sitting by himself sipping an orange juice, which definitely wasn't his normal drink. When I asked why, he muttered, 'I don't know. I just feel totally drained and want to take it easy for a while.' So I left him to it. Then the bulk of the players began filing in. When the doors closed, there were just the 31 players, the manager Dr Charles ('Chilla') Wilson, Jonesy and his assistant

OPPOSITE *Alan Jones (above) succeeded Bob Dwyer as Wallaby coach in 1984 and enjoyed phenomenal success. Simon Poidevin (below) played under three national coaches, including Alan Jones from 1984 to 1987.*

Alex Evans, the medical officer Dr Syd Sugerman and Graham Short our baggage man.

Normally on those occasions, Jonesy gets up and says his piece about the game and where we went right or wrong. His speeches were always clipped and emphatic. But this time there was an entirely different tenor to what he had to say, and it showed in his voice. He spoke quietly and with far deeper emotion than I've ever heard from him. It had been a week he'd never forget. He'd been crippled the whole week with a back injury, but had struggled along with that enormous disability and had finally had everything he'd ever dreamed of in rugby come true.

When he finished you could hear a pin drop. Then he mentioned that our skipper, Andrew Slack, might like to save his comments for the official dinner that evening and sat down. But Slacky wouldn't have a bar of that. Suddenly, he was on his feet. He's a pretty emotional sort of person, and as he also tried to get across to the rest of us what winning the Grand Slam meant to him, he had to stop. The words were there, but there was a lump in his throat stopping them coming out. Again, the room was suddenly full of silence.

Then, simultaneously it seemed, we all heard the sniffle and looked around to see Topo Rodriguez, our mighty prop, someone feared and respected by every rugby forward in the world, quietly crying. The tears were trickling down his cheeks and into the tips of his shiny black moustache.

Topo's emotion was infectious. No sooner had we seen him crying than almost everyone else in the team started shedding tears too, some more than others. It went on for some minutes.

Nobody outside that room will ever know or fully understand why that extraordinary outpouring of emotion happened. Many will scarcely believe it; a team of international footballers weeping! Others will paint us as a bunch of nancies. I often wonder what the reaction might have been if the masses of joyful Aussies who were choking all the bars and pubs and watering holes in Edinburgh at that very moment (some had obviously made it, judging from the noise, to the corridor outside our meeting room) had suddenly walked in. Fairly perplexed I'd suggest. All I can say is that had you been through what all the people in that room had been through, worked as hard and wanted something as badly as we had, then you'd understand.

At the end of every happy hour, the team always stood and sang the national anthem. It always gave us a sense of pride, and reminded us that we were playing for Australia. Well I don't think I've ever sung 'Advance Australia Fair' with as much pride as I did on that occasion, knowing we'd not only done so much for ourselves but also for everybody back home who would get such a fantastic lift out of this Grand Slam.

Had my rugby career ended then and there I'd have had much to be thankful for. But I'm a pretty lucky Australian. I lived to fight more wars and two more great and successful battles.

Two years later I found myself in the midst of another jubilant dressing room on the other side of the world, sharing another great victory with many of those same teammates and the same coach. We'd just beaten the New Zealand All Blacks at Eden Park in Auckland by 22–9 to win the series against them by two Tests to one and regain possession of the Bledisloe Cup.

I'd been in Test teams which had previously beaten the All Blacks, and was part of the team which took the Bledisloe Cup from them back home in 1980. But this was the first and only time in my long career that we'd ever beaten them in a series in New Zealand. On their own dungheap; right in their own backyard!

A fortnight before we'd been beaten in the second Test by 13–12 after winning the first by the same score, and in the eerie silence of that dressing room at Carisbrook Park in Dunedin every player had vowed that we'd not lose the third and deciding Test. Defeat would not be considered.

Now we'd succeeded and, take it from me, there's no sweeter smell of success in all of rugby than beating the All Blacks in a series on New Zealand soil. They're an arrogant team and have every right to be, because they're so damned successful. But this arrogance, and the competitiveness of both nations at any sport, has festered into an absolute blind hatred between our national rugby teams. I stress that it's between the teams, because there's a great deal of underlying respect and, in some cases, even friendship among the players. But put the teams on opposite ends of a rugby paddock and it's like two bull mastiffs going at each other to the death.

The New Zealand crowds also stir up a lot of the hatred from the Australians. They're fanatical and terribly parochial. While that's understandable, and the support they give their team is something our crowds could learn from, they're also very unfair in that they're reluctant to acknowledge the outstanding qualities or play of rival teams the same way that crowds do at the major British grounds or even in France. That really gets to us and makes us want to humble their precious All Blacks in front of them more than ever.

I remember that very day before we ran out onto Eden Park. The walls of the dressing rooms have louvre windows between the players and the public outside. The locals know that, and the rude and barbed jibes that drifted through as we prepared for that deciding Test worked better than a blow-torch to the stomach in getting us stirred up for the conflict. As I recall, there wasn't much noise coming from outside those windows about 4.45 that afternoon.

Then again, we probably wouldn't have heard it. The dressing room was packed with people, there were television lights and photographic flashes, Jonesy was running around shouting hoarsely (who ever thought he'd go hoarse!) that this was 'bigger than *Quo Vadis*', we had our arms around each other singing and congratulating ourselves, and every now and then you'd be passed the massive Bledisloe Cup, take a swig of champers from it, and pass it on.

Here we were deep in enemy territory and we were the champions. We were absolutely racked with exhaustion, but it's remarkable what that euphoria did for all those aches and pains.

I spared a thought for Andrew Slack, as he'd achieved another great victory as captain. Slacky had been around for a few years longer than me and to be still playing centre for Australia as well as he was, and leading us so well, was a fantastic achievement. He was always vastly underestimated and this further success should have finally changed a lot of people's opinions of him.

Another I thought of was Jeff Miller, who'd played such gutsy football in the second and third Tests. What a little dynamo he'd proved to be. And Mark Hartill, who'd been brought in from nowhere to fill the shoes of Andy McIntyre. He'd been under intense pressure in the three Tests but had never buckled. And Steve Cutler and Bill Campbell, who had dominated the line-outs so much during the series. Many thought a team couldn't afford to carry beanstalks like these two in the pack. But we had, and they'd done a fantastic job for us in securing possession.

Amidst all the dressing room din, in walked Brian Lochore, the All Black coach. This was akin to Rommel suddenly appearing in the doorway of Monty's headquarters at El Alamein. But Brian's big in humility as well as size. The noise quietened at his presence. Then, choosing his words carefully, he warmly congratulated Australia on the way they had played. Lochore had been my coach during the International Rugby Board Centenary matches earlier that year in Britain, and I had come to know and respect him as a great coach and a fantastic person. As Brian spoke, I could see the great sadness in his eyes and I felt very sorry for him, for it was only the fourth time this century the All Blacks had lost a series at home and he was going to have to bear the brunt of that humiliation.

Often I'm asked to compare the two occasions – winning the Grand Slam and taking that series from the All Blacks.

A tour of the British Isles is certainly the most interesting a rugby player can make, moving as you do through four different countries, experiencing the history and contrasting cultures, and playing on such famous grounds as Twickenham and Cardiff Arms Park. For those reasons alone, such a tour is very absorbing, a great experience in itself. To have won the Grand Slam made it even more memorable and highly emotional.

Scaling Mount Everest

In contrast, a tour of New Zealand is where the commitment to the game of rugby is more intense and the basic principles of winning and losing are honed more sharply than anywhere else on earth. Therefore, winning a series there is really the ultimate in terms of pure footballing satisfaction. I remember Greg Growden from the *Sydney Morning Herald* asking me that afternoon in the Eden Park dressing room what winning that 1986 series meant. I replied, 'Now I can live life in peace.' It meant that much to me.

A product of St Patrick's College, Goulburn, Simon Poidevin played 59 Tests for the Wallabies between 1980 and 1991. He made 13 overseas tours with Australia, was the first Wallaby to win 50 caps and played in 11 Sydney 1st-grade grand finals with Randwick for eight victories. He is now a senior commentator with the Seven Network and a managing director of stockbroking conglomerate Salomon Smith Barney.

Kindred spirits

You'll need to have a pretty good long-term rugby memory to recall what David Campese and former dynamic Easts open-side flanker Dirk Williams have in common. It's that they both played their first big game at the SCG in 1982 – the trans-Tasman Under 21 curtain-raiser for the second Test between the Wallabies and Scotland.

No fewer than 16 future internationals came out of that match. Campo's teammates in the Australian side included Michael Lynagh, Steve Tuynman and Tommy Lawton. Among Dirk's colleagues facing the young Aussies across the sacred old SCG turf were budding All Black greats Grant Fox and Steve McDowell. The Australian colts downed their New Zealand counterparts 36–12 and the teenage Campese so dazzled the selectors that his inclusion in the Wallaby team headed for NZ later that month was a mere formality. The rest is the stuff of rugby folklore.

From that day at the SCG 15 years ago the fortunes of the two rugby stalwarts took contrasting courses, but they came together again in the 1996 Wallabies' unbeaten tour of Europe. Campo played two Tests, while Williams served as fitness coach and even got a game in the green and gold when the side was decimated by injuries. He scored Australia's first try against a Scottish selection in Perth.

1984 Grand Slam heroes: the mercurial David Campese (centre) is supported by dashing full-back Roger Gould (left) and inspiring skipper Andrew Slack. Seven years later in Britain, Campo was judged Player of the 1991 World Cup, won so handsomely by the Wallabies.

Frank Keating

A free spirit – Mark Ella

'Improvement makes straight roads; but the crooked roads without improvement are the roads of genius.'

– William Blake

Gordon Bray writes: *Perhaps once, maybe twice, and, improbably, thrice in a lifetime, a rugby player arrives from heaven by 'special delivery'. A player with unique vision, instinctive reaction, a daring spirit and one-of-a-kind talent. A player who makes you, as a follower, feel privileged and fulfilled to have seen him perform first-hand.*

For me, Mark Ella was such a player. The spearhead of the historic 1984 Grand Slam tour under Alan Jones, his remarkable style and talents restructured the coaching manual for back-line play. In five eventful seasons of Test rugby, he always did things his way. Ella had his critics, but in truth his self-effacing approach was actually geared to satisfy appreciative spectators and fuel their continuing enjoyment of the game.

One such ardent fan was Frank Keating, the revered UK sports writer and unashamed rugby nut. He penned this tribute to Mark Ella in his 1993 book The Great Number Tens.

It is difficult, from this distance, to realise that [Stuart] Barnes' first one-off cap for England before [Rob] Andrew succeeded him was won at Twickenham against Australia on 3 November 1984, in direct confrontation with arguably the most regal and majestic No. 10 of all time. If Barry John was called, with reason, 'the king', then Mark Ella was the very 'prince' of fly-halves. Within a month, Ella's 1984 Wallabies inflicted a glorious whitewash on the four British Isles national teams. It was a voluptuous spasm in which the young Aboriginal – who, uniquely, scored tries in all four Tests – set coruscating new standards for the position.

And, in doing so, he preached what he practised. I was privileged to follow him throughout the tour. From Twickenham the Wallabies went to Belfast to prepare for the Dublin international. The touring team came in from practice at Ulster's ancient old club, Malone. It was bucketing down. The others returned, pronto, to the team hotel. Mark Ella stayed – to conduct a seminar. It was quite, quite memorable, and one recalls it like it was the day before yesterday.

He looks out at the rain, and shrugs and smiles: 'Sure, at home we only play in the rain two or three times a year. But we have to continue telling ourselves that our running game is suited to all conditions. Okay, it's wet – so you play your natural game and we'll play ours. Of course. We'll keep running the ball and, you'll see, it can be done. You have to make an effort to play good rugby. So often in Britain, I guess, three-quarters trot out and say: "Oh, its raining so let's just leave it to the forwards to slurp around."

'If backs don't try anything what are they out there for?'

There are more things in the philosophy of young Mark

Ella than are dreamed of by the majority of greybearded, clipboard-screaming coaches in Britain. For almost an hour he sat on a table in the Malone RFC clubroom and talked without a note to an entranced group of 60 or so of Ulster's leading coaches, schoolmasters and players.

'What I'm about to tell you,' he began, 'is not meant to degrade your British style of play at all: I just think it is worth it to compare it with my own attitude towards rugby . . .' He was received in awed silence, except for the odd scratching of a pen as a coach scribbled notes. Talk about the infant preaching to the wise men in the temple.

His arms were folded across his green national sweater as he extemporised, with insight and no little wit, his brown leather lace-up shoes gently rocking from the table. Behind him the usual clubhouse plaques in signwriter's gilt named the captains and the cups and the caps. The legendary Ernie Crawford played for Malone in the '20s, Jimmy Nelson in the '40s . . . those old-timers would have been awestruck at the aplomb of this young man – even more so by the content of his tutorial.

The dark-skinned handsome native boy from the Aboriginal mission station was himself that missionary now. He was born into poverty in La Perouse, which the rich whites of Sydney scornfully call 'Larpa – our Soweto'. They don't look down from the aircraft window for shame when they fly into Sydney airport over Botany Bay. It has been an Aborigine compound since Captain Cook hit land.

May and Gordon Ella brought up their 12 children in a shanty hut, which a nailed-up plyboard partition turned into a two-roomed job. They daily slept on shared mattresses on the floor; no privacy, no sewerage; there was one cold tap; a bath and a communal trough in the yard; a shower was when it rained, for the roof was a sieve.

Yet it was, the boy will tell you, a home with a lot of love and laughter. May was the adored, feared matriarch; Gordon, whose white grandfather had married an Aboriginal girl, was the romantic who loved to catch mullet off the cliffs when he had time away from the factory night shift.

But at least – as ghettoes go – the compensation was the sea down the lane and the sun on their backs. And 'La Pa' had a junior rugby and cricket team, so the children knew more than the rudiments when they were admitted to Matraville High School – since when Mark with his brothers, Glen and Gary, first inspired the Australian Schoolboys XV to a thrilling walkabout round the world before graduating, each one, to the full national side.

Mark won his first cap for Australia in 1980. He was 20. The torch he carried became brighter with every appearance. In 1983 he was elected Young Australian of the Year.

I sat there in Belfast, listening to him, and musing . . . I had seen the languid, outside-body swerve of Richard Sharp; the carefree, waiflike insouciance of Barry John; the hopscotch of [Phil] Bennet; the vim, dash and control of young [Mike] Gibson; the dozy skill and awareness of [Hugo] Porta . . . this boy here is in that classic line. But he is a revolutionary within it.

He scarcely fits into the canon. An original. It is worth rereading the description of the old-time Australian player and visionary coach Cyril Towers. He had written in the Twickenham program a week before: 'Ella runs from the shoulders down, with the fingers, hand and arms completely relaxed; he takes the ball on one side and passes before the foot comes down again; his concept of the fly-half position is that it is semi-restricted – the attack must begin further out; he is very difficult to think against – if you think ahead of him, he will slip inside, and it's no good thinking four or five moves ahead, because he hasn't invented them yet.'

Ella sits on the clubhouse table. No side, no swank. Only his soft voice, and the coaches' pencils frantically scratching at their notebooks. Many of them must have been coaching rugby for over 20 years. They were not going to miss these revelations from the 25-year-old prophet: 'You Irish have particularly impressed me that you are trying at least. But it's still dull football. You have got out of the habit of entertaining and running with the ball – it's an attitude which has evolved over the years. In Australia, we have been playing running football for a long time. I grew up playing that way. But here, the natural ability has been coached out of the players. You are playing too basic a game, concentrating on the physical aspect rather than moving the ball. Everybody says Britain has potentially the best backs but they only turn it on for five minutes in an entire match. That's no good. We have already lost count of the number of occasions teams started to run the ball against us when we are out of sight and the match won. Only then would you Brits move it.'

Above the scrape of the scribbling hieroglyphics, the packed room of rugby elders were murmuring enthused murmurs which seemed to mean a mixture of mea culpas and eureka.

'Fly-half play,' Ella went on, 'was more speed of thought than foot. Look at little me. I'm not fast. I'm not a stepper. I can run a bit, but I've no idea of a jink either off left or right.

And you know I can't kick for peanuts. At set pieces, no, I never run up in defence – simply because no one runs the ball at me; and in Britain they nearly always simply kick. A breakaway wing-forward has honestly never touched me in years – and I think that might be something to do with the secret . . .

'The crucial thing must be the speed of the ball through the hand. The quicker you get it, the quicker you can pass it on. The nearer you play on the opposition and the straighter you run, the better. It's common sense. Then, the shorter the pass, the quicker you can decide your options. Then, you can think of carrying the length of your passes.'

It was stunning stuff. No note, no prompt. Out of the mouths of babes . . . I wished Percy Bush could have been listening from heaven; or Adrian Stoop. Perhaps they were. Or Carwyn James, the coaching genius and old fly-half, who had, alas, died the year before, mourned by the game. How proud Carwyn would have been of this Aboriginal boy's clean mind and logic. On he went:

'British coaches must let young players read the game themselves and think for themselves on the field. That is non-existent in British rugby at this time. You are over-coached and the emphasis is far too much on winning – in any way. Your teams would rather defend than attack because it has become natural to them. As much as they are trying to say it's changing, I don't see it. Your teams have no imagination. They have been taught the same old moves with the same old patterns. They continually keep on call-ing the set moves.'

Nor was he finished, and I hugged myself again for being the only journalist who had bothered to turn up. And all

OPPOSITE *Mark Ella – fly-half extraordinaire. Although his Test career was way too short (1980–84), Ella established himself as one of the greatest running number 10s of all time.*

taking place on Dr Jack Kyle's patch and parish. The British fly-half disease, said young Ella, was reliance on the boot. 'Kicking away possession is absolutely crazy. To score a try you have to have the ball in your hands. I say to my scrum-half: "I'm calling the shots – give me the ball however bad it is!" All this British business of kicking for 20 minutes to size up the opposition!

'If in the first 20 minutes my scrum-half puts up one kick himself, then okay, I suppose; if he puts up two, I'll go over and hit him. His job is to get the ball to me any way he can. I call the moves, I distribute to those outside me and then, with the ball in their hands, they can put the pace on it. I know a lot of our fancy moves cause us Wallabies to make mistakes; we try everything and aren't quite getting the points on the board, but at least we try and we'll keep on trying. If not, isn't the whole thing totally boring for every-one concerned? How can you go out there and have the feeling: "If I try something and it works, then we're going to win"?'

It was still bucketing down outside; no matter, Ella was smiling – and so was every utterly refreshed fellow in the room as they turned another page in their notebooks and queued, to a man, for Mark Ella's autograph. There is, in fact, not much more one needs to log about Ella's fly-half play. Simply, as he talked that day, so he played.

On the following Saturday, Ireland were well beaten in Dublin – Ella dropping two goals and dapping down a blinding, 'loop-the-loop' try at the corner flag. Within the next three weeks, Wales and Scotland were both compre-hensively smithereened by the Australians by an aggregate score of 65–21. Both times, Ella was an inspiration and a joy.

Then, just like that – still 25, and two years younger even than Barry John had been – he retired. Rugby league, understandably, offered him a fortune; he declined it firmly and positively, with a gracious smile – and became a businessman and an unofficial, worldwide diplomat and distinguished human-rights activist for the cause of Aboriginals. I was next to meet him four years later, in 1988, when he was the enchanting manager of the commemorative centenary cricket tour of England by a team of Australian Aboriginals. He remembered how he had preached his gospel to the rugby elders of Ulster.

'That was an apocalyptic rainstorm, wasn't it?' he recalled. 'Apocalyptic' in more ways than one, said I.

Frank Keating has won a barrowload of Fleet Street awards in his capacity as feature sportswriter for the Guardian. *His autobiography,* Half-time Whistle, *was runner-up in the William Hill Sports Book of the Year award. He is also a columnist for the internationally renowned UK monthly magazine* Rugby World.

Peter Jenkins

Wallaby gold – the top ten

Ten classic matches from the author of *Wallaby Gold*

'An unbiased opinion is always absolutely valueless.'
                                    – Oscar Wilde

Like an addicted sweet tooth struggling to choose from the delights on a restaurant dessert trolley, selecting the best ten Australian Tests was an almost painful pleasure. The list was endlessly reviewed, revised, rewritten. But I did, in the end, make room for two matches the Wallabies lost – the 2000 Bledisloe Cup clash won by the All Blacks at Stadium Australia and the magnificent 1987 World Cup semifinal at Concord Oval won by France.

Elsewhere, I placed major emphasis on the significance of an occasion – a great victory of the time, or the turning point for future achievements. Many will argue with my top ten, but here they are, complete with a tie for the last spot.

1. Australia 16 New Zealand 6 – Dublin, 1991

In essence, this was the match that won Australia its first World Cup – a semifinal decided by two moments of magic in the first half by winger David Campese. Campo drifted off his blind wing after 12 minutes, took the first pass off the ruck and angled himself to the left corner, turning rival John Kirwan inside out before touching down.

But his solo effort was later upstaged by a blind over-the-shoulder pass for centre Tim Horan to cross in the 35th minute. Campese gathered a well-weighted chip kick from five-eighth Michael Lynagh, avoided one defender and drew two others before the famous offload. 'I knew Tim was there,' said Campese. 'I was just trying to suck the winger in and next thing I knew I was looking up off the ground to see Tim put the ball down.'

Australia had defeated the World Cup favourites and would, a week later, beat England to take the title. But this was the key match in the campaign and the Australian first-half display, led by Campese's attacking genius and an impregnable defence, was arguably its finest 40 minutes under Bob Dwyer's coaching. 'It was the most important game for Australia I've ever played in,' recalled flanker Simon Poidevin, a battle-scarred survivor of the 1984 Grand Slam and 1986 Bledisloe Cup wins.

2. *Australia 12 New Zealand 6 – Sydney, 1979*

The scenes at the SCG were unprecedented in the history of the Bledisloe Cup – the Wallabies, including their jubilant coach, Dave Brockhoff, running a victory lap after winning the oversized trophy of trans-Tasman dominance. But the joy was justifiable. This was the Wallabies' first seizure of the cup from All Black hands since Trevor Allan's side whitewashed a two-Test series in 1949. On this occasion, it was a one-off match. It was far from spectacular on the field, with Australia winning a tryless encounter courtesy of three penalty goals from full-back Paul McLean and a dropped goal from five-eighth Tony Melrose. However, the very reversal of the long-standing New Zealand monopoly on the Bledisloe Cup made it forever memorable. As respected Kiwi journalist Don Cameron penned, 'It will remain one of the vivid memories of sport.'

The win was achieved on the back of a marauding pack. Coach Brockhoff remembered: 'We had taken them on, we had beaten them at their own game. We had a low, vicious pack and they were magnificent. We didn't have the pretty backs but everyone played it perfectly.'

3. *New Zealand 39 Australia 35 – Sydney, 2000*

It has been dubbed 'the greatest Test of all time' but fails to take top billing on my list because, firstly, the Wallabies were beaten and, secondly, the match did not influence where the Bledisloe Cup or Tri Nations trophies would eventually be housed. However, for thrills, skill, entertainment and a lashing of the on-field bizarre (with a world-record crowd of 109 874 and a television audience of 2.8 million to boot), this was a special night unsurpassed in event magnitude. After just eight minutes the All Blacks had raced to a lead of 24–0 through three converted tries and a penalty goal. Australia hadn't touched the ball other than to kick off. When they did finally receive possession, a try to winger Stirling Mortlock followed. Ten minutes later Mortlock was over again: 19 minutes played, the All Blacks leading 24–12. Further tries to full-back Chris Latham and winger Joe Roff allowed Australia, miraculously, to go to the break on even terms. Seven minutes after the break, Mortlock kicked a penalty and Australia led for the first time. The tryfest continued apace until, in injury time with Australia leading 35–34, the ball was speared to the All Black left wing. Jonah Lomu went over wide out and the biggest name in the game had decided the biggest game. Ten tries in all were scored, five to each side.

4. *Australia 29 Lions 23 – Sydney, 2001*

While people will always remember THAT tackle by George Gregan to win a Bledisloe Cup in 1994, they will also recall THAT line-out steal when reminiscing about a Lions tour that surpassed expectations on all counts and came down to this series decider. Second-rower Justin Harrison had been brought into the side for his Test debut with David Giffin sidelined by injury. His job in the line-out was to mark the lion of the Lions, their skipper, Martin Johnson. Better than that, he pinched the ball thrown for Johnson in the closing stages of the Test as the tourists attacked, looking for the try that would surely kill off their hosts. The pressure had been building on the Wallabies and a score looked inevitable – until Harrison intervened.

This Test was the last for coach Rod Macqueen, who left the scene as the most successful Australian coach in history. It also completed a Grand Slam of major titles for the side he had guided since the final months of 1997. They had won a World Cup, a Tri Nations trophy and a boatload of Bledisloe Cups. But a series win over the British and Irish Lions was the last Holy Grail. No Wallaby side could boast a Lions series scalp and, long before this game, it seemed the 'Class of 2001' would finish empty-handed as well. The Lions creamed the world champions 29–13 in the first Test and led 11–6 at half-time in the second before the turnaround started.

5. Australia 11 South Africa 9 – Johannesburg, 1963

The historical importance of this win was illustrated with one statistic: South Africa, that proud rugby nation of behemoth forwards where the Springbok jumper ensures lifelong celebrity status, had never been beaten in successive home Tests since 1896. The Wallabies, humiliated on their 1961 tour, had lost the first of four Tests on this trip but sprang an upset in the second and backed it up with this one-try-to-nil effort. The side boasted Phil Hawthorne and Ken Catchpole in the halves, Greg Davis and Jules Guerasimoff in the back row and a well-credentialled tight-five of Jon White, Peter Johnson, skipper John Thornett, Rob Heming and Peter Crittle.

The Boks led 9–6 before winger John Williams scored for Australia with 13 minutes to play after good lead-up work from Crittle and centre Dick Marks. The most bizarre moment came in the final seconds, with Australia having a scrum feed on their own quarter and hooker Johnson petrified of being penalised for striking early. 'I told Catchy to make sure he put the ball in slowly. I knew their hooker wouldn't strike, hoping when I did it would look like I was early. So he held back, so did I, and there we were, our faces an inch off the ground and the ball sitting there'. Bok prop Hannes Marais reached out with a foot, mistimed his strike and kicked the ball back on the Australian side. Catchpole sent it to Hawthorne and his kick went out. Game over.

6. Australia 16 New Zealand 9 – Auckland, 1949

It remains one of the great debates of trans-Tasman competition. How good were the 1949 Wallabies? Or, more to the point, how good were the All Blacks they beat in successive

OPPOSITE *Wallaby heroes from the 1963 tour of South Africa, skipper John Thornett (in car, right) and mercurial scrum-half Ken Catchpole, are feted by the Sydney public at Hyde Park. David v. Goliath: Jonah Lomu (below right) runs amok in the 'greatest Test of all time' at Stadium Australia in 2000. This desperate tackle by George Gregan (left) saved a certain try.*

Tests to become the first Australian team to win the Bledisloe Cup in New Zealand – the only side to do so until Alan
Jones's outfit of 1986 returned home with a 2–1 series win?
New Zealand, when the Wallabies arrived in '49, had 30
players touring South Africa. But Australian captain Trevor
Allan, 50 years later, said it was wrong to imply that the best
All Blacks were overseas at the time. The NZ Rugby Union
president Don Max told Allan at a reception: 'You won't
beat us. I believe the best team is sitting here. The Maoris
were not allowed to go and quite a few of them should be
in South Africa. There are also a couple of forwards who
should have gone across.'

But the Australians did win, taking the first Test 11–6
in Wellington and following up with this victory at Eden
Park where one of Australia's greatest-ever flankers, Col
Windon, scored one of three tries. Windon had now scored
a try in five successive Tests. Second-rowers Rex Mossop
and Nick Shehadie dominated the second half line-outs and
five-eighth Nev Emery played with aplomb, while Allan's
tackling in the centres was, as usual, devastating.

7. *France 30 Australia 24 – Sydney, 1987*

French number 8 Laurent Rodriguez knocked on, the handling lapse was missed by Scottish referee Brian Anderson
and the play swept left. Two minutes to go, scores locked at
24-all in the World Cup semifinal of 1987 at the compact sub-
urban Sydney ground then known as Concord Oval. Through
11 pairs of French hands the ball travelled before the brilliant
Serge Blanco, the French full-back, made a graceful, effortless
run for the corner. He was all poise, and the defence was
in panic. Wallaby hooker Tom Lawton, somehow calling on

massive, weary thighs to carry him across in cover, made a desperate dive. Winger David Campese was also in on the chase. But Blanco was just out of reach.

How quickly it had turned sour for the Wallabies. With seven minutes remaining they had led 24–21 despite a day when the gods of injury were against them. Both centre Brett Papworth and second-rower Bill Campbell had made their exits with knee damage before the clock had passed 17 minutes. Australia led 9–6 at half-time and the lead was swapped on five occasions after the break. But the crucial play came just before the interval. The home side was up 9–0 when French second-rower Alain Lorieux stole a line-out on the Australian line and dived across. It breathed life into the French.

8. *Australia 27 New Zealand 23 – Christchurch, 1998*

This was a performance befitting the occasion and a display of sustained excellence as the Australians won on New Zealand soil for the first time since 1990. It ended a 40-year hoodoo at Lancaster Park and sealed the Bledisloe Cup series, decided that year over three Tests played on both sides of the ditch. Despite the final margin of four points, the Test was over when the Wallabies raced to a 27–9 lead during the second half. On an afternoon when the go-forward of the pack coupled with inspirational defence was crucial to Australia's success, the highlight was an ensemble try – one of the finest ever scored by a Wallaby side.

For three minutes and 10 seconds late in the first half, the Wallabies retained and controlled possession through 17 rucks and one maul before full-back Matt Burke scored. It was the hallmark of the Australian side under coach Rod

Macqueen: their ability to constantly recycle possession, mistake-free, until they suffocated an opposition. Second-rower Tom Bowman sidestepped Jonah Lomu on the way to a first-half try, but the star of the Australian victory was Jason Little, formerly a first-choice centre but now a utility player who was called onto the wing in place of the injured Ben Tune. Little scored one try and had a hand in three others.

9. *Australia 15 New Zealand 13 – Sydney, 1929*

They remain one of the most exclusive clubs in Australian rugby, the band of 23 players, including two run-on replacements, who took part in the three Tests against the All Blacks in 1929. In making a clean sweep of three matches, the Australians became the first nation to impose such a humiliation on the All Blacks. They are also, along with the 1998 side, the only Australian team to complete a three-Test series whitewash of the trans-Tasman neighbours.

Australia had won the first two Tests 9–8 and 17–9 before playing the third at the SCG in late July. The home side included two back-line legends, five-eighth Tom Lawton and centre Cyril Towers; one of Australia's greatest back-rowers in Jack Ford; and the infamous 'Wild' Bill Cerutti at prop. There was still a healthy contingent of the 1927–28 Waratahs in the team, but where that side was revered for its scintillating back-line play, this 1929 outfit also had a pack capable of outplaying the All Blacks up front. Yet, at half-time in this Test, the All Blacks led 13–9 after scoring three tries to nil. After the break the green-clad Australians took over, with Towers setting up the first of two tries, scored in the corner by Jack Ford. Centre Syd King scored the decider

12 minutes from time after taking a pass from his midfield partner, Towers.

Tied 10. Australia 27 France 14 – Sydney, 1986

Under the coaching of Alan Jones, the Wallabies enjoyed the greatest golden period Australian rugby had witnessed until the early 1990s triggered further waves of success. In 1984, a first-ever Grand Slam was achieved in the UK and Ireland with Mark Ella scoring a try in each Test, and in 1986 the Wallabies won the Bledisloe Cup in New Zealand. But sandwiched between those two successes was one of the most overlooked performances from the Australian side of the time. The forward performance at the SCG against the French, six weeks before the Wallabies embarked on their NZ tour, was complete. Skipper Andrew Slack considered it the best he had seen, superior even to the 1984 crushing of Wales that had included a pushover try at Cardiff Arms Park, and the 1979 shutdown of the All Blacks pack in Sydney.

The French were favourites after destroying Queensland with 10 tries, but the Australian forwards and a watertight midfield defence, where Michael Cook and Slack teamed in the centres, brought the joint Five Nations champions undone. Five-eighth Michael Lynagh controlled the game with his tactical kicking, second-rowers Steve Cutler and Bill Campbell made the line-outs their own domain, and the scrum pinched two tight heads.

Tied 10. Australia 20 New Zealand 5 – Wellington, 1964

Conditions were unusually calm for the Windy City as the All Blacks kicked off, but the on-field storm had yet to hit. Midway through the first half, Australian hooker Peter

241

Johnson won a tight head and half-back Ken Catchpole darted to the blind-side before sending winger Stewart Boyce over in the corner. By half-time it was still the only score: Australia 3–0 ahead. Full-back Terry Casey landed a penalty after the break for 6–0 before the All Blacks, leading the series 2–nil, scored from a high ball.

But the Australian halves, Catchpole and Phil Hawthorne, and flankers Greg Davis and Jules Guerasimoff, were inspired. Hawthorne landed a drop goal for a 9–5 lead, Casey kicked two penalties for 15–5, and then the All Blacks turned over possession inside their half. Catchpole, ever the opportunist, made another rapier dash to the blind, found Boyce, and his chip and regather brought him a second try. It also gave the Australians a 15-point victory, their biggest win over the All Blacks and the worst defeat New Zealand had suffered since going down 0–17 to South Africa in 1928. And the Australian side, while in the midst of a successful era, could have been even more effective if former Wallabies Michael Cleary, Jim Lisle, Arthur Summons, Dick Thornett and Kevin Ryan had stayed in the game. They were now playing rugby league and toured with the 1963 Kangaroos.

Peter Jenkins is the senior rugby correspondent for the Daily Telegraph. *He is the author of the magnificent chronicle* Wallaby Gold, *which celebrates 100 years of Australian Test rugby.*
A former 1st-grade fly-half with Parramatta, he has been covering rugby for the News Limited group since 1985.

RICOH CAPLIO RR1. THE WORLD'S MOST STUNNING DIGITAL CAMERA
STEAL THE LIMELIGHT WITH THE STAGGERING DESIGN AND SOPHISTICATION OF THE RICOH CAPLIO RR1

4.1 MILLION PIXEL RESOLUTION•
PRINT HIGH QUALITY A3 PICTURES•
10.8x ZOOM (3 X OPTICAL/ 3.6 X DIGITAL)•
STILL, MOTION, SOUND, TEXT RECORDING•
1CM MACROS•
FLEXIBLE MULTI-ANGLE MONITOR•

RICOH
Image Communication
WWW.RICOH.COM.AU

Live with one of Australia's Greatest Sporting Teams.

Pacific Bay Resort at Coffs Harbour is the official 'Base Camp'
where the Wallabies live and train before tackling the world's leading rugby teams.
Pacific Bay offers both first class resort accommodation and facilities,
and a unique opportunity to own a wide range of properties
which are for sale through our on site office.
For more information please call 1300 363 360 to secure your place… with the Wallabies.

PACIFIC BAY
COFFS HARBOUR

PREMIER PROPERTY DEVELOPMENT

Charlesworth Bay Road Charlesworth Bay
PO Box 6725 Park Beach Plaza Coffs Harbour NSW 2450
Phone: (02) 6652 7333 **Fax:** (02) 6650 9011
www.pacificbay.com.au

Home
of the
Wallabies

THAKRAL HOLDINGS GRO

Olympic glory

The historical sporting curiosity of Australia's Olympic gold medal for rugby at the London Games in 1908 is well documented. The Wallabies beat English county champions Cornwall, representing the UK, 32–3, but only after surviving a half-time protest from a Pommy official who reckoned our lads were wearing running spikes.

What is not commonly known about that contest is that we could never have done worse than the silver medal. Australia and Cornwall were the only two teams to take part.

Rugby first made the Olympic program in 1900 in Paris when introduced by Baron Pierre de Coubertin, who, incidentally, refereed the first-ever French championship final. Paris also staged the last Olympic tournament, in 1924, when the USA team, comprising mainly students from Stanford University, scored an upset victory over the home nation in front of 40 000 fans on 18 May at Colombes Stadium. It was not a popular victory. One US player did not receive his medal at the ceremony after being felled by the umbrella of an irate Frenchwoman.

Australian Dan Carroll has the unique distinction of winning Olympic rugby gold medals for two countries. He was a member of the 1908 Wallabies and in 1920, at Antwerp, pulled on a USA jumper.

The Olympic-champion Wallabies take the field against Devon in their opening game in Britain. The Australians finished with an impressive tour record: played 38, won 32, lost 5, drew 1.

H.M. Moran

Men, rough men and rugby

Adapted from the memoirs of Herbert 'Paddy' Moran, captain of the 1908–09 Wallabies

'This story shall the good man teach his son.'
— Shakespeare, *Henry V*

At Sydney University there was almost no chance for a mediocre or an inexpert player to get a game. I was interested in sport but already at 17 had become an onlooker. Then, a man who used to come to our house and sing sentimental songs in a poor but manly voice chided me one evening on my slackness.

I was a miserable, stooped, poring introspective sort of fellow in my third year of university. Whatever he said stung. When he ended up his castigation by offering to get me a game the next day, I accepted it. Five years later I captained the first Australian rugby team which visited England. I owe all of that to him, and to my momentary resentment.

In that first match I wore a pair of hastily cut down trousers, a pair of old boots on which bars in front, and sprigs on the heels, had been feverishly hammered; also an

244

ancient sweater. The team was the Rose Bay F.C. – it consisted of men from offices and banks who played in no competition and for no cup. It was the very essence of sporting rugby. We trained occasionally, before an important match, but usually we got our wind with a preliminary down the field just before the game began. We were beaten more often than not, but from the noisy laughter and rude guffaws which could be heard later in the nearest bar, you might have thought we had won some glorious victory.

For the following season I was invited to play for the university's second team. Gone now was the cheery irresponsibility of play: this grade football was a serious business. We must win the premiership! There was now something in the games entirely new to me, and for which such terms as 'vigour' or 'robustness' were a euphemism. When you sank on the ball to stop a dribbling rush half a dozen feet raffled on you like heavy knocks at a door which would not open.

This of course was not the sport for a purist, but for a timid lad like myself it had its value. When professionalism was established later on, the game became cleaner because we lost some of the rougher element, but it was not all gain for us.

In 1904, amateur rugby was still a game for all the classes. There were no social distinctions nor any systematic professionalism. We all stood on a level of equality and since we played only on Saturday afternoons no one lost money by playing. Those who later became professionals changed their status, not as a rule from any dire necessity, but out of a desire to gain their living more pleasantly. It was they themselves who created a social discrimination in Australian rugby.

We tussled with factory hands and firemen, with miners,

wharf labourers and carters. These players might have rougher manners but in many of the elementary virtues of life they were our superiors. Above all they had a hard edge to their characters and a robuster humour. By contact with them we gained immeasurably more than they. When professionalism came, university players were shut out from friendships with men in ranks called lower and their education suffered by it. Whatever polite scholarship they might possess they were now sentenced to be weaker in humanity.

The next year I was in the university first team and won my 'blue'. In this grade the player was on a higher plane of organised roughness. It was, however, largely a good-natured violence. There were only a few vicious players who would deliberately do a man harm although grade matches were always a form of local warfare. None of the very nice refinements of sportsmanship were observed and yet the hard code was not without its chivalries. In the Decalogue of our rugby, there were two commandments on which you were judged and condemned. There were: 'Thou shalt not squib it', and again: 'Thou shalt not squeal'. In some clubs the front-row forwards used to let their beards grow for two or three days before a match, and thus armed at all points would rub their faces against the tender newly shaven cheeks of their opposite numbers.

University players had a reputation for good sportsmanship, although some of our enemies said we hit first and apologised afterwards. In 1906 I went to Queensland with the New South Wales team. In the first match at Brisbane one of our hulking big forwards jumped in the air and kicked the Queensland full-back on the chest. I was horrified. There were angry shouts from the crowd and the referee coming up ordered the wrong player off. It was an amazing situation. Many of us New South Welshman gathered round a red-faced and angry referee and supporting the alibi of the innocent player while the real culprit hid away. In the end no one left the field.

None of us enjoyed that first experience of a representative game. As a horse-drag was taking us from the ground to our hotel, stones were thrown by the crowd and one struck 'Bluey' Burdon, but no one complained. Somehow we were all feeling relieved that we had not been pelted with rocks on the ground itself. Some of our team had deserved it.

The outstanding player in the Australian season in 1906 was H.H. 'Dally' Messenger, one of the great three-quarters of all time. His play was full of surprises, unorthodox, flashy. His game was directed largely by the unconscious mind. He did not, like lesser players, have to think it all out deliberately. In rugby we still neglect too much the element of surprise in all our attacks. Our methods are too fixed and too stereotyped. Messenger never became a slave to copybook practices. He was a natural player whose instinct enabled him to see and take an opening in that operative second which is all-important. He was like Bradman in cricket: sensory impressions took a shortcut in his brain so that coordination was almost instantaneous. If you watch Bradman you will find him balanced in the correct position, apparently seconds before the ball arrives. Yet he has assumed that stance only after the bowler has begun his action.

Messenger had a brilliant career both in the rugby union and the northern (rugby) league games but somehow all the world went wrong with him, and later, while his name still lingered on footballs and football boots, the man himself was

247

Rugby Union Football Team for England.

S. A. Middleton
(Glebe).

M. M'Arthur
(Eastern Suburbs).

Dr. H. M. Moran (Captain)
(Newcastle).

C. A. Hammond
(University).

N. Row
(Eastern Suburbs).

F. Wood (Glebe).

Mr J. M'Mahon (Manager).
(Photo by Wiley, Brisbane.)

P. M'Cue (Newtown).

C. M'Murtrie (Orange).

F. Bede Smith (Macquarie).

Ward Prentice (Western Suburbs).

C. E. Murnin (Eastern Suburb

Rugby Union Football Team for England.

J. T. Barnett (Newtown).

P. Burge (South Sydney).

T. Griffin (Glebe).

E. Maudible (Sydney).

P. Flanagan (Queensland).

T. Richards (Queensland).

H. Daly (Mudgee).

C. H. M'Kivat (Glebe).

E. Parkinson (Queensland).

P. Carmichael (Queensland).

D. B. Carroll (St. George).

J. Hickey (Glebe).

E. M'Intyre (Orange).

C. Russell (Newtown).

W. Dix (Armidale).

Sydney's Town and Country Journal *published these pictures of the first Wallabies on 5 August 1908 in the lead-up to their tour of Britain. Captained by Herb Moran (opposite, top row centre), the team won Australia's lone Olympic gold medal for rugby, downing England's representative, Cornwall. They also beat the English at Twickenham but lost a torrid international against Wales.*

forgotten and fell upon hard times. Like a great catherine-wheel he had flared and spluttered in a dazzling white light and suddenly faded out, a dark thing lost in the darkness.

Many years afterwards he came along one day when by chance I had stopped my car in the street to talk of football days to a great little player named Jimmy Clarken. The three of us loitered there, lost in reminiscence of this and that footballer who had feinted or fended his way to a goal line when, a little hurt that his own feats were being neglected, Messenger said simply: 'I was a pretty fair player myself, in those days.'

We hastened to repair our omission of tribute and turn the kaleidoscope of our memories to days when, emulating A.E. Stoddart, he leapt over a full-back, or scored amazing tries. We left him lost in a reverie, his eyes shining. He was hearing again the rapturous applause of the great multitudes who, still remembering his deeds, had now forgotten him.

In those days in Sydney were many picturesque types. There was a fruit dealer who played three-quarter in an old brown cap pulled rakishly down on one side. Since he was given to drink, his teammates often had to seek for him on the morning of a match in the back streets of a dingy suburb. Then after a cold shower and a rub-down, untrained as he was, he would go out on the field and surprise everyone with a sparkling, individual game, full of delightful impromptus. He had that faculty possessed by some untutored players of scoring unexpected tries. But then he went through life always snatching at something, spasmodically.

There are tragic figures as well as ludicrous in that old gallery of portraits. We had for a contemporary a big chunk of a man whom we admired for his qualities of grit and rugged determination. He was not a great exponent, lacking the speed and cleverness necessary for the first flight, but in a tight corner he shone resolute and inspiring. When the war came he responded promptly, displaying the same qualities in the ranks as with his team. What a great try-out is the football ground! How well we got to know the shiner who was brilliant when all was going well and easy, but who was missing – hanging out on the outskirts of the ruck – when our horny-handed opponents were 'putting it in'.

For rugby is a great game, not ending with the blown whistle. Years after we see again the rift in the opposing defences. We get ready to break through with a sudden flash of speed. Long after the events we still stretch ourselves full-length barely to reach the heels of a flying three-quarter, drag them to ourselves and him to the ground. We leap, once more, higher than the others on a long line-out, gather the ball on our fingertips, marvellously, and head the rush onward.

We sink at the feet of dribbling forwards and gather the ball as the attacking force tumbles pell-mell upon us; the situation is saved! We feel the joyous rapture of massed forwards taking it on in a fierce irruption, or of centre-threes swerving through and just reaching the white line as they hit the green turf. The earth trembles but a try has been scored.

Herb Moran released his memoirs, Viewless Winds, *in 1939. His passion for the game and his respect for those who played rugby in the true spirit, as demonstrated in this extract, would be just as appropriate had it been written today.*

He who doth all things well

For sheer excellence in an incredible number of sports, it's hard to imagine anyone surpassing our own Reginald 'Snowy' Baker. In 1904, Snowy was capped twice at scrum-half against the touring British team. He also represented Australia in boxing, polo, swimming and diving, as well as competing in top-level rowing, wrestling, surfing and equestrian events. Before graduating to a career as a star of silent films, Baker fought for the middleweight boxing gold medal at the 1908 Olympics. His opponent was the future England cricket captain, J.W.H.T. Douglas. The crowd agreed Snowy had won the bout fair and square, but he lost the gold medal on points. The 'man in the middle' (who had scored the fight) just happened to be Douglas's father!

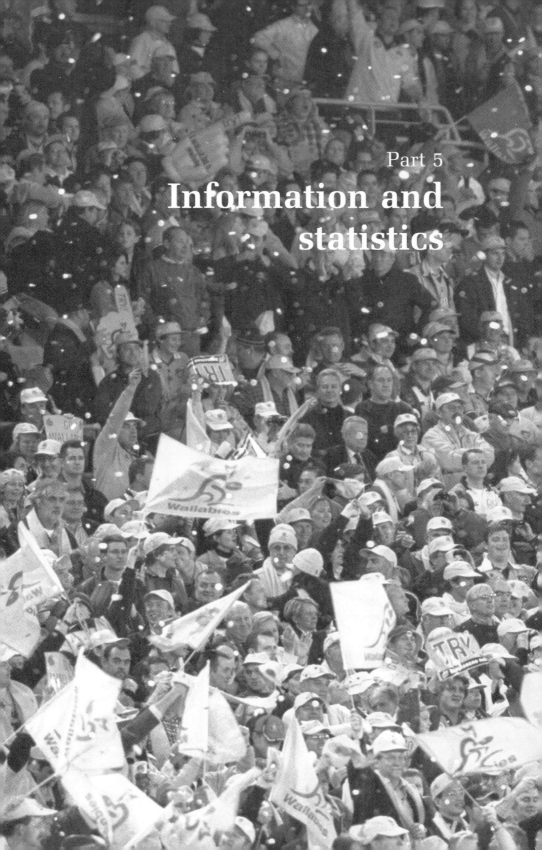

Part 5
Information and statistics

Channel Seven's televised rugby schedule: Internationals 2002

As the free-to-air TV rights holder in Australia, the Seven Network televises all domestic rugby Test matches live. Details of the end-of-2002 Wallaby tour telecasts are yet to be confirmed. Please check TV guides for accurate times.

2002 BUNDABERG RUM RUGBY SERIES

15 June Australia v. New Zealand Maori – Subiaco Oval, Perth

RESULT   Australia............................. New Zealand ....

22 June Australia v. France – Colonial Stadium, Melbourne

RESULT   Australia............................. New Zealand.............................

29 June Australia v. France – Stadium Australia, Sydney

RESULT   Australia............................. France ....

TRI NATIONS SERIES

13 July New Zealand v. Australia – Jade Stadium, Christchurch

RESULT   New Zealand .... Australia ....

20 July New Zealand v. Sth Africa – Westpac Trust Stadium, Wellington

RESULT   New Zealand .... Sth Africa ....

Channel Seven's televised rugby schedule

27 July Australia v. South Africa – The Gabba, Brisbane

RESULT   Australia............................ South Africa ....

3 August Australia v. New Zealand – Stadium Australia, Sydney

RESULT   Australia............................ New Zealand.............................

10 August South Africa v. New Zealand – ABSA Stadium, Durban

RESULT   South Africa .... New Zealand.............................

17 August South Africa v. Australia – Ellis Park, Johannesburg

RESULT   South Africa .... Australia ....

END OF SEASON TOUR

2 November Argentina v. Australia – Buenos Aires

RESULT   Argentina........................... Australia....................................

9 November Ireland v. Australia – Lansdowne Road, Dublin

RESULT   Ireland............................... Australia....................................

16 November England v. Australia – Twickenham, London

RESULT   England............................. Australia....................................

23 November Italy v. Australia – Genoa

RESULT   Italy .... Australia ....

Seven's rugby production team is led by producer Niki Hamilton. The director is Greg Clarke, technical director is Gavin Romanis and associate producers are Jacqui Powell and Matt Gray. Harold Anderson is Network Director of Sport and the Olympics. Seven's 2001 Bledisloe Cup telecast won a Logie for 'Most Outstanding Sports Coverage'.

Australian rugby
Test stadiums

Ground capacity determines which stadiums are used for Test matches in Australia; the standard minimum for a major game is 40 000. Stadium Australia, with its new capacity of 80 000, will be the signature venue for the 2003 World Cup. With all 48 matches to be staged in Australia, every mainland capital will host games, along with selected regional centres.

THE GABBA, Brisbane

Capacity: 37 000
Australian Test record at the ground: Played 3, won 0, lost 3

The Brisbane Cricket Ground, or 'The Gabba' as it is more widely known, takes its name from the suburb of Woolloongabba, where it is located. There are two theories as to the meaning of the Aboriginal words from which 'Woolloongabba' is derived – it either means 'whirling water' or 'fight talk place'. The ground dates from 1895, when the land was designated as the site for a cricket ground. The Gabba was first used for Test cricket in 1931, when Don Bradman christened the ground with an innings of 236 – still the highest Test innings at the Gabba. In 1960–61 the ground saw the famous 'tied Test' between Australia and the West Indies.

The Gabba has been used for much more than just cricket: athletics, Aussie Rules, greyhound racing, soccer, concerts and rugby. Today the ground is home to the Pura Cup side the Queensland Bulls, as well as the 2001 AFL premiers, the Brisbane Lions. In 2000 it was used as an Olympic soccer venue, hosting seven matches.

Rugby returned to the Gabba in 2001 for the first time in 50 years, when the Wallabies played the Lions in the First Test. The game set a new modern-day attendance record of 37 460. The ground has now seen three Test matches, but the Wallabies are yet to record a victory there.

STADIUM AUSTRALIA, Sydney

Capacity: Before reconfiguration 110 000; after reconfiguration 85 000

Australian Test record at the ground: Played 6, won 5, lost 1

Stadium Australia was the main venue for the Sydney 2000 Olympic Games. In less than three years the site had been remarkably transformed from a crumbling abattoir and stockyard into the largest stadium ever built for an Olympics. An estimated 4.5 billion people around the world watched the opening ceremony staged at the stadium. It is located at the demographic heart of Sydney: half of the city's four-million population live within a 30-minute drive of the Homebush Bay site.

257

Since the stadium opened in 1999, some epic rugby Test matches have been played on the ground. In 2000 a world-record rugby crowd of 109 874 turned out to watch the All Blacks beat the Wallabies 39–35 in what was later described as the greatest rugby game ever played. In 2001 the Wallabies beat the Lions in the Third Test to win the Tom Richards Cup for the first time. Later that year they defeated the All Blacks when Toutai Kefu scored in injury time – the try that gave the retiring John Eales a fairy-tale finish to his career.

The atmosphere, and just about everything about the stadium, is enormous. During the 1999 Bledisloe Cup game, 180 000 beers were poured and 16 000 pies were eaten.

Stadium Australia has been used for a wide variety of events, including soccer and rugby league. Following the Olympics the stadium was reconfigured and it is now able to host cricket and Aussie Rules games.

COLONIAL STADIUM, Melbourne

Capacity: 52 000
Australian Test record at the ground: Played 2, won 2, lost 0

Colonial Stadium is one of the most recent and most advanced rugby stadiums in the world. It has a retractable roof that is capable of closing in eight minutes. Sections of movable seating enable the stadium to be reconfigured to suit many sports.

The stadium is the home ground for three AFL clubs: Essendon (the Bombers), St Kilda (the Saints) and the Western

258

Bulldogs. It is also the former home of the city's rugby league side, the Melbourne Storm. The ground has hosted soccer matches and in 2000 successfully staged a one-day international cricket series between Australia and South Africa. When not hosting sports events, Colonial Stadium has been used for concerts including Bon Jovi, Barbra Streisand and Ricky Martin.

Despite its location in the AFL heartland, the stadium is quickly building a tradition as one of the great rugby stadiums in Australia. In 2000 the Wallabies played the First Test on the ground, defeating the Springboks to win the inaugural Mandela Cup. The following year the ground was used for the Second Test against the touring British and Irish Lions. With the roof closed and a roaring capacity crowd, the atmosphere was incredible. The rugby played was also memorable, with the Wallabies recording a series-levelling win to remain undefeated at Colonial.

SUBIACO OVAL, Perth

Capacity: 43 513
Australian Test record
at the ground: Played 3, won 1, lost 1, drawn 1

Subiaco Oval, home of AFL clubs the Fremantle Dockers and the West Coast Eagles, has for many years been Western Australia's football headquarters. The first recorded game played on the site was back in 1896, when the Subiaco Football Club met the Fremantle Imperials. Once known as 'the sand patch', the ground has a rich history in Aussie Rules, having hosted the WAFL competition, State of Origin games and, more recently, AFL matches. The attendance record was established in 1970, when 52 322 people turned out to watch the local grand final between West Perth and South Fremantle.

During the 1950s and '60s the ground hosted professional tennis matches. Concert presentations have ranged from Nat King Cole in 1956 to Elton John and Led Zeppelin in the 1970s. Recently the stadium has hosted soccer matches, including the 2002 National Soccer League Grand Final between the Perth Glory and the Sydney Olympic Sharks.

Subiaco has also built a reputation as a great stadium for rugby Test matches. The first international was played on the ground in 1998, when the Wallabies met the Springboks. The venue again hosted Test rugby in 1999, when Ireland played the Wallabies. In 2001 the Springboks returned to contest a nail-biting draw with Australia. The public in the West has warmed to the 15-man code and each match has attracted large crowds and been played in a tremendous atmosphere.

Gordon Bray's Wallaby profiles: 2002 Wallabies

The following pool of players, with a few exceptions, are on Australian Rugby contracts. Some new players will be added to the list in 2002/2003 based on performances in Super 12 and other major domestic competitions, and more major signings from rugby league are possible before the start of the 2003 domestic season.

GRAEME BOND

Position	Centre/Wing
Height	180 cm
Weight	95 kg
Date of birth	21 May 1974
Nicknames	Bondy, The Iceman
Club	Northern Suburbs
State	ACT
Tests	5
Test points	5 [1t]
Test debut	2001 v. South Africa, Subiaco Oval, Perth
Honours	NSW Country U19s; NSW Country 21s; NSW U19s; NSW U21s; NSW; ACT; Australian U19s; Australian U21s; Australian Barbarians; Australian Wallabies
Senior tours	2001 – Europe

Graeme Bond is an elusive running utility back who can play either in the centres or on the wing. He had a superb season with the victorious Brumbies in 2001, paving the way for his selection in the Wallabies squad. A try against the Maori in his first game for the Wallabies was soon followed by a Test cap, when he came off the bench against the Springboks in Perth.

Injuries have plagued his career and prior to season 2001 he had not played an injury-free season since 1993. Two shoulder reconstructions, numerous knee problems, broken hands, hamstring strains as well as a crippling back injury have all interrupted his progression in representative rugby. This constant battle with injury has tormented Bond so much that he now avoids wearing the number 13 jersey for superstitious reasons.

Raised near an active volcano on the isolated Duke of York Island in Papua New Guinea, Graeme wasn't even aware of rugby's existence until he moved to Brisbane at the age of 13. Attending Marist Ashgrove, he played in the same teams as Dan Herbert and Pat Howard. In his first year at school he was also ball boy to John Eales. From selection in the 1992 Australian Schools side he progressed through the ranks to play Australian U19s and U21s and then with the NSW Waratahs in 1995. After being overlooked by the Waratahs in 1998, he moved to the Brumbies in 1999 where he has proved to be a major attacking weapon, as shown by his hat-trick of tries against the Sharks in 2002. Bond has also broadened his experience by playing with Southland in New Zealand's NPC competition.

TOM BOWMAN

Position	Lock
Height	201 cm
Weight	117 kg
Date of birth	13 July 1976
Nickname	Disaster
Club	Eastern Suburbs
State	NSW
Tests	16
Test points	10 [2t]
Test debut	1998 v. England, Ballymore
Honours	NSW; NSW U19s; Australian Schools; Australian U19s; Australian U21s; AIS Australian Barbarians; Australian Wallabies
Senior tours	1997 – Argentina; 1998 – France, England; 1999 – World Cup (UK); 2001 – Europe

Tom Bowman burst onto the international stage as a 22-year-old when he played 12 of the 13 Tests in 1998. He proved to be a valuable member of the Wallaby side with his strong line-out play and devastating running with the ball. He was subsequently named Wallaby Rookie of the Year. One of the highlights of 1998 was his runaway try against the All Blacks in Christchurch, an effort that helped Australia secure the Bledisloe Cup.

Since that dream year of 1998 he has been dogged by a succession of injuries, leading to his apt nickname of 'Disaster'. The Bowman injury list includes a number of knee problems as well as a troublesome ankle. This has made it difficult for Tom to return to his best form and his outings in the Wallaby jumper have been limited. His disastrous luck was highlighted when he was once forced to miss a Super 12 game after he lacerated his oesophagus when eating a steak sandwich.

A product of the Scots College in Sydney, Tom's rugby career developed along traditional lines via the Australian Schools, Australian U19s and two years in the Australian U21s. His two seasons with the U21s side yielded two victories in the Southern Hemisphere Championship.

MATTHEW BURKE

Position	Full-back
Height	184 cm
Weight	97 kg
Date of birth	26 March 1973
Nickname	Burkey
Club	Eastwood
State	NSW
Tests	58
Test points	723 [24t, 87c, 143pg]
Test debut	1993 v. South Africa, Sydney Football Stadium
Honours	Sydney; NSW; Barbarians; Australian Schools; Australian U21s; Australian Sevens; AIS Australian Barbarians; Australian Wallabies
Senior tours	1993 – World Cup Sevens (Scotland), North America, France; 1995 – World Cup (South Africa); 1996 – Europe; 1999 – World Cup (UK); 2000 – Japan, France, UK; 2001 – Europe

Matt Burke is Australia's most capped full-back and has been a prolific points scorer for both the Waratahs and the Wallabies. Second only to Michael Lynagh on Australia's all-time Test-scoring list, he holds numerous individual records, including most points in a single Test by an Australian (39 points against Canada in 1996).

Raised just up the hill from where Granny Smith grew her famous apples, Matt began his sporting career with the Carlingford Redbacks soccer club. His rugby career blossomed while boarding at the famous St Joseph's College in Sydney, where he won selection in the 1990 Australian Schools team. His brilliant athleticism meant that he also enjoyed success at cricket and athletics, where he was GPS champion in both hurdles and long jump.

Burke's fast-maturing talent gained him selection for Eastwood's 1st side in his first year out of school. He went on to make the Australian U19s and U21s teams before being selected for his Test debut in 1993 against the Springboks as a replacement for Damian Smith on the wing. He has now played over 50 Tests, including two World Cup campaigns. A number of serious injuries have sidelined Matt over the last few years, but each time he has managed to fight back and reclaim his Wallaby jersey. He is now a senior member in the Wallabies side and captain of the Waratahs. In the 2002 Super 12 Matt successfully made the transition to outside centre, where he enjoyed an outstanding season.

BRENDAN CANNON

Position	Hooker
Height	187 cm
Weight	107 kg
Date of birth	5 April 1973
Nicknames	Maximus, Canno
Club	Sydney University
State	NSW
Tests	5
Test points	0
Test debut	2001 v. British and Irish Lions, Colonial Stadium, Melbourne
Honours	Queensland U19s; Queensland; Australian Schools; Australian U19s; AIS Australian Barbarians; Australian Wallabies
Senior tours	1997 – Argentina; 2001 – Europe

Often mistaken for movie star Russell Crowe, Brendan Cannon emerged on the Wallaby scene in 2001 following two consistent years as hooker with the NSW Waratahs. After playing understudy to Michael Foley at the Reds for five years, Brendan moved south at the end of the 1999 season. His move proved fruitful when an injury to Jeremy Paul in the 2001 Lions series paved the way for him to win his first Test cap in the Second Test in Melbourne.

Brendan's rugby career began with the Souths under 7s in Brisbane even though he was only four years old at the time. Playing flanker at school, he went on to win selection in the Australian Schools and then the Australian U19s. In 1993 a serious car accident threatened to end his rugby career, but he made a remarkable comeback and was playing again by the end of the season. After much encouragement from former Wallaby hooker Chris Carberry, Cannon turned out as a hooker the following year. The move proved a master-stroke and he soon found himself in the Reds squad. Two years later he was sitting on the Wallaby bench in the Test against Canada.

Brendan has a degree in communications and also holds a real estate licence. In his spare time he works for a firm of property consultants, and he is planning to do his Masters in commerce and property economics.

MATT COCKBAIN

Position	Blind-side flanker/ Lock
Height	197 cm
Weight	105 kg
Date of birth	19 September 1972
Nickname	Labbie
Club	GPS
State	Queensland
Tests	46
Test points	5 [1t]
Test debut	1997 v. France, Ballymore
Honours	Queensland Country U19s; Queensland; AIS Australian Barbarians; Australian Wallabies
Senior tours	1997 – Argentina, UK; 1998 – France, England; 1999 – World Cup (UK); 2000 – Japan, France, UK; 2001 – Europe

Matt Cockbain did not play his first game of rugby until he was 16 years old, in the North Queensland schools trials while he was attending Innisfail High School. Incredibly, he won selection in the team. Matt then went on to be picked for the Queensland Country U21s and the Queensland Country senior side. In 1994 he moved to Brisbane and in 1995 won selection in the Queensland side and was named Reds Rookie of the Year.

After a strong season in the 1997 Super 12 with the Reds, Matt was rewarded with his first Test cap against the French at Ballymore. Since then he has been a regular member of the Wallaby side, either in the back row or second row. Best known for his punishing defence, Matt also provides an extra option in the line-out. He is now close to reaching 50 caps for Australia. Cockbain joined elite company when he captained the Wallabies in their tour game against Oxford during the 2001 European tour.

Matt is a draughtsman by trade, having completed an Associate Diploma in Civil Engineering. He also has a passion for electronic equipment, owning a massive stereo system and a Sony PlayStation that is popular with the other players on tour. His brother Brent also plays rugby, having appeared for the Australian U21s. Brent is currently playing with Pontypridd in Wales.

MARK CONNORS

Position	Lock/Blind-side flanker
Height	196 cm
Weight	101 kg
Date of birth	17 May 1971
Nickname	Buzzard
Club	Souths
State	Queensland
Tests	20
Test points	10 [2t]
Test debut	1999 v. South Africa, Lang Park, Brisbane
Honours	Queensland; AIS Australian Barbarians; Australian Wallabies
Senior tours	1996 – Europe; 1999 – World Cup (UK); 2000 – Japan, France, UK; 2001 – Europe

A product of St Laurence's College in Brisbane, Mark Connors made his Queensland debut on the Reds' end-of-season tour to Argentina in 1994. By 1996 he was a regular member of the side and was on the verge of Wallaby selection for the UK tour when he unluckily injured his knee. He then had to wait until 1999 before winning his first Test cap when he came off the bench against the Springboks at Lang Park. Later that same year he played an important role in the Wallabies' success in the World Cup.

Mark is a strong, athletic footballer who can play either in the back row or second row. His line-out play is also a feature of his game, most notably when he pinched a throw-in off the All Blacks in the closing seconds of the Test in Wellington in 2000. The ensuing play led to John Eales kicking the winning penalty goal to retain the Bledisloe Cup. Having now played over 100 games for his state, Mark's wise rugby head offers plenty of experience to any side he graces.

As a schoolboy, he was a promising Australian Rules footballer and at just 15 was playing first grade in the QAFL. Outside rugby, Mark is a practising solicitor, having completed his law degree at the Queensland University of Technology.

DAVID CROFT

Position	Flanker
Height	185 cm
Weight	98 kg
Date of birth	22 January 1979
Nickname	The Prawn
Club	Brothers
State	Queensland
Tests	0
Test points	0
Test debut	Uncapped
Honours	Queensland Schools; Queensland U19s; Queensland U21s; Australian U21s; Queensland; Australian Barbarians
Senior tours	2000 – Queensland to Argentina

Educated at St Joseph's Gregory Terrace, David Croft began his rugby career at fly-half with Souths juniors in the under 8s. His inside-centre partner was none other than Steve Kefu, but the pair soon swapped positions and David remained there until a move to open-side flanker was suggested in U15s. An all-round sportsman at school, he rowed in the 2nd VIII and ran in the 4 × 400 m relay.

David has never played against Phil Waugh in Super 12 but packed against him at school in the annual interstate clash (won, of course, by the Reds). His uncle is former Wallaby lock Peter Reilly, brother of David's mother, Jenny.

David enjoyed a spectacular first season for the Reds in 2001 and was named Australian Rookie of the Year. Running on for his debut in Rotorua against the Chiefs alongside Toutai Kefu and John Eales remains his most cherished rugby memory. He had another brilliant Super 12 campaign in 2002 and was consistently one of the best on the field.

Careerwise, David is studying for a Bachelor of Business Administration at the University of Queensland.

BEN DARWIN

Position	Tighthead prop
Height	186 cm
Weight	115 kg
Date of birth	17 October 1976
Nickname	Robo
Club	Northern Suburbs
State	ACT
Tests	9
Test points	0
Test debut	2001 v. British and Irish Lions, The Gabba, Brisbane

Honours   Australian U21s; Australian Barbarians; ACT;
           Australian Wallabies
Senior tours   2001 – Europe

Ben Darwin's rugby career began with the Beecroft under 9s in Sydney. Packing behind him was a dynamic little girl named Michelle Ryan. 'She made me look good,' Ben recalls. From that moment his dream was to play with the Wallabies, a dream realised in 2001 when he burst onto the scene after an outstanding season with the victorious ACT Brumbies. He made his Test debut as a replacement against the Lions in the First Test at the Gabba and by the end of the season had won himself a starting role in the Wallabies side that toured Europe.

A product of Barker College in Sydney, Ben played in the same school side as former Wallaby Nathan Spooner. In 1997 he played for the Australian U21s and the following year was selected in the ACT Brumbies squad. His 1999 season was ruined when a collision with Jonah Lomu broke his arm. After serving an apprenticeship behind Patricio Noriega, he eventually earned his chance in 2001 and formed a formidable combination with Bill Young and Jeremy Paul. Ben has had some celebrated mentors in his front-row education, including World Cup-winning props Ewen McKenzie and Andrew Blades. At just 25 years of age, he has a big and bright future.

MATT DUNNING

Position	Loosehead prop
Height	184 cm
Weight	122 kg
Date of birth	19 December 1978
Nickname	–
Club	Eastwood
State	NSW
Tests	0
Test points	0
Test debut	Uncapped
Honours	Australian Schools; NSW U19s; NSW U21s; Australian U19s; Australian U21s; NSW
Tours	–

Matt Dunning burst onto the Waratah scene in 2001 and attracted so much media attention that his teammates quickly dubbed him 'the human headline'. Born in Calgary, Canada, Matt moved to Sydney as a youngster and started his sporting career as a representative soccer goalkeeper. He took up rugby when he attended Northolm Grammar and gained selection in the Australian Schools side. He also excelled at cricket and represented NSW as a wicket-keeper in the same team as Phil Waugh.

Following school, Matt progressed through the Australian U19s and U21s. Making his Waratah debut in 2000 he made an impact in just his third game, against the touring Argentines, when he became famous for his right hook. Shedding 6 kg and 6 cm around the waist before season 2001, Matt returned in superb form and became a crowd favourite with Waratah fans. His speed off the mark

THE fabric OF AUSTRALIAN rugby.

Australian rugby is the best in the world. Our game is uncompromising, intelligent, innovative and as hard as it gets.

Canterbury. Developing and making the world's toughest rugby gear right here in Australia for the best team on earth - the Wallabies.

Official sponsors of the World and Super 12 Champions.

w w w . c a n t e r b u r y n z . c o m

Available at all leading Canterbury stockists.

and incredible skills soon became trademarks. An injury later in the season harmed his chances for selection with the Wallabies but he made a comeback to win a premiership with the Eastwood 2nd-grade side. Matt is an exciting footballer with tremendous athleticism and is working hard on his scrummaging technique.

FLETCHER DYSON

Position	Tighthead prop
Height	183 cm
Weight	116 kg
Date of birth	27 May 1973
Nickname	Fletch
Club	University
State	Queensland
Tests	10
Test points	0
Test debut	2000 v. Argentina, Ballymore
Honours	NSW U19s; NSW Country U19s; NSW U21s; NSW; Queensland; Australian U19s; Australian U21s; Australian Wallabies
Senior tours	2000 – Japan, France, UK

Originally from Queensland, where he attended John Paul College in Brisbane, Fletcher Dyson spent six years in NSW studying at Armidale University and then playing rugby in Sydney. After gaining a degree in philosophy and politics, Fletcher moved to Sydney in 1994 where he played for Norths and Randwick. After winning selection for both the Australian U19s and U21s, he made his debut for the

Waratahs in 1998. In two years with NSW he played only six games and his game time totalled just seven minutes of Super 12 football.

Fletcher moved back home to Brisbane in 2000 for what turned out to be a dream year. He played every Super 12 game for the Reds and was voted Rookie of the Year. Then, in a selection surprise, he was picked in the Wallabies run-on side and made his debut against the Pumas at Ballymore. Despite throwing up on the morning of the Test, he more than held his own and started all 10 Test matches for the year. Unfortunately, a severe back injury sustained in the last Test against England kept him sidelined for much of 2001 and he subsequently lost his Wallaby number 3 jumper.

Away from rugby, Fletcher works as a sales consultant for a Brisbane car dealership.

MANUEL EDMONDS

Position	Fly-half
Height	183 cm
Weight	92 kg
Date of birth	12 April 1977
Nickname	Manny
Club	Warringah
State	NSW
Tests	2
Test points	23 [2t, 5c, 1pg]
Test debut	1998 v. Tonga, Bruce Stadium, Canberra

Honours	ACT U16s; ACT B; NSW U21s; NSW;
	Australian Schools; Australian U19s;
	Australian U21s; Australian Barbarians;
	Australian Wallabies
Senior tours	1998 – France, England; 2001 – Europe

Kiwi-born Manny Edmonds started his rugby career at the age of five in Ashburton, south of Christchurch. His family later moved to Canberra, where he played his junior rugby as a scrum-half with the Royals club. He won selection in the Australian Schools side where he partnered Elton Flatley in the midfield. As an 18-year-old, he played in an ACT side alongside George Gregan and Joe Roff.

Manny's career really took off in 1998 after he took a dominant role in the Australian U21s victory in the Southern Hemisphere tournament in South Africa. He then made his Super 12 debut for the Waratahs and later in the same year was called into the Wallabies squad. He made a sensational debut against the Tongans in a World Cup qualifier in Canberra, where he racked up 20 points, including two tries. After a frustrating two-year battle with Christian Warner for the starting fly-half spot with the Waratahs, his 2001 form once again elevated him to the Wallaby squad. A strong game for Australia A in their victory over the Lions led to Manny winning his second Test cap when he came off the bench against South Africa in Pretoria.

The Australian Rugby Companion

OWEN FINEGAN

Position	Flanker/Lock
Height	197 cm
Weight	119 kg
Date of birth	22 April 1972
Nickname	Melon
Club	Randwick
State	ACT
Tests	44
Test points	30 [6t]
Test debut	1996 v. Wales, Ballymore
Honours	NSW U19s; NSW U21s; NSW; ACT; Australian U21s; Australian Barbarians; Australian XV; Emerging Wallabies; Australian Wallabies
Senior tours	1994 – Emerging Wallabies to Southern Africa; 1996 – Europe; 1997 – Argentina, UK; 1998 – France, England; 1999 – World Cup (UK); 2001 – Europe

The big, blockbusting back-rower from the Randwick club enjoyed a super season in 2001 with both the ACT Brumbies and then the Wallabies, playing in all 11 Tests. His exceptional form was recognised by his teammates, who voted him Player of the Year.

As a seven-year-old, Owen played in three rugby league grand finals in the one day: the under 7s, under 8s and under 9s. The next day the *Daily Telegraph* proclaimed him the next whiz-kid of rugby league. Luckily for the Wallabies, he also played rugby union while attending Waverley College and went on to gain selection with the NSW U19s

278

and then the Australian U21s. After eight games with the Waratahs he moved to Canberra in 1996 to become a foundation member of the ACT Brumbies. He has been integral to the success of that team ever since. Owen is now an important part of the leadership team for both the Brumbies and the Wallabies. He is also one of the jokers in the Wallaby side and is responsible for collecting fines from his teammates for any misdemeanours they commit when in camp. In his spare time he works as a property consultant for a firm in Sydney and runs a preschool with his mum.

ELTON FLATLEY

Position	Fly-half/Centre
Height	178 cm
Weight	87 kg
Date of birth	7 May 1977
Nickname	Flats
Club	Brothers
State	Queensland
Tests	12
Test points	8 [4c]
Test debut	1997 v. England, Twickenham
Honours	Queensland; Australian Schools; Australian U21s; AIS Australian Barbarians; Australian Wallabies
Senior tours	1997 – Argentina, UK; 2000 – Japan, France, UK; 2001 – Europe

Raised on the Isle of Capri on the Gold Coast, Elton Flatley is regarded as one of the greatest schoolboy rugby players

Australia has ever produced. He played a remarkable four years in the 1st XV at famous Nudgee College, culminating in his captaining the Australian Schools side in his last year at school.

Following his brilliant school career Elton was pursued by the Canterbury Bulldogs but decided to stick with union. It was a wise choice as in 1996 he became the youngest player to play for Queensland since Michael Lynagh in 1982. Just over a year later he found himself chosen in the Wallaby team for the end-of-year tour and went on to make his debut against England when David Knox was forced to pull out with a broken hand. Elton's fortunes fluctuated until 2000, when he won his first cap in three years. Solid form with the Reds in 2001 has seen him return to the Wallaby fold, where he played an important part in their successes in 2001. He enjoyed a strong finish to Super 12 and was a leading point-scorer on 148.

DAVID GIFFIN

Position	Lock
Height	198 cm
Weight	107 kg
Date of birth	6 November 1973
Nicknames	Giff, Hubble
Club	Canberra
State	ACT
Tests	34
Test points	0
Test debut	1996 v. Wales, Cardiff Arms Park

| Honours | Queensland B; Queensland; ACT; Barbarians; Australian U21s; Australian XV; Australian Wallabies |
| Senior tours | 1996 – Europe; 1999 – Rugby World Cup (UK); 2000 – Japan, France, UK; 2001 – Europe |

David Giffin, a graduate of the Redeemer Lutheran College in Brisbane, played three games for Queensland before he decided to move to Canberra in order to put some space between himself and Eales, McCall and Morgan. He was a foundation member of the Brumbies in 1996 and has played a part in all three of their finals campaigns.

His good form at the Brumbies was rewarded when he won his first Test cap in 1996 against the Welsh at Cardiff Arms Park. In so doing he became the first Wallaby to have come from the Sunnybank club in Brisbane. The next few years of his career were frustrated by a string of injuries that saw him receive the cruel nickname of '60 Minutes' because he rarely finished a full game. The injuries included broken feet and broken hands as well as a broken back. David fought his way back into the Wallaby side and didn't miss a Test in 1999 and 2000, playing 25 consecutive Tests. Among them were all of the World Cup games, in which he played an important role in the Wallabies' win. Now, with the retirement of John Eales, his leadership in the Wallaby forward pack has become crucial. David missed the entire 2002 domestic season after undergoing shoulder surgery.

GEORGE GREGAN

Position	Scrum-half
Height	173 cm
Weight	80 kg
Date of birth	19 April 1973
Nickname	Guv
Club	Randwick
State	ACT
Tests	72
Test points	55 [11t]
Test debut	1994 v. Italy, Ballymore
Honours	ACT U21s; ACT; Australian U19s; Australian U21s; Australian Sevens; Australian Wallabies
Senior tours	1995 – World Cup (South Africa); 1996 – Europe; 1997 – Argentina, UK; 1998 – France, England; 1999 – World Cup (UK); 2001 – Europe

Australia's most capped scrum-half and second only on the world list behind Springbok Joost Van Der Westhuizen, George Gregan has been among the first players picked in the Wallaby side for the past five years. Vice-captain of the Wallabies since 1997, he has now taken over as captain following the retirement of John Eales.

Born in Zambia and given the middle name of Musarurwa ('the chosen one'), George's family moved to Canberra when he was one year old. He began his rugby career at St Edmond's College. An all-round sportsman, he also played golf at a high level and was a middle-order batsman in the ACT cricket side.

George broke onto the Wallaby scene in 1994 when he made his debut against the touring Italians. In only his fourth Test he became a household name with '*that* tackle' on Jeff Wilson. It stopped a certain try and enabled Australia to win back the Bledisloe Cup. Since then he has been named Australian Super 12 Player of the Year, won an Australian Players' Player award and a World Cup, and captained the Brumbies to victory in the Super 12.

NATHAN GREY

Position	Inside centre
Height	185 cm
Weight	94 kg
Date of birth	31 March 1975
Nickname	Crazy Greysie
Club	Manly
State	NSW
Tests	30
Test points	25 [5t]
Test debut	1998 v. Scotland, Ballymore
Honours	Queensland U19s; Queensland U21s; Queensland B; Queensland; NSW; Australian U19s; Australian U21s; Australian Universities; Australian Sevens; Australian Wallabies
Senior tours	1998 – France, England; 1999 – World Cup (UK); 2000 – Japan, France, UK; 2001 – Europe

While his father worked in the timber industry Nathan Grey moved between Gosford, Papua New Guinea and Fiji before settling in Queensland, where he attended the Southport School. He enjoyed three years in the school's 1st XV, spending his last season in the number 8 jumper. He then went on to make his 1st-grade debut as a 17-year-old at Wests, where he partnered Jim Williams in the centres.

After winning selection in the Australian U19s and U21s, Nathan's promotion to senior level was blocked at Queensland by Horan, Little and Herbert. He won two caps with the Reds but moved south to the Waratahs, where he was an immediate success. In 1998 he played in all of NSW's Super 12 games and had his good form rewarded with a first Test cap against Scotland at Ballymore. Since then he has been regularly picked in the Wallaby side and played an important part in the series victory over the Lions in 2001. Nathan is best known for his brutal defence as well as his hard, straight running in attack. A serious knee injury sustained in Super 12 put him out for the rest of the 2002 season

Off the field Nathan has gained a Diploma in Business Management and works part-time as an investment salesperson for a real estate firm.

SEAN HARDMAN

Position	Hooker
Height	180 cm
Weight	102 kg
Date of birth	6 May 1977
Nicknames	Labels, Hardy
Club	Brothers
State	Queensland
Tests	0

Test points	0
Test debut	Uncapped
Honours	Australian Schools; Queensland U21s;
	Australian U21s; Queensland
Tours	–

A product of the Reds 'Rugby College', Sean Hardman has emerged as an exciting young hooker with a big future. After touring South Africa with the Australian U21s, Sean went on to make his debut for the Reds in 1999. For the past two years his Super 12 game time has been limited due to the presence of veteran Michael Foley. With the retirement of Foley, Sean will be looking to take over as the number-one hooker in Queensland. He is a strong all-round player, but has impressed many rugby critics with his ball-running talents in particular.

Sean follows a long line of famous Nudgee College old boys to play for Queensland, including Mark Loane, Paul McClean, Glenn Panoho and Elton Flatley. He will be hoping to follow their lead and go one step further by gaining selection with the Wallabies. He gained valuable experience as back-up to Tom Murphy, and with further natural improvement will be in contention for the World Cup squad.

SAM HARRIS

Position	Inside centre
Height	191 cm
Weight	105 kg
Date of birth	30 January 1980
Nickname	–
Club	Warringah
State	NSW
Tests	0
Test points	0
Test debut	Uncapped
Honours	Australian Schools; NSW U19s; Australian U19s; NSW U21s; Australian U21s
Tours	–

Sam Harris is a powerful centre and a strong runner of the ball with a no-nonsense defence. NZ-born Sam grew up on Sydney's northern beaches, where he plays for the Warringah Rats. He has followed the classic representative path with Australian Schools, U19s and U21s. He had an outstanding 2000 with the Rats, winning the Catchpole Medal for the best and fairest player in the Sydney club competition.

Harris made his Waratah debut in 2001 on the trip to South Africa. His Super 12 opportunities were limited due to Nathan Grey, but he always played strongly when given the chance. He seized his opportunity against the touring Lions and had a great game, including a try.

Sam lists Tim Horan as his role model and claims to be the best backgammon player on Sydney's northern beaches. He also leads the Waratah board-riders club in between training sessions.

JUSTIN HARRISON

Position	Lock
Height	203 cm
Weight	110 kg
Date of birth	20 April 1974
Nickname	Googy
Club	Canberra
State	ACT
Tests	7
Test points	0
Test debut	2001 v. British and Irish Lions, Stadium Australia, Sydney
Honours	ACT U21s; ACT; Australian U21s; Australian Universities; AIS Australian Barbarians; Australian Wallabies
Senior tours	2001 – Europe

Justin Harrison is a fiery lock from the ACT Brumbies who was once described by a South African commentator as 'a stampeding giraffe on steroids'. Raised on an Aboriginal settlement in the Northern Territory, Justin grew up playing Aussie Rules as a ruckman. It wasn't until he left school that he enjoyed his first taste of rugby when he played for the Gold Rats at the Southern Cross University in Lismore.

Scouted by Tuggeranong Vikings coach Chris Hickey, Justin arrived in Canberra weighing a mere 90 kg. His size and skill improved and after winning selection in the Australian U21s side he served an apprenticeship behind Langford, Waugh and Giffin at the Brumbies. He eventually got his chance in the 1999 Super 12 and by 2001 was one of the outstanding members of the Brumbies' championship-winning team. Harrison then made a memorable debut for the Wallabies in the Third Test with the Lions in Sydney. His line-out steal from Martin Johnson in the final minute helped Australia hold on to win the Tom Richards Cup. With the retirement of John Eales, Justin can look forward to more chances playing for Australia in the future.

DANIEL HERBERT

Position	Outside centre
Height	188 cm
Weight	100 kg
Date of birth	6 February 1974
Nickname	Herbie
Club	GPS
State	Queensland
Tests	57
Test points	50 [10t]
Test debut	1994 v. Ireland, Sydney Football Stadium
Honours	Queensland; Barbarians; Australian U19s; Australian U21s; Emerging Wallabies; Australian Wallabies
Senior tours	1994 – Emerging Wallabies to Southern Africa; 1995 – World Cup (South Africa); 1996 – Europe; 1997 – Argentina, UK; 1998 – France, England; 1999 – World Cup (UK); 2000 – Japan, France, UK; 2001 – Europe

Dan Herbert has been an integral part of the Wallaby side for many years. Now, as vice-captain, he is a senior member of the team. Originally known as the little brother of 10-Test veteran Anthony, Dan broke through onto the Wallaby scene as a 20-year-old in 1994, when he scored a try on debut against Ireland with his first touch of the ball.

Dan has an incredibly strong physique and his powerful play has been a highlight of his game in both attack and defence. He has missed only four Tests in the last four years. In 2001 he celebrated his 50th cap for Australia and his 100th for Queensland, where he is now the Reds captain. Dan is also eligible to play in the Australian Deaf rugby side, having lost the hearing in his left ear due to mumps he contracted as a baby. As a youngster he also showed great promise as a junior Queensland tennis player. Dan had a quiet Super 12 in 2002 but finished strongly and, as always, led the Reds stylishly.

JAMES HOLBECK

Position	Outside centre
Height	182 cm
Weight	94 kg
Date of birth	10 July 1973
Nickname	Bone
Club	Randwick
State	ACT
Tests	7
Test points	0
Test debut	1997 v. New Zealand, Lancaster Park, Christchurch
Honours	Australian Schools; Australian U21s; Australian Wallabies
Senior tours	1997 – Argentina

James Holbeck's strength, pace and versatility make him a highly valuable back-line player. However, a shocking run of injuries has severely limited his time on the field in recent seasons. Born in Ipswich like Joe Roff, he attended the Armidale School in northern NSW. James played in the 1992 Australian Schools side and then went on to win selection in the Australian U21s. In 1996 he was signed to the Brumbies after Pat Howard and Adam Magro suffered early-season injuries.

The 1997 season proved to be a big one for James. After helping the Brumbies reach the Super 12 final, he won his first Test cap when he came on as a replacement against the All Blacks in Christchurch. Although he played five more Tests that year and toured Argentina with the Wallabies, Holbeck was left out of the reduced squad that went on to England and Scotland. After a strong season with the Brumbies in 2001 he again won selection in the Wallaby squad and gained one more cap when he came on as a replacement against the Lions in the Third Test.

PAT HOWARD

Position	Centre
Height	178 cm
Weight	87 kg
Date of birth	14 November 1973
Nickname	Paddy
Club	Sydney University
State	ACT
Tests	20
Test points	10 [2t]

Test debut	1993 v. New Zealand, Carisbrook, Dunedin
Honours	Queensland U19s; Australian U19s;
	Queensland; ACT; Australian Wallabies
Tours	–

Pat Howard is a centre with impeccable bloodlines. Both his father, Jake, and grandfather, Cyril Towers, were Wallabies. Born in Brisbane, Pat played with Queensland before heading down to Canberra to join the Brumbies for their initial season in 1996. After coming through the Australian U19s, just one year later he found himself making his Test debut against the All Blacks as a tender 20-year-old. Despite a shaky start to his Wallaby career, his class could not keep him down and he went on to play 19 more Tests before he decided to move to England in 1998 to play with the Leicester Tigers.

Pat played in three consecutive premiership sides with Leicester and in 2000 was named English Premiership Player of the Year. He captained the Premiership All Stars XV in England's 1999 World Cup warm-up match and had a number of games with the Barbarians, including one opposing the Wallabies at the Millennium Stadium in 2001.

With his exceptional skills and experience in the midfield, Pat is a welcome returnee to Australian rugby. His creativity and vision definitely kept him under notice for a recall to the Wallaby jumper. A pharmacist by profession, Pat also enjoys backpacking with his wife, Bess.

STEVE KEFU

Position	Centre
Height	187 cm
Weight	95 kg
Date of birth	16 December 1979
Nickname	Little Kef
Club	Souths
State	Queensland
Tests	1
Test points	0
Test debut	2001 v. Wales, Millennium Stadium, Cardiff
Honours	Queensland U19s; Queensland U21s; Queensland Reds; Australian U19s; Australian U21s; Australian Wallabies
Senior tours	2001 – Europe

Steve Kefu has now emerged from the shadow of his older brother, Toutai, after winning his first Test cap in the match against Wales at the Millennium Stadium on the end-of-season tour in 2001. (That match saw the Kefus become the first brothers to play in a Test for Australia since the Blades boys achieved the feat against England in 1997.) Steve was voted by his teammates as Newcomer of the Wallaby Tour to Europe and was rewarded with the honour of playing alongside Toutai in the centres in the tour finale against the Barbarians.

Steve has followed the traditional rugby representative path of the Australian Schools, Australian U19s and then Australian U21s, with whom he played for two years. In his first year out of school he remarkably helped Souths take out the 1st-grade premiership in Brisbane. With the retirement of Tim Horan in 2000, Steve stepped into the Reds starting side and played every Super 12 game in 2001. One of five brothers, there is a chance he will not be the last Kefu to play for the Wallabies.

TOUTAI KEFU

Position	Number 8
Height	191 cm
Weight	113 kg
Date of birth	8 April 1974
Nickname	Kef
Club	Souths
State	Queensland
Tests	44
Test points	40 [8t]
Test debut	1997 v. South Africa, Loftus Versfeld, Pretoria
Honours	Queensland Sevens; Queensland B; Queensland; Australian U19s; Australian U21s; Australian Wallabies
Senior tours	1996 – Europe; 1997 – Argentina; 1998 – France, England; 1999 – World Cup (UK); 2000 – Japan, France, UK; 2001 – Europe

Born in Tonga but raised in Queensland, Toutai Kefu is the son of Fatai, who was a member of the famous Tongan touring team that defeated the Wallabies in 1973. After coming through the Australian U19s and U21s, Toutai made his Queensland debut in 1995 and scored a try with his first touch. Despite touring with the 1996 Wallabies he didn't win his first Test cap until 1997, when he came on as a centre to replace James Holbeck against South Africa in Pretoria.

Toutai is now closing in on Tim Gavin's Australian record of caps at number 8. He has become a world-class forward and reached national hero status when he scored a try in injury time to beat the All Blacks in 2001 and sent retiring captain John Eales out on a high.

Toutai almost took up a career in basketball when he signed as a 17-year-old with the AIS. However, inspired by fellow Tongan Willie O's performance during the 1991 World Cup, he stuck with rugby. Toutai has a long list of achievements in the game and was once quoted as saying, 'The three things I care about in rugby are winning the Bledisloe Cup, beating New South Wales and winning grand finals with the Magpies.' He has achieved all three.

STEPHEN LARKHAM

Position	Fly-half
Height	189 cm
Weight	88 kg
Date of birth	29 May 1974
Nickname	Bernie
Club	Canberra
State	ACT
Tests	46
Test points	77 [14t, 2c, 1dg]
Test debut	1996 v. Wales, Sydney Football Stadium
Honours	ACT Schools; ACT U19s; ACT U21s; ACT; Australia B; Australian Sevens; Australian Wallabies

Gordon Bray's Wallaby profiles

Senior tours   1996 – Europe; 1997 – World Cup Sevens
               (Hong Kong), Argentina, UK; 1998 –
               France, England; 1999 – World Cup (UK);
               2001 – Europe

Stephen Larkham continues to amaze with his remarkable feats on the rugby field. He began his career as a nine-year-old prop but was soon moved to scrum-half, growing up with Nick Farr-Jones as his hero. His dad, Geoff, who played over 300 games for the Wests club in Canberra, built his son a footy field at home where Steve practised his kicking for hours on end. In 1995 he was still playing reserve grade as a scrum-half, but the following year he switched to full-back and found himself in the Brumbies side. To complete a dream year, he then went on to make his Test debut as a replacement on the wing against Wales in Sydney.

Stephen moved into the Wallaby starting line-up in 1997 at full-back after Matt Burke was sidelined with injury. He proved a more than capable replacement and scored two memorable tries against Scotland in Edinburgh. However, coach Rod Macqueen had different ideas for Stephen and in 1998 he turned out as the Wallaby fly-half. The move was an instant success. He scored three tries in the first Test he played against England and it wasn't long before many were rating him as the best fly-half in the world. 'Bernie', as he is affectionately known to his teammates, reached national hero status after he kicked a miraculous 45-metre drop goal in injury time to down the Springboks in the 1999 World Cup semifinal. Although he tends to be injury-prone, Stephen Larkham still plays an integral role in the Wallaby side.

CHRIS LATHAM

Position	Full-back
Height	192 cm
Weight	99 kg
Date of birth	8 September 1975
Nickname	Latho
Club	Wests
State	Queensland
Tests	26
Test points	70 [14t]
Test debut	1998 v. France, Stade de France, Paris
Honours	NSW; Queensland; Barbarians; Australian U21s; AIS Australian Barbarians; Australian Wallabies
Senior tours	1998 – France, England; 1999 – World Cup (UK); 2000 – Japan, France, UK; 2001 – Europe

Despite attending the same school in Narrabri as former Wallabies Scott Gourley and Michael Brial, Chris Latham did not play his first game of rugby until he was 17. (He was talked into playing as a way of having a day off classes.) He then moved to Sydney and joined the Randwick Club. During that time he also completed his apprenticeship as a motor mechanic.

In 1997 Chris made his debut with the Waratahs on the wing because Matt Burke was blocking his chance at full-back. The following year he signed with the Reds and hasn't looked back since. He has even been quoted as referring to himself as 'a born and bred Queenslander'. Strong form with the Reds in 1998 prompted his selection for the

Wallaby tour to Europe, where he went on to make his debut against the French.

Latham's career really matured in 2000 when he was named Reds Player of the Year for the second year in a row. With Matt Burke injured, he played all 10 tests with the Wallabies and scored no less than eight tries, including a record four against Argentina, and was subsequently named Test Player of the Year. His speed, superb kicking game and strong defence make him a valuable member of the Wallaby squad. Chris emerged as Player of the Tournament in Super 12 2002, scoring 10 dashing tries.

DAVID LYONS

Position	Blind-side flanker/ Number 8
Height	191 cm
Weight	116 kg
Date of birth	16 June 1980
Nickname	Mini Melon
Club	Sydney University
State	NSW
Tests	4
Test points	0
Test debut	2000 v. Argentina, Ballymore
Honours	NSW Schools; NSW U19s; NSW; Australian Schools; Australian U19s; Australian Wallabies
Senior tours	2000 – Japan, France, UK; 2001 – Europe

The rapid rise of David Lyons through the ranks of Australian rugby has been extraordinary. Until the last two

years of school David played hockey in his home town of
Molong. He first played rugby as a centre when he boarded
at Hurlstone Agricultural College and only moved to
number 8 when one of his teammates was injured. Incredibly, by the end of the year David had won selection in the
Australian Schools side. The next year he backed up, was
named captain of the side and led them on their undefeated
tour of the UK.

His first playing year out of school was cut short by
injury, but not before he had been selected in the NSW and
Australian U19s sides. The year 2000 proved another big
one for David when he played in every game of the Super 12
series with the Waratahs. His strong form led to selection in
the Wallabies and he made his debut off the bench against
Argentina at Ballymore. Unbelievably, Lyons had represented both his state and his country before he had even
played a game of 1st-grade club rugby. However, he made
amends the following year when he helped Sydney University to capture their first premiership since 1972.

During his spare time David is studying science at
Sydney University, with an emphasis on agriculture and
environment.

ROD MOORE

Position	Tighthead prop
Height	186 cm
Weight	118 kg
Date of birth	6 January 1972
Nickname	Panda
Club	Eastwood
State	NSW
Tests	11
Test points	0
Test debut	1999 v. United States, Thomond Park, Limerick
Honours	NSW U19s; NSW U21s; NSW; ACT; Australian U19s; Australian U21s; Australian Wallabies
Senior tours	1999 – World Cup (UK); 2001 – Europe

Rod Moore is a gentle giant off the field but the complete opposite on the paddock. He is a strong scrummager, but belying his 118 kg frame he is also very mobile around the field. His rugby career started at the North Rocks rugby club in Sydney while he was still attending Carlingford High School. His representative career began when he toured the UK with the 1990 Australian Schools side. He then went on to play for NSW U19s and the Australian U21s.

Rod's Super 12 career began with the ACT Brumbies in 1997 but lack of game time behind Patricio Noriega prompted him to move back to Sydney at the end of 1999. That same season he teamed with Bill Young and Josh Cullen in the Eastwood front row to help them to their first premiership in the club's 52-year history. The Eastwood scrum dominated their opponents and proved to be perhaps the most significant factor in the win. On the same day of that premiership victory, Rod received his call-up to the Wallaby World Cup squad to replace the injured Noriega. A week later he made his Test debut against the USA.

Rod enjoyed a sensational year in 2001. He played in every Super 12 game for the Waratahs and then went on to earn selection again with the Wallabies. He won 10 caps in the year and played an important role in the wins over the Lions and All Blacks. Away from rugby, Rod is a trained accountant and enjoys riding his Malibu surfboard.

STIRLING MORTLOCK

Position	Centre/Wing
Height	191 cm
Weight	100 kg
Date of birth	20 May 1977
Nicknames	Stirlo, Beavis
Club	Gordon
State	ACT
Tests	10
Test points	122 [7t, 9c, 23pg]
Test debut	2000 v. Argentina, Ballymore
Honours	ACT; Australian U19s; Australian U21s; Australian Wallabies
Senior tours	1997 – Argentina; 2000 – Japan, France, UK

Stirling Mortlock is a talented centre who is also accustomed to the roles of full-back and winger. He forced his way into the Gordon 1st-grade side in 1997 after leading the

Colts to a premiership win in the previous year. After playing with the Australian U21s he then toured with the Wallabies to Argentina, playing two games. All this occurred before he had played in the Super 12 competition.

Stirling made his ACT debut in 1998 and by 2000 was a key player in the Brumbies' star-studded back line. His Test debut came on the wing against Argentina in Brisbane, the start of an extraordinary season with the Wallabies. He became the fastest Australian to reach both 50 and 100 Test points, including a world-record 29 against the Springboks in Melbourne. To cap off 2000 (he was named Rookie of the Year), he kicked a freakish last-minute penalty goal from the sideline to clinch our first Tri Nations trophy.

Stirling played a crucial role in the winning Brumbies Super 12 campaign in 2001 but a shoulder injury in the semifinal game against the Reds required reconstructive surgery and he did not play another match that year. In 2002 he enjoyed another spectacular Super 12 campaign as one of the stand-out line-breakers.

PATRICIO NORIEGA

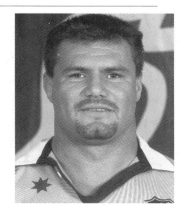

Position	Prop
Height	185 cm
Weight	117 kg
Date of birth	22 October 1971
Nickname	Pato
Club	Eastern Suburbs
State	NSW
Tests	9 for Australia; 22 for Argentina

Test points	0 (Aust.); 5 [1t] (Arg.)
Test debut	1992 v. Spain (Arg.);1998 v. France (Aust.), Stade de France, Paris
Honours	Buenos Aires; ACT; Argentina; Australian Wallabies
Senior tours	1995 – World Cup (South Africa); 1998 – France, England; 1999 – World Cup (UK)

Patricio Noriega's international career started as a 21-year-old when he made his debut with the Argentine Pumas against Spain. He played in the 1995 World Cup and during the same year toured Australia, where he propped against a future teammate, Dan Crowley. After playing 22 Tests with the Pumas, Patricio made the decision to settle in Canberra. He joined the ACT Brumbies in 1996 and went on to play over 50 Super 12 games with them. After gaining his Australian residency he made his Test debut for the Wallabies in 1998 against the French in Paris.

The following year he lost 9 kg in the off-season after cutting back his red meat diet from twice a day to only a few times per week. He was selected in the World Cup squad but withdrew without playing a game due to a shoulder injury. Patricio bounced back to play every Super 12 game in 2000 and help the Brumbies reach their second final. However, an injury in the Super 12 final meant he missed the Wallabies' 2000 campaign. He departed Australia to play with John Connolly's Stade Français. Patricio returned to Australia in 2001 and signed with the Waratahs. He is renowned for his strong scrummaging and has received the nickname Pato, which means 'the great man'.

GLENN PANOHO

Position	Prop
Height	183 cm
Weight	120 kg
Date of birth	12 May 1971
Nicknames	Pancho, Texas
Club	Brothers
State	Queensland
Tests	19
Test points	0
Test debut	1998 v. South Africa, Ellis Park, Johannesburg
Honours	Queensland; Australian U19s; Australian U21s; AIS Australian Barbarians; Australian Wallabies
Senior tours	1998 – France; 1999 – World Cup (UK); 2000 – Japan, France, UK

Glenn Panoho, an outstanding loose forward at schoolboy level, moved to the front row after school and went on to represent Australia in both the U19s and U21s. In 1993 he made his Queensland debut as a 22-year-old but then spent five long years grafting out his apprenticeship sitting on the bench. Glenn started 1998 much fitter and stronger and had a sensational season with the Reds in the Super 12. His good form was finally rewarded when he won his first Test cap as a replacement against the Springboks at Ellis Park.

Glenn is a highly versatile player who can be used on either side of the scrum. He has often been utilised as an impact player coming off the bench and in 2000 was used in this capacity in nine of the 10 Tests. Unfortunately, a

303

shoulder injury against the Lions in the First Test in Brisbane ended his season with the Wallabies.

Glenn grew up in Northland, New Zealand, and is the son of Brian Panoho, who coached the Whangarei 1st XV. When Glenn was 13 years old, Brian moved the family to Australia after accepting an offer to coach rugby at Nudgee College.

JEREMY PAUL

Position	Hooker
Height	186 cm
Weight	102 kg
Date of birth	14 March 1977
Nickname	JP
Club	Canberra
State	ACT
Tests	25
Test points	25 [5t]
Test debut	1998 v. Scotland, Sydney Football Stadium
Honours	Queensland U19s; ACT; Australian U19s; Australian U21s; Australian Wallabies
Senior tours	1999 – World Cup (UK); 2000 – Japan, France, UK

Son of slaughterman David Paul, Jeremy was raised in the Waikato and still holds a New Zealand passport. Moving to Brisbane when he was 13, he took up rugby league at his school, Capalba High, but when the school was banned from the Commonwealth Bank Cup competition for brawling, he decided to take up rugby union. As a 16-year-old he began as a flanker but then moved to hooker because of his height.

Jeremy represented Queensland and Australia at both U19s and U21s level and helped his club side, Easts, win the 1997 Brisbane club premiership when he was just 20 years old. Yet he was still ranked as only the sixth-best hooker in Queensland. So, at the end of the year, he packed his bags for Canberra and the ACT Brumbies.

Although Jeremy began as understudy to Marco Caputo at the Brumbies, the Wallaby selectors spotted his potential and he made his Test debut against Scotland later that year. In 1999 he moved into the starting line-up at the Brumbies and was soon playing a major role with the Wallabies in the World Cup campaign. In 2000 he figured in every Test as a replacement for Michael Foley and eventually won the starting spot in 2001 after a sensational Super 12 season with the Brumbies. Sadly, Jeremy ruptured his anterior cruciate ligament in the First Test against the Lions and surgery kept him out for the rest of the season. He is an exceptionally mobile hooker with outstanding ball skills and will be around the Australian team for many years to come.

MAT ROGERS

Position	Utility back
Height	182 cm
Weight	87 kg
Date of birth	1 February 1976
Nickname	Rat
Club	Randwick
State	NSW
Tests	0
Test points	0

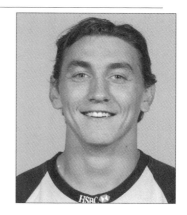

The Australian Rugby Companion

Test debut	Uncapped
Honours	Australian Schools; Barbarians
Tours	—

Mat Rogers is an exciting new signing for both Waratah and Australian rugby, having made the move across from rugby league. However, he is no stranger to rugby union, having played the game as a youngster when he attended the Southport School in Brisbane, the same school as Nathan Grey. As a fly-half he won selection in the Australian Schools team and played alongside Ben Tune and Joe Roff.

Following school, Mat walked in the footsteps of his famous father, Steve, and joined the Cronulla Sharks Rugby League Club. At the Sharks Mat enjoyed a distinguished career as a prolific point-scoring winger, representing Queensland in the State of Origin and also being selected for the Kangaroos. He made his return to rugby union when he played for the Barbarians against the Wallabies in Cardiff at the end of 2001. Coming off the bench for the last 30 minutes, he impressed at outside centre. His speed and skills will make him a valuable player at almost any position in the back line.

WENDELL SAILOR

Position	Wing
Height	191 cm
Weight	106 kg
Date of birth	16 July 1974
Nickname	–
Club	Gold Coast Breakers
State	Queensland
Tests	0
Test points	0
Test debut	Uncapped
Honours	Queensland
Tours	–

Wendell Sailor caused a sensation when he decided to make the switch from rugby league in 2001. The immense publicity he attracted was a reflection of his status in the 13-man code as one of that sport's greatest-ever wingers. His achievements include numerous premierships with the Broncos, State of Origin successes with Queensland and World Cup glory with the Kangaroos.

Wendell is determined to succeed in rugby union and has set himself the goal of becoming a dual international before the 2003 World Cup. His athleticism and powerful running will be his major assets as he makes the transition, and he has also worked hard on his kicking game. Wendell had his first taste of rugby when he played 20 minutes off the bench for the Reds in their game with NSW to celebrate Federation late in 2001. Many fans will eagerly await a possible confrontation between Wendell and New Zealand's colossus Jonah Lomu.

Wendell is lighter than he has been in several seasons and

has vowed to give up all alcohol until he clinches a Wallaby jumper. He has had an early feel of the famous gold jersey, representing the national seven-a-side team.

> 'Take good care of these. They're worth a lot of money.'
>
> Wendell Sailor to the Reds trainer as he handed over his gold chains and earrings before a mauling session.

NATHAN SHARPE

Position	Lock
Height	200 cm
Weight	113 kg
Date of birth	26 February 1978
Nickname	Calfie
Club	University
State	Queensland
Tests	0
Test points	0
Test debut	Uncapped
Honours	Australian U19s; Australian U21s; Queensland
Tours	–

Nathan Sharpe grew up in Wagga Wagga, where his first sporting love was Aussie Rules. However, when he moved to Queensland and attended the Southport School his rugby career was under way. He represented Australian U19s in his first two years out of school and then backed up with another two years in the U21s side. During his first year in the U21s he partnered Tom Bowman in the second row, and in the second year he was captain of the side.

Nathan was named Queensland Colt of the Year in 1997 and in 1998 made his debut for the Reds. In the absence of John Eales in 1999 he played a full season of Super 12 and rose to the challenge. In 2001 his strong form kept Wallaby veteran Mark Connors out of the Reds' starting line-up.

Nathan has shown great potential over the last few years and is not far away from a Wallaby berth. Interestingly, he is also eligible to play for Wales through a Welsh grandparent, and is a nephew of former ACT Brumbies and Wallaby lock John Langford.

GEORGE SMITH

Position	Open-side flanker
Height	180 cm
Weight	97 kg
Date of birth	17 July 1980
Nickname	Jackal
Club	Manly
State	ACT
Tests	14
Test points	5 [1t]
Test debut	2000 v. France, Stade de France, Paris
Honours	NSW U19s; ACT; Australian U16s; Australian Schools; Australian U19s; Australian U21s; Australian Wallabies
Senior tours	2000 – Japan, France, UK; 2001 – Europe

Born in Manly to an Australian dad and a Tongan mum, George Smith is one of nine children. His rise to the top of Australian rugby has been incredibly rapid, going from

309

playing in the Manly Colts to playing with the Brumbies and then the Wallabies all in the space of a year.

A product of Cromer High School, George played two years in the Australian Schools team and was named Player of the 1998 Tour to the UK. He rejected offers from both the Manly and Balmain league clubs to stick with rugby. Eddie Jones spotted Smith's talents and brought him to the Brumbies as a 19-year-old, where he scored a try in the 2000 Super 12 final. With the retirement of David Wilson, George made his Test debut against the French in Paris. He took the rugby world by storm with his speed to the breakdown and ability to steal opposition ball, frustrating many teams. He played every Test in 2001 and was named Wallaby Rookie of the Year. On his 21st birthday George was voted Man of the Match in the Wallabies' Third Test win over the Lions in Sydney.

George may not be the last of the Smith clan to represent the Wallabies – many of his brothers have shown promise in junior representative rugby.

SCOTT STANIFORTH

Position	Wing
Height	186 cm
Weight	100 kg
Date of birth	12 December 1977
Nickname	Spanner
Club	Eastwood
State	NSW
Tests	1
Test points	10 [2t]

Test debut   1999 v. United States, Thomond Park,
                Limerick
Honours   NSW U19s; NSW U21s; NSW; Australian
                Schools; Australian U19s; AIS Australian
                Barbarians; Australian Wallabies
Senior tours 1998 – France, England; 1999 – World Cup
                (UK); 2001 – Europe

Scott Staniforth, the try-scoring winger from West Wyalong, comes from a rich rugby background. His father, Peter, is a former captain of West Wyalong and his uncle, Anthony Gelling, a former Wallaby back-rower from the 1970s, while his three brothers – Mitch, Graydon and Nigel – have all played representative rugby.

Scott grew up playing Aussie Rules with his brothers for Girral-Wyalong. He made the switch to rugby when attending All Saints College in Bathurst and gained selection in the 1995 Australian Schools side. He progressed through the Australian U19s and U21s before being selected for the Waratahs, where he scored two tries on debut in 1997.

Scott made an impressive start to his Wallaby career when, as he had done for NSW, he scored two tries on debut against the USA in the 1999 World Cup. His next appearance in the green-and-gold jersey was not until 2001, when he played against Oxford on the Wallabies' end-of-year tour to Europe. Voted Man of the Match, Scott again scored two tries. His good form on tour was rewarded with a start in the Barbarians game in Cardiff, where he went one better with three tries. A powerful runner with strong defence and an uncanny ability to score tries, Scott has a big future in representative rugby.

NICK STILES

Position	Loosehead prop
Height	183 cm
Weight	112 kg
Date of birth	17 October 1973
Nickname	Stilesy
Club	University
State	Queensland
Tests	11
Test points	5 [1t]
Test debut	2001 v. British and Irish Lions, The Gabba, Brisbane
Honours	Queensland Schools; Queensland U21s; Queensland; Australian Schools; Australian Wallabies
Senior tours	2000 – Japan, France, UK; 2001 – Europe

Nick Stiles is a mobile loosehead with a high work rate who has been a prolific try-scorer at club level. A product of Brisbane's St Gregory Terrace, Nick captained the 1992 Australian Schools side. After a quick stint playing under Alec Evans at Cardiff in 1993, he then turned out for the Queensland U21s in 1993 and 1994. Four years later Nick was selected for the Reds and made an immediate impact, scoring a try two minutes into his debut game against Hong Kong.

After captaining the Reds on their 2000 tour to Argentina, Nick gained selection in the Wallabies' end-of-year tour to France and the UK. However, he didn't get his chance in the national jersey until the following year, when he played for the Wallabies against the Maori. As he had done for

Queensland five years earlier, Nick scored a try on debut. He then made his Test debut against the Lions and went on to play in all 11 Test matches for the year. He scored a memorable try in the Test against Spain when he ran 25 metres to go over under the posts.

BEN TUNE

Position	Wing
Height	185 cm
Weight	93 kg
Date of birth	28 December 1976
Nicknames	Flute, Looney
Club	GPS
State	Queensland
Tests	41
Test points	115 [23t]
Test debut	1996 v. Wales, Sydney Football Stadium
Honours	Queensland; Australian Schools; Australian U19s; Australian Sevens; Australian Wallabies
Senior tours	1996 – Europe; 1997 – Argentina, UK; 1999 – Rugby World Cup (UK); 2000 – Japan; 2001 – Europe

Ben Tune burst onto the Wallaby scene in 1996 as a 19-year-old after he scored an eye-catching 10 tries in 13 games with the Reds. He is brilliant to watch when in full flight, and backs up his scintillating running with devastating defence. Unfortunately, a long list of injuries, including a broken jaw, knee tendonitis, a knee infection and a damaged shoulder, has meant that his appearances in the Wallaby jersey have been limited in the last few years. Some of the problems Ben has experienced with his left knee stem from a childhood cycling accident.

One of the positives to come out of the 2001 Wallaby tour of Europe was Ben's return to top form. He scored a try in his first game back against the French. Ben attended St Paul's College in Bald Hills, where he managed to run the 100 metres in 10.8 seconds and also gained selection in the Australian Schools side. He played a year of Colts and was voted QRU Colt of the Year in the same year he made his debut for the Reds against Otago.

DAN VICKERMAN

Position	Lock
Height	204 cm
Weight	115 kg
Date of birth	4 June 1979
Nickname	Japie
Club	Sydney University
State	ACT
Tests	0
Test points	0
Test debut	Uncapped
Honours	Australian U21s
Tours	–

At a towering 204 cm, Dan Vickerman is one of the tallest players in the Super 12. Born and schooled in Cape Town, South Africa, Dan accepted an invitation from Bob Templeton to come and play rugby in Brisbane once he had left school. Playing for the University of Queensland Colts, he went on to play with the state U19s, then returned to Cape Town, where he won selection in the South African U21s and was called in as a train-on member of the Stormers squad in 1999.

In 2000 Dan returned to Australia and joined the Sydney University club. He became a 'dual' international when he was selected in the Australian U21s, having qualified on the basis of an Australian grandparent. He was a stand-out player for the Australians in the Southern Hemisphere Championships played in New Zealand. Eddie Jones quickly signed Dan up for the Brumbies and he made his debut in 2001. His opportunities were limited but his size and skills make him an exciting prospect for the future. He capped off the season by helping Sydney University win their first premiership since 1972.

ANDREW WALKER

Position	Utility back
Height	177 cm
Weight	81 kg
Date of birth	22 November 1973
Nickname	Walks
Club	Canberra
State	ACT
Tests	7
Test points	11 [1t, 2pg]
Test debut	2000 v. New Zealand, Stadium Australia, Sydney
Honours	NSW Country; ACT; Australian U17s;

Australian U21s; Australia (rugby league);
Australian Wallabies

Senior tours   2000 – Japan, France, UK

Andrew Walker became the first dual international since Scott Gourley when he made his Wallaby Test debut against the All Blacks at Stadium Australia in 2000. Andrew also played one Test with the Kangaroos, after a lengthy league career with Sydney's St George Dragons and Easts Roosters.

Originally from Bomaderry on the south coast of NSW, Andrew grew up as the youngest of 13 in the Walker family. He played 1st grade at Randwick as a 16-year-old and won selection in the Australian U21s side. While at Randwick he and Eddie Jones were teammates in the 1991 2nd-grade premiership side. After a nine-year absence Andrew returned to rugby in 2000, when he joined the ACT Brumbies. Scoring two tries on debut, he proved a sensation and ended the season with 13 tries from the 13 Super 12 games played. Earning just one Test cap in 2000, he came back in 2001 and put in another sublime season with the Brumbies. This secured him a starting spot in the Wallabies side for the Lions series. He scored a brilliant try in the First Test and his uncanny skills proved a handful for all opponents in the six Tests he played during the year. However, he mysteriously left a Wallaby training camp before the Springbok Test and was subsequently dropped from the team. When a similar thing happened later in the year, he was dropped from the Wallaby tour squad to Europe.

Andrew runs a sheep farm on 100 hectares at Dalton. Outside rugby, he simply lives for his wife and four kids.

PHIL WAUGH

Position	Open-side flanker
Height	182 cm
Weight	94 kg
Date of birth	22 September 1979
Nickname	Devon
Club	Sydney University
State	NSW
Tests	8
Test points	5 [1t]
Test debut	2000 v. England, Twickenham
Honours	NSW U19s; NSW; Australian Schools; Australian U19s; Australian U21s; Australian Sevens; Australian Wallabies
Senior tours	2000 – Japan, France, UK; 2001 – Europe

Phil Waugh's speed, skill and strength have made him a world-class flanker despite his tender age. A product of the Shore School in Sydney, Phil enjoyed two years in the Australian Schools and was named captain of the side in 1997. His talents were not limited to rugby: he also represented in the NSW U17s cricket team as a wicket-keeper and was a member of Shore's 4 × 100 m team that won the GPS championship.

Waugh made his Waratah debut in 1999 and the following year was named Australian Super 12 Rookie of the Year. His Test debut came against the English at Twickenham on the end-of-year tour. Phil's 2001 season was nothing short of sensational. Besides captaining the Waratahs – as a 21-year-old – when Matt Burke was injured, he was voted the Australian Super 12 Player of the Year. He stepped up his appearances in the Wallaby jersey and by season's end had won the coveted starting spot at open-side flanker. Phil has an enormous future with the Wallabies and his battles with George Smith and David Croft will no doubt inspire all three players to new levels.

CHRIS WHITAKER

Position	Scrum-half
Height	179 cm
Weight	84 kg
Date of birth	19 October 1974
Nickname	Whits
Club	Randwick
State	NSW
Tests	10
Test points	10 [2t]
Test debut	1998 v. South Africa, Ellis Park, Johannesburg
Honours	NSW U21s; NSW; Australian Universities; AIS Australian Barbarians; Australian Wallabies
Senior tours	1998 – France, England; 1999 – World Cup (UK); 2000 – Japan, France, UK; 2001 – Europe

Chris Whitaker is a tenacious scrum-half with a slick pass and strong defence. Beginning his career as a seven-year-old, he worked his way through the ranks at the Randwick rugby club before gaining selection with the NSW U21s in 1995. He made his Waratah debut in 1997 and began a five-year battle with Sam Payne for the starting scrum-half spot. Winning that battle in 1998, he had a marvellous year and was subsequently named Australian Super 12 Rookie of the Year.

Chris made his Test debut in 1998 against the Springboks in Johannesburg, when he came off the bench to replace Stephen Larkham at fly-half. Since then his chances for further honours with the Wallabies have been limited due to the commanding presence of George Gregan. At the close of the 2001 season Chris had been selected in 39 Test teams for a modest total of 10 caps, being named in the starting line-up just twice. For a while he struggled under the cruel nickname of 'Armageddon' after Rod Macqueen stated, 'There would have to be an Armageddon before Whits came on'.

Chris enjoys surfing and his brother Tom is a professional surfer.

BILL YOUNG

Position	Loosehead prop
Height	188 cm
Weight	108 kg
Date of birth	4 March 1975
Nickname	Youngie
Club	Eastwood
State	ACT
Tests	3
Test points	0
Test debut	2000 v. France, Stade de France, Paris
Honours	NSW B; ACT; Australian U21s; Australian Universities; AIS Australian Barbarians; Australian Wallabies
Senior tours	2000 – Japan, France, UK; 2001 – Europe

Bill Young is renowned for his high work rate, skill with ball in hand and speed around the field. After the retirement of Richard Harry, Bill came into the Wallaby team on the end-of-year tour in 2000 and made his Test debut against the French in Paris. Despite an outstanding season with the champion Brumbies in 2001, a knee injury in the Super 12 final forced him out of the remainder of the domestic season.

Bill was a late bloomer in rugby and played in the St Joseph's College 2nd and 3rd XVs as a second-rower. His focus at the time was more on rowing, where he represented the school in the First VIII. Moving to prop after school, Bill won selection in the Australian U21s and in 1998 joined the Brumbies, making his debut against Wellington. The following year he played a vital role in Eastwood's initial premiership win before crossing the Tasman to gain further experience playing with Otago in the NPC. He formed a formidable combination with Jeremy Paul and Patricio Noriega for the Brumbies in 2000 and was rewarded with selection in the Wallaby squad. When not playing rugby, Bill works as a hotelier at Concord in Sydney.

SANZAR referees

SANZAR (South African, New Zealand and Australian Rugby) was formed in 1995 to represent the joint interests of the rugby unions of South Africa, New Zealand and Australia in the new professional era. SANZAR's showpiece competitions are the Tri Nations (home and away Tests between the three countries) and the Super 12 (a round-robin provincial tournament), which both began in 1996. Each of the three SANZAR unions employs full-time referees who officiate in the Super 12 and Tri Nations. As required, these referees are appointed to overseas Test matches by the International Rugby Board.

AUSTRALIA

ANDREW COLE

Date of birth	1 October 1960
Previous job	Dentist
Test debut	1997 – Samoa v. Tonga
Tests	14
Rugby province	Queensland

The Brisbane dentist started his refereeing career back in 1977 as a

17-year-old, soon after leaving Marist Brothers Ashgrove, the alma mater of John Eales, Dan Herbert and Pat Howard. Twenty years of hard work paid off when, in 1997, he made his Test debut. Since then he has refereed an All Blacks–Springbok Test and Six Nations Tests and, in 1999, officiated in two World Cup games. He started 2002 off with the appointment to the England–Wales Six Nations game at Twickenham. Andrew enjoys competing in triathlons and masters athletics over 1500 and 3000 metres. He runs Cole Dental with his wife, Anne-Maree; their practice has won two national business awards for family-friendly work initiatives.

STUART DICKINSON

Date of birth	19 July 1968
Previous job	Transport manager
Test debut	1997 – PNG v. Tahiti
Tests	13
Rugby province	NSW

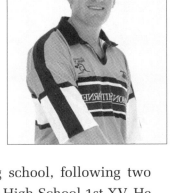

Stuart Dickinson started his rugby-playing career as a four-year-old and ended it shortly after finishing school, following two years at full-back in the Epping Boys High School 1st XV. He started his refereeing as a junior in the Eastwood District in Sydney and after progressing through the ranks is now an experienced Test referee. His résumé includes the 1999 World Cup, an All Blacks–France Test and numerous Six Nations games. The year 2001 was a big one for Stuart: he officiated in no fewer than four Tests, including the England–South

Africa clash at Twickenham. Stu completed a degree in sports administration last year after studying by correspondence through Southern Cross University at Lismore.

WAYNE ERICKSON

Date of birth	8 March 1959
Previous job	Operations Manager, ARU
Test debut	1994 – Argentina v. Scotland
Tests	21
Rugby province	NSW

Having retired from a distinguished career as a player, Wayne Erickson took up refereeing at the age of 27. As a tighthead prop he played over 100 1st-grade games for Eastern Suburbs and UNSW in Sydney and was selected to play for the Sydney representative side in 1983. As a referee, his career has been equally impressive. He has been to two World Cups, officiated in a Lions–Springbok Test and refereed the All Blacks in eight Test matches. 'Gus', as Wayne is more commonly known, is one of the characters of the international game. He also plays cricket for Briars in the municipal and shires masters competition and was a NSWCA umpire before taking up refereeing.

PETER MARSHALL

Date of birth	28 July 1955
Previous job	Administration manager
Test debut	1993 – Fiji v. Tonga
Tests	22
Rugby province	NSW

Peter Marshall is a former 1st-grade player from the Manly club in Sydney. He started his career as a referee in 1986 as a 36-year-old and rose to Test status seven years later. Peter refereed two games at the 1999 World Cup, both involving South Africa. In 2000 he suffered a debilitating knee injury that forced him to have surgery and kept him on the sidelines for some time. Making a remarkable comeback in 2001, his consistent performances throughout the Super 12 saw him voted Referee of the Series by a panel of international journalists. He then refereed the Springboks–All Blacks game in Auckland later that year – the fifth time he had refereed these two old rivals. Peter started 2002 with the England–Ireland clash at a packed Twickenham and is Australia's most experienced Test referee. He enjoys riding his surf ski and plays touch football when time permits.

SCOTT YOUNG

Date of birth	4 July 1965
Previous job	Project Manager, AMP
Test debut	1994 – Japan v. Chinese Taipei
Tests	11
Rugby province	Queensland

Scott McGilvery Young played as a winger while attending Toowoomba Grammar School. Continuing his career at university, he switched to refereeing at the age of 22 in 1987. He made his Test debut in 1994 in Kuala Lumpur, taking charge of Japan and Chinese Taipei. Despite a knee reconstruction in 1997, Scott has emerged as one of Australia's leading referees. He enjoyed many highlights in 2001, including the Sevens World Cup in Argentina, a Six Nations game in Dublin, the now-infamous bloody battle between the Waratahs and Lions in Sydney, and the New Zealand–South Africa Tri Nations clash in Cape Town. Scott holds an arts degree from Queensland University, majoring in economics, and is currently studying for a diploma in finance through Deakin University in Victoria. His passion away from professional refereeing is public speaking, where he likes to specialise in sporting and corporate themes.

SOUTH AFRICA

TAPPE HENNING

Date of birth   6 June 1961
Referee since   1987
Test debut   1995 – Scotland
                Samoa

William Taljaard Stopforth Henning, better known as Tappe Henning, is one of the leading referees in SANZAR. A former Pretorian policeman, Tappe began refereeing in 1987 as a 25-year-old after a successful playing career, including honours with the Northern Transvaal U20s. The year 2001 was a big one for Tappe despite an unfortunate early injury that saw him replaced at half-time in the England–France Test at Twickenham. He ended the year on a high when he officiated the now-famous Bledisloe Cup Test at Stadium Australia, where Toutai Kefu's injury-time try helped John Eales retire from the game in fairytale fashion.

JONATHAN KAPLAN

Date of birth   7 November 1966

Referee since   1984

Test debut   1996 – Zimbabwe v. Namibia

Jonathan Kaplan, although still young by refereeing standards, has already gained a wealth of big-time Test experience as a whistleblower. He started his career as an 18-year-old in 1984 and made his Test debut 12 years later at the age of just 30. He has recently refereed two Test matches involving the Wallabies: in 2000 he officiated in the Bledisloe Cup clash at Wellington where John Eales' penalty goal in extra time won the game for Australia (the extreme amount of injury time played in that match attracted some controversy, at least from the Kiwis!), and in 2001 he refereed the Second Test between the Wallabies and Lions in Melbourne, again won by Australia.

MARK LAWRENCE

Date of birth   16 June 1965

Referee since   1990

Test debut   2000 – Fiji v. Samoa

Mark Lawrence is an up-and-coming referee whom some wags may say is ideally suited for the job because of his background in optometry. He played in the Highbury School 3rd XV and then in the 2nd XV at Wits Technikon University before becoming a referee in 1990. In 2001 he refereed the highly entertaining Wallabies–Maori clash in Sydney. Mark started off 2002 with an appointment to referee the Italy–England Six Nations clash in Rome.

ANDY TURNER

Date of birth   25 December 1963
Referee since   1989

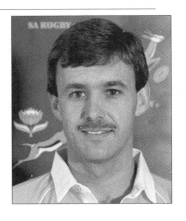

Born on Christmas Day in 1963, Andy Turner is another South African referee rising rapidly through the ranks. An administration manager for Panorama Medi-Clinic, Andy played for four years in the 1st XV of his club Gordon's Bay. He lists his top match as the 1998 Commonwealth Games Sevens Final between Fiji and New Zealand.

ANDRE WATSON

Date of birth	24 April 1958
Referee since	1986
Test debut	1996 – Australia v. Canada

Currie Cup finals, Super 12 finals, Six Nations Test matches, Lions Test matches and the 1999 World Cup final all sit proudly on the resume of Andre Joseph Watson. His big-match experience is now unrivalled by any referee in the world. Perhaps his greatest performance came in 2000 when he officiated in the Bledisloe Cup Test at Stadium Australia, won by the All Blacks 39–35. The game has been widely acclaimed as the greatest ever played – surely the highest praise a referee can be given. Before becoming a professional referee, Andre worked as an engineer as well as filling the role of CEO at the Falcons RFU. He also enjoyed success as a player, winning selection for the Transvaal Schools and going on to play at the famous Stellenbosch Gauteng University.

NEW ZEALAND

KELVIN DEAKER

Date of birth	19 October 1965
Referee since	1991
Test debut	2001 – Japan v. Wales
Tests	2

Kelvin Deaker is a referee to watch. Having only turned professional in 2001, he made his Test debut in Tokyo during the same year. From Hawkes Bay, Kelvin played as a centre until he was 22, when he turned his attention to refereeing. He began 2002 with the appointment for the Six Nations game between Italy and Scotland in Rome. The recent retirement of Colin Hawke means Kelvin will be looking for more opportunities in the future.

PAUL HONISS

Date of birth	18 June 1963
Referee since	1984
Test debut	1997 – Tahiti v. Cook Islands
Tests	17

Despite his relative youth, Paul Honiss has already gained considerable experience refereeing at Test level. Hailing from Hamilton on the North Island of

New Zealand, Paul had a promising career as a fly-half, representing Waikato Schools in 1981. Despite his success as a player, he quit the same year and three years later decided to take up refereeing. In 2001 he controlled the Australia A–Lions game in Gosford, which the Australians won. His most admired referee is the late Australian Kerry Fitzgerald.

PADDY O'BRIEN

Date of birth	27 July 1959
Referee since	1984
Test debut	1994 – Japan v. Hong Kong
Tests	25

Patric Dennis O'Brien, the former police detective from Invercargill, is New Zealand's most experienced referee. He has controlled a Super 10 final and two Super 12 finals, including the 2001 final won by the ACT Brumbies. To climax a fine 2001 he also refereed the 3rd Test between Australia and the Lions at Stadium Australia. Like most referees, his career has included the odd disappointment, particularly during the 1999 World Cup, where he endured criticism after the controversial game played between France and Fiji. However, Paddy is the ultimate professional and employs a sports psychologist and fitness trainer to ensure he stays at the top of his form. He kicked off 2002 with a big game in Paris between France and Ireland.

STEVE WALSH

Date of birth   24 February 1973
Referee since   1987
Test debut   1998 – Argentina v.
                             France
Tests   6

Steve Walsh, from Auckland's North Shore, is one of the rising stars in international refereeing circles. He began his career as 'Steve Walsh Jnr' to distinguish himself from an unrelated referee of the same name. He has been refereeing since he was 16, when a spine condition ended his career as a back-row forward. Before he turned professional he was a customs agent for a freight forwarding company. In 2001 Steve refereed the Wallabies–Springboks Test in Perth and in early 2002 he had the honour of refereeing the Calcutta Cup match between England and Scotland at Murrayfield. He lists his most admired referee as Wayne Erickson.

Australian Test records
(as at 21 June 2002)

Australia played its first-ever Test match against the touring Great Britain team in 1899. Seven's rugby statistician, Matt Gray, has compiled the following detailed records, which encompass all internationals involving Australia since then.

Most tries by Australia in a Test
13 v. South Korea (65–18), 1987, Brisbane
13 v. Spain (92–10), 2001, Madrid

Most tries conceded by Australia in a Test
9 by New Zealand (13–38), 1936, Dunedin

Most points in Tests
911 by Michael Lynagh in 72 matches (1984–95)

Most points in a Test
39 by Matthew Burke v. Canada, 1996, Brisbane

Most tries in Tests
64 (world record) by David Campese in 101 matches (1982–96)

The Australian Rugby Companion

Most tries in a Test
4 by Greg Cornelsen v. New Zealand, 1978, Auckland
4 by David Campese v. USA, 1983, Sydney
4 by Jason Little v. Tonga, 1998, Canberra
4 by Chris Latham v. Argentina, 2000, Brisbane

Most conversions in a Test
10 by Matthew Burke v. Spain, 2001, Madrid

Most penalty goals in a Test
8 by Matthew Burke v. South Africa, 1999, London

Most dropped goals in a Test
3 by Phil Hawthorne v. England, 1967, London

Largest crowd for a Test involving Australia
109 874 at Stadium Australia, Sydney, 2000, Australia v.
New Zealand (35–39)

Most Tests as captain
55 by John Eales (1996–2000)

Most consecutive Test wins by Australia
10 – from 1991 v. Argentina until 1992 v. New Zealand
10 – from 1998 v. New Zealand until 1999 v. South Africa
10 – from 1999 v. New Zealand until 2000 v. South Africa

Most consecutive Test losses by Australia
10 – from 1937 v. South Africa until 1947 v. New Zealand

Youngest player on debut
Brian Ford – 18 years 90 days – v. New Zealand, Brisbane
(Ex), 1 June 1957

Oldest player in his last match
Anthony 'Slaggy' Miller – 38 years, 113 days – v. New
Zealand, Wellington, 19 August 1967

Longest career
15 years, 193 days – Graham Cooke (played 13 matches
from 2 July 1932 until 11 January 1948)

Sent off
David Codey v. Wales, Roturua, 1987 (referee: F.A. Howard)

Most points on debut
21 by David Knox v. Fiji, Brisbane, 1985 (won 52–28)

Most consecutive Tests
62 by Joe Roff (1996–2001)

Most capped player
David Campese 101 (1982–96)
Full-back Matt Burke 50 (1993–2001); has also played
2 Tests at centre and 6 as a winger
Wing David Campese 85 (1982–96); has also played
16 Tests at full-back
Centre Tim Horan 69 (1989–2000); has also played 2 Tests
on the wing and 9 at fly-half
Fly-half Michael Lynagh 64 (1984–95); has also played
7 Tests at centre and 1 at full-back

Scrum-half George Gregan 72 (1994–2001)
Number 8 Tim Gavin 44 (1988–96); also played 3 Tests at lock
Flanker David Wilson 79 (1992–2000)
Lock John Eales 84 (1991–2001); also played 2 Tests at number 8.
Prop Ewen McKenzie 51 (1990–97)
Hooker Phil Kearns 66 (1989–99); also played 1 Test as a flanker

TOP 10 TEST CAPS		
	Tests	Test career
David Campese	101	1982–96
John Eales	86	1991–2001
Tim Horan	80	1989–2000
David Wilson	79	1992–2000
Jason Little	75	1989–2000
George Gregan	72	1994–
Joe Roff	72	1995–
Michael Lynagh	72	1984–95
Phil Kearns	67	1989–99
Nick Farr-Jones	63	1984–93

TOP 10 CAPTAINS

	Tests as captain	Total Tests	Year first captain
J.A. Eales	55	86	1996
Nick Farr-Jones	36	63	1988
A.G. Slack	19	39	1984
G.V. Davis	16	39	1969
J.E. Thornett	16	37	1962
M.P. Lynagh	15	72	1987
A.A. Shaw	15	36	1976
K.W. Catchpole	13	27	1961
A.S.B. Walker	11	15	1918
T. Allan	10	14	1947

LEADING TRY-SCORERS

	Tests	Tries
David Campese	101	64
Tim Horan	80	30
Joe Roff	72*	26
Matt C. Burke	58*	24
Ben Tune	41*	23
Jason Little	75	21
Michael Lynagh	72	17
Matt P. Burke	23	15
Brendan Moon	35	14
Stephen Larkham	37*	14
Chris Latham	26*	14

*Still playing

The Australian Rugby Companion

LEADING POINT-SCORERS

	Tests	Career	Tries	Cons	PGs	DGs	Total
Michael Lynagh	72	1984–95	17	140	177	9	911
Matt Burke	58	1993–2001	24	87	143	0	723
David Campese	101	1982–96	64	8	7	2	315
Paul McLean	30	1974–82	2	27	62	4	260
John Eales	86	1991–2001	2	31	34	0	173
Joe Roff	72	1995–2001	26	10	6	0	168
Tim Horan	80	1989–2000	30	0	0	0	140
Stirling Mortlock	10	2000	7	9	23	0	122
David Knox	13	1985–97	2	19	21	2	117
Marty Roebuck	23	1991–93	5	12	23	0	115
Ben Tune	41	1996–2001	23	0	0	0	115

Powerful Queensland Reds centre Steve Kefu had big shoes to fill in Super 12 2001 as heir to Wallaby great Tim Horan. One of five brothers (Toutai is the senior member), the skilful youngster looks set to play a lead role at the 2003 World Cup.

A noble Pacific Islands tradition continues: blockbusting All Black Jonah Lomu (above) is fiercely proud of his Tongan heritage.

Lomu's exciting teammate Tana Umaga (above) has Samoan heritage.

Former Wallaby Willie 'O' Ofahengaue moved from Tonga to New Zealand before becoming a proud Australian.

Australian women's rugby is on the rise. Flanker Bronnie Mackintosh (above) plays for the Warringah Rats in Sydney and has been a permanent fixture in the Wallaroo team.

NSW scrum-half Cheryl Soon offloads in the Second Test against England at TG Millner Field in 2001. She scored Australia's only try in the hard-fought 5–15 loss.

Wallaroo hooker Louise Cooke charges ahead in the Second Test in 2001. The Wallaroos also competed with distinction at the 2002 World Cup in Barcelona, Spain.

Brilliant Brumbies winger Joe Roff spent the 2002 domestic season with Biarritz in France.
Fatigued after seven straight seasons of top-level football in Australia, 'Smokin' Joe' enjoyed his
sabbatical and will be welcomed back in 2003. He should be a key performer at the World Cup.

Thrills and spills at the 2002 Brisbane International Sevens: outstanding Aussie captain Richard Graham (left) shows how to fell a rampant Kiwi.

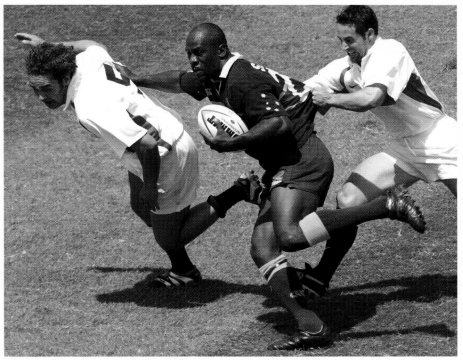

'Big Dell', Wendell Sailor (centre), made a smashing debut in the Brisbane tournament. His powerful fend and lethal running caused major headaches for England's defence.

Dynamic Queensland Reds flanker David Croft (partly obscured, right) spends a lot of time at the bottom of pile-ups due to his exceptional ability to be first man at the breakdown.

Star rugby league recruit Mat Rogers displayed dynamic form in Super 12 in his debut union season at full-back for the Waratahs to stake a strong claim for Wallaby selection.

PROTEIN BARS

40 grams of protein

Three delicious flavours

Enriched with EFAs + Calcium

Slathered in milk chocolate

MOST POINTS IN A TEST MATCH

Points	Player	Opponent	Venue	Score	Date
39 (3t, 9c, 2pg)	Matt Burke	Canada	Brisbane	74–9	26 June 1996
29 (2t, 2c, 5pg)	Stirling Mortlock	South Africa	Melbourne	44–23	8 July 2000
28 (2t, 3c, 4pg)	Michael Lynagh	Argentina	Brisbane	53–7	30 April 1995
25 (2c, 7pg)	Matt Burke	France	Cardiff	35–12	6 November 1999
25 (1t, 4c, 4pg)	Matt Burke	Scotland	Sydney	45–3	13 June 1998
25 (1t, 1c, 6pg)	Matt Burke	Lions	Melbourne	35–14	7 July 2001
24 (6c, 4pg)	Michael Lynagh	France	Brisbane	48–31	24 June 1990
24 (2t, 8c)	Michael Lynagh	USA	Brisbane	67–9	8 July 1990
24 (2t, 1c, 4pg)	Matt Burke	New Zealand	Melbourne	24–16	11 July 1998

TEAM RECORDS

HIGHEST SCORE

92 v. Spain (92–10), 2001, Madrid

v. individual countries

53 v. Argentina, 1995 (53–7) and 2000 (53–6), Brisbane

35 v. British and Irish Lions (35–14), 2001, Melbourne

74 v. Canada (74–9), 1996, Brisbane

76 v. England (76–0), 1998, Brisbane

66 v. Fiji (66–20), 1998, Sydney

48 v. France (48–31), 1990, Brisbane

46 v. Ireland (46–10), 1999, Brisbane

55 v. Italy (55–6), 1988, Rome

50 v. Japan (50–25), 1975, Brisbane

35 v. New Zealand (35–39), 2000, Sydney

57 v. Romania (57–9), 1999, Belfast (World Cup)

73 v. Samoa (73–3), 1994, Sydney

45 v. Scotland (45–3), 1998, Sydney

44 v. South Africa (44–23), 2000, Melbourne

65 v. South Korea (65–18), 1987, Brisbane

92 v. Spain (92–10), 2001, Madrid

74 v. Tonga (74–0), 1998, Canberra

67 v. USA (67–9), 1990, Brisbane

63 v. Wales (63–6), 1991, Brisbane

BIGGEST WINNING MARGIN

82 v. Spain (92–10), 2001, Madrid

v. individual countries

47 v. Argentina (53–6), 2000, Brisbane

21 v. British and Irish Lions (35–14), 2001, Melbourne

65 v. Canada (74–9), 1996, Brisbane

76 v. England (76–0), 1998, Brisbane

46 v. Fiji (66–20), 1998, Sydney

23 v. France (35–12), 1999, Cardiff (World Cup)

36 v. Ireland (46–10), 1999, Brisbane

49 v. Italy (55–6), 1988, Rome

30 v. Japan (37–7), 1975, Sydney

21 v. New Zealand (28–7), 1999, Sydney

48 v. Romania (57–9), 1999, Belfast (World Cup)

70 v. Samoa (73–3), 1994, Sydney

42 v. Scotland (45–3), 1998, Sydney

26 v. South Africa (32–6), 1999, Brisbane

47 v. South Korea (65–18), 1987, Brisbane

82 v. Spain (92–10), 2001, Madrid

74 v. Tonga (74–0), 1998, Canberra

58 v. USA (67–9), 1990, Brisbane

57 v. Wales (63–6), 1991, Brisbane

HIGHEST SCORE BY AN OPPOSING TEAM

61 by South Africa (22–61), 1997, Pretoria

By individual countries

27 by Argentina (19–27), 1987, Buenos Aires

31 by British and Irish Lions (0–31), 1966, Brisbane

16 by Canada (43–16), 1993, Calgary

28 by England (19–28), 1988, London

28 by Fiji (52–28), 1985, Brisbane

34 by France (6–34), 1976, Paris

27 by Ireland (12–27), 1979, Brisbane

20 by Italy (23–20), 1994, Brisbane

25 by Japan (50–25), 1975, Brisbane

43 by New Zealand (6–43), 1996, Wellington

9 by Romania (57–9), 1999, Belfast (World Cup)

13 by Samoa (25–13), 1998, Brisbane

24 by Scotland (15–24), 1981, Edinburgh

61 by South Africa (22–61), 1997, Pretoria

18 by South Korea (65–18), 1987, Brisbane

10 by Spain (92–10), 2001, Madrid

16 by Tonga (11–16), 1973, Brisbane

19 by USA (55–19), 1999, Limerick (World Cup)

28 by Wales (3–28), 1975, Cardiff

BIGGEST LOSING MARGIN

39 by South Africa (22–61), 1997, Pretoria

By individual countries

15 by Argentina (3–18), 1983, Brisbane

31 by British and Irish Lions (0–31), 1966, Brisbane

17 by England, 1973 (3–20) and 1976 (6–23), London

2 by Fiji, 1952 (15–17) and 1954 (16–18), Sydney

28 by France (6–34), 1976 Paris

15 by Ireland (12–27), 1979, Brisbane

37 by New Zealand (6–43), 1996, Wellington

9 by Scotland (15–24), 1981, Edinburgh

39 by South Africa (22–61), 1997, Pretoria

5 by Tonga (11–16), 1973, Brisbane

25 by Wales (3–28), 1975, Cardiff

Note: Australia has never lost to Canada, Italy, Japan, Romania, Samoa, South Korea, Spain or the USA.

Australian Schools tour November–December 2001: Tracking future Wallabies

The Australian Schools team first toured overseas in 1969, to South Africa, following which a national schoolboy squad has been picked every year since 1973. Historically, the team has been an extremely productive nursery for future Australian international players. More than 70 national schoolboy representatives have graduated to Wallaby status.

AUSTRALIAN SCHOOLS SQUAD		
Ole Avei	The Southport School	QLD
Rodney Blake	Homebush Boys High School	NSW
Richard Brown	St Joseph's College Nudgee	QLD
Mitchell Chapman (captain)	Brisbane Grammar School	QLD
Josh Clements	Hurlstone Agricultural College	NSW
Jon Collignon *Replaced Henari Veratai (Scots NSW) due to rugby league contract*	St Edmund's College	ACT
David Dillon	St Edmund's College	ACT
Josh Graham	The Southport School	QLD
Simon Hockings	Parkes High School	NSW
Luke Holmes	Narrabeen Sports High School	NSW

343

Jonathon Hoy	Narrabundah College	ACT
Junior Hunt	St Francis College	QLD
Chris Kennedy	The Southport School	QLD

Replaced Jarrod Saffy (St Joseph's NSW),

who was injured in camp

Gordon Kome	Punchbowl Boys High School	NSW
Saul Lilomaiava	Noble Park Secondary College	VIC
Chris Lyons	St Joseph's College Nudgee	QLD
Kieran Massey	Homebush Boys High School	NSW
Kit Maulio	The Southport School	QLD
Hugh McMeniman	St Joseph's College Nudgee	QLD
Drew Mitchell	St Patrick's College	QLD
Rowen Pearce	Parkes High School	NSW
Ian Potter	St Joseph's College Nudgee	QLD
Alex Quinlivan	St Ignatius College	NSW
Chris Siale	St Patrick's College	NSW
Joel Slater	Narrabeen Sports High School	NSW

Replaced Tyrone Smith (St Edmund's ACT)

due to rugby league contract

Lei Tomiki	The Scots College	NSW
Joe Tufuga	St Francis College	QLD
Josh Valentine	Narrabeen Sports High School	NSW

Mr Glen Cronan (manager)	St Joseph's College Nudgee	QLD
Mr Peter Gledhill (coach)	St Joseph's College Nudgee	QLD
Mr John Reed (assistant manager)	Oakhill College	NSW
Mr Patrick Langtry (assistant coach)	St Edmund's College	ACT
Mr Brad Harrison (physiotherapist)		NSW

MATCH REPORTS

GAME 1

Date	Sunday 25 November 2001
Opponent	Japan U19
City	Tokyo
Field	Prince Chichibu Stadium
Kick-off	12.15 p.m. local time
Weather	Clear
Ground	Good
Result	Australia 77 (Hunt 2, Siale 2, Kome, Mitchell, Blake, Clements, Valentine, Maulio, Quinlivan tries; Dillon 8, Lyons 3 conversions) defeated Japan 5 (Kubo try)

Under clear skies at Tokyo's Prince Chichibu Stadium the 2001 Australian Schools kicked off their overseas tour with a comprehensive 77–5 win over the Japanese U19 team. After some early nerves and difficulty with interpretation of laws in a different country, the Australian team settled down to play some well-structured and entertaining rugby, running in 11 tries and converting them all.

After a week-long preparation the boys were keen to play a match and were committed and determined in all aspects of play. The most pleasing aspect was the successful transfer, into a game situation, of the structure and pattern worked on during the preparation. Continuity and ball control were a feature and, combined with some brutal and uncompromising defence, laid the foundation for the win.

After receiving the kick-off and being held in their quarter by a string of penalties, the Australians had to wait until the 10-minute mark for their first scoring opportunity. A turn-over of possession and quick ball led to the first try and then confidence grew. As they got into a rhythm, the holes opened and by half-time it was 35–0. From there the platform was set and the impetus was carried through the second half to record a further six tries. With both goalkickers on target, all conversions were successful and a big scoreline resulted.

Team Pearce, Holmes, Blake, Clements, McMeniman, Tomiki, Brown, Chapman, Valentine, Dillon, Siale, Hunt, Graham, Kome, Mitchell.
Reserves Tufuga, Hoy, Kennedy, Hockings, Avei, Maulio, Lyons, Quinlivan.
Replacements Hockings for Chapman, Quinlivan for Kome, Tufuga for Pearce, Hoy for Holmes, Avei for Brown, Lyons for Dillon, Maulio for Valentine.

GAME 2

Date	Saturday 1 December 2001
Opponent	Welsh Schools
City	Llanelli
Field	Stradey Park
Kick-off	2.30 p.m. local time
Temperature	8°C
Weather	Cold and windy
Ground	Muddy and heavy
Score	Australia 22 (Blake 2, McMeniman tries; Dillon 1 penalty, 2 conversions) defeated Welsh Schools 9 (Aled Thomas 3 penalties)

Under clear blue skies, the Australian Schools team successfully started the UK leg of their tour with a 22–9 victory against Welsh Schools at famous Stradey Park in Llanelli. Australia got off to a good start from the kick-off, taking play down to the Welsh end of the field. A penalty ensued and after just three minutes a successful kick from fly-half David Dillon had Australia in front 3–0.

The Welsh came back hard from the restart and threatened on a couple of occasions, challenging the Australian defensive line both in close and out wide. Australia soon turned defence into attack with some crucial turnovers. A decision to kick for the line and take an attacking line-out, rather than the three points on offer from a penalty, proved fortuitous. Clean ball at four was driven 10 metres and tighthead prop Rodney Blake crashed over almost untouched to come up with the try. After a successful conversion from Dillon, the visitors led 10–0 at the midway point of the half.

With a scoreline of 10–6, the match was well and truly in the balance at the 10-minute mark of the second half. A penalty to Australia about 40 metres out saw Dillon elect to take a shot from long range. This proved to be the turning point of the match because, while the kick was unsuccessful, its ricochet off the crossbar was regathered by a vigilant and purposeful chase from lock Hugh McMeniman, who subsequently crashed over under the posts from 10 metres out. Another driving line-out in the attacking quarter saw Blake secure a second try on 25 minutes and, despite a missed conversion, the result was now beyond doubt, with a 16-point lead and less than 10 minutes remaining.

Overall, it was a hard-fought contest with not a lot of free-flowing play. The defensive effort of the Australians to keep the opposition scoreless was a feature of the victory.

Team Pearce, Holmes, Blake, Clements, McMeniman, Tomiki, Brown, Chapman, Valentine, Dillon, Siale, Hunt, Graham, Kome, Mitchell.
Reserves Tufuga, Hoy, Kennedy, Potter, Avei, Maulio, Lyons, Quinlivan.
Replacements Quinlivan for Mitchell, Tufuga for Pearce, Hoy for Holmes, Potter for Clements, Avei for Brown, Maulio for Valentine and Kennedy for Blake.

GAME 3

Date	Wednesday 5 December 2001
Opponent	Welsh President's XV
City	Swansea
Field	St Helen's
Kick-off	7.15 p.m. local time
Temperature	9°C
Weather	Cool with a light wind
Ground	Good
Result	Australia 23 (Potter try; Lyons 5 penalties, Slater 1 penalty) defeated Welsh President's XV 22 (Matt Nuttall 2 tries; Matt Jones 4 penalties)

Australian Schools finished the Welsh leg of their tour in style, with a courageous and well-constructed 23–22 victory over a Welsh President's XV that was made up of the nucleus of the Welsh FIRA Cup squad to contest the U19 Championships in Italy. Coming off the Australian victory over Welsh Schools, it was always going to be a big challenge to get up for this difficult fixture. Due to the vagaries of touring, playing time needs to be shared among the 28 players in the squad and untested combinations are often used. In this game, Saul Lilomaiava and John Collignon made their debuts for Australia; Joe Tufuga, Jonnie Hoy, Ole Avei, Kit Maulio, Chris Lyons, Kieran Massey and Alex Quinlivan secured their first run on jerseys; and Jonnie also captained the side for the first time.

Some strong play from both teams between the 22s characterised the middle stages of the first half before a sickening head clash involving Josh Graham led to him being forced off to the blood bin with his opponent sustaining a broken jaw. Not long after, Australia received another penalty and Lyons converted from long range for the visitors to lead 6–3 after 18 minutes. Again the Welsh came back, harder than ever, and put together enough phases to take advantage of the reshuffle in the Australian back line due to Graham's departure. They scored a well-constructed try out wide in the 21st minute. The conversion was unsuccessful and the home side led for the first time, 8–6. Australia replied with a penalty, but with five minutes left before the break the tourists relaxed and allowed the Welsh to again enter the attacking half and slot a penalty on the stroke of half-time, for the home side to lead 11–9.

In the 12th minute a possible turning point emerged when Lyons was sin-binned for slowing down the home team's ball at the breakdown. The ensuing penalty meant a 17–12 Welsh lead. Both sides exchanged tries, but after a series of forays into Welsh territory the break finally came on 32 minutes with a penalty 40 metres out and 45 degrees to the uprights.

Back on the field after his earlier sin-binning, Lyons elected to take his chances with the penalty goal and under pressure delivered with a high standard kick that sneaked inside the left-hand post. Australia led by a point at 23–22, with three minutes plus injury time remaining.

A gutsy and skilful performance had maintained the Australian Schools' proud record of never having lost on Welsh soil in seven tours, dating back to 1973–74.

Team Tufuga, Hoy, Blake, Potter, Hockings, Avei, Tomiki, Lilomaiava, Maulio, Lyons, Massey, Slater, Graham, Collignon, Quinlivan.
Reserves Kennedy, Holmes, Chapman, McMeniman, Brown, Valentine, Dillon, Hunt.
Replacements Hunt for Graham, Valentine for Maulio, Chapman for Lilomaiava, McMeniman for Potter.

GAME 4

Date	Monday 10 December 2001
Opponent	Scotland 'A' U19
City	Edinburgh
Field	Murrayfield
Kick-off	7.00 p.m. local time
Temperature	−4°C
Weather	Clear and cold
Ground	Icy
Result	Australia 26 (Massey, Collignon, Slater, Dillon tries; Lyons 3 conversions) defeated Scotland 6 (Sam Hendry 2 penalties)

In one of the great ironies of Northern Hemisphere rugby, fine weather and a lack of cloud and rain nearly caused the cancellation of the touring Australian Schools first match in Scotland. At lunchtime on the day of the match the Bridge-haugh Ground in Stirling was deemed unsafe due to its frozen surface. The match was shifted to Murrayfield in Edinburgh, where the No. 2 Field was used.

In near-freezing conditions the match commenced as scheduled. After winning the toss, the Scottish team chose to kick off and gave Australia first use of the ball. This proved an important factor as the visitors controlled the ball well and recycled good possession early before left-winger Kieran Massey beat two defenders to score the first try after two minutes. The conversion from fly-half Chris Lyons put Australia in front 7–0.

After this initial incursion Scotland regrouped and both teams shared the spoils over the next quarter of an hour as they attempted to impose their preferred style of play on the match. Shoulder injuries to full-back Drew Mitchell and number 8 Saul Lilomaiava during this time demon-strated the physical nature of the game and Scotland took advantage of a penalty in the 14th minute to get their first points on board and trail 3–7. Right-winger John Collignon then scored out wide for the visitors' second try. A tough conversion was successful from Lyons and after 18 min-utes Australia led 14–3. The home side let their guard down in injury time and centre Joel Slater crossed for Australia's third try in the 36th minute. An unsuccessful conversion from Lyons saw the half-time score read Aus-tralia 19 Scotland 'A' 3.

The Australian Rugby Companion

A number of changes at half-time resulted in a major reshuffle to the Australian team and this, combined with a fired-up Scottish team after the break, saw the momentum swing somewhat in the early stages of the second half. The revamped Australian back line also began to click and this led to a fourth try to scrum-half replacement David Dillon. Lyons again converted the try for Australia to make the match safe at 26–6 after 22 minutes.

Team Tufuga, Hoy, Kennedy, Potter, Hockings, Avei, Brown, Lilomaiava, Maulio, Lyons, Massey, Slater, Hunt, Collignon, Mitchell.
Reserves Pearce, Holmes, Blake, Clements, McMeniman, Tomiki, Valentine, Dillon.
Replacements Tomiki for Lilomaiava, Valentine for Dillon (blood bin) and Maulio, Holmes for Hoy, Clements for Potter, McMeniman for Hockings.

GAME 5

Date	Thursday 13 December 2001
Opponent	Scotland U19
City	Greenock (transferred from Glasgow)
Field	Fort Matilda (transferred from Burnbrae, West of Scotland RFC)
Kick-off	1.10 p.m. local time (put back from 12 noon)
Temperature	1°C
Weather	Cold
Ground	Icy and muddy
Result	Scotland 3 (Andrew McLean penalty) defeated Australia 0

Very cold conditions continued to wreak havoc with the Scottish leg of the Australian Schools tour, with frozen grounds not only causing another reshuffle of venue but this time a delayed kick-off. The match was transferred further west two days prior to kick-off due to frozen fields in Glasgow and a chance of softer fields near the coast. Despite this, continued cold weather still left the match in doubt as the alternative venue was quite hard on the surface when the teams arrived. Both sides expressed concern and the referee agreed it was unplayable at match time. Despite requests not to play for safety reasons, the referee decided to start the match with the proviso it be called off if he believed it was too dangerous to continue.

The game commenced an hour and a quarter after the scheduled time, with both sides hesitant in the opening encounters. It became clear very quickly that conditions dictated this would be a match in which very few points would be scored. A muddy ball and heavy field contributed to a lot of turnovers, and some baffling interpretations of the ruck and maul by the Welsh referee added to the frustration of both teams. Any attempt at creativity in the backs was stifled by the man in the middle, who deemed that decoy runners, no matter how far away from the ball, were automatically interfering with the defence and therefore to be penalised. A penalty next to the posts in injury time was converted by the Scottish fly-half and the home team went to the break with a 3–0 advantage.

The second half saw the game ebb and flow between the 22-metre zones in the early stages before the Australians began to control possession a bit better. Some sustained pressure midway through the half forced the home team to defend grimly, but they held firm and gave away some penalties rather than continue to defend. The visitors chose to ignore the three points on offer in search of a try, which was to prove costly in the final analysis. A curious loss of the scrum feed while in possession and a disallowed try for offside from a grubber kick released the pressure on the Scottish try line and from there they played field position to consolidate their lead. A missed penalty from the Scottish fly-half from long range bounced off the crossbar and nearly led to a lucky try for the home side, but other than this the game was closed down and, despite the Australians' attempts to open things up in the final 10 minutes, little continuity was allowed and the game ended at Scotland 3 Australia 0.

Team Pearce, Holmes, Blake, Clements, McMeniman, Tomiki, Brown, Chapman, Valentine, Dillon, Massey, Hunt, Graham, Kome, Siale.
Reserves Tufuga, Hoy, Kennedy, Potter, Avei, Maulio, Lyons, Slater.
Replacements Tufuga for Pearce, Lyons for Dillon, Avei for Tomiki, Potter for Clements.

GAME 6

Date	Saturday 15 December 2001
Opponent	Ulster Schools
City	Belfast
Field	Ravenhill
Kick-off	6.00 p.m. local time
Temperature	4°C
Weather	Clear and cool

Ground   Perfect
Result   Australia 25 (Siale, Kennedy, Slater tries;
            Lyons 2 penalties and 2 conversions)
            defeated Ulster Schools 0

After the frozen grounds debacle in Scotland, the Australian squad commenced the Irish leg of their tour in absolutely perfect conditions against Ulster Schools at the famous Ravenhill Ground in Belfast. This was always going to be a crucial match after the loss in Scotland, and in effect the remainder of the tour hinged on how the boys would bounce back from the disappointment of Fort Matilda.

Ulster won the toss and elected to kick off and it was evident from the first chase that the home side were keen for a big performance in their final match together. The Australians had control of the match but let themselves down by failing to capitalise on a number of opportunities being created by good lead-up work. Some good passages of play in the final 10 minutes by the tourists provided good field position, and successful penalty kicks to Lyons at 32 and 35 minutes sent Australia to the break with a 6–0 advantage. In truth it should have been much more, however – while they were competing well enough, the boys looked tired and their concentration was faltering.

After some soul-searching in the huddle at half-time, the visitors came out with a new sense of purpose in the second stanza. Good ball control and structure led to an easy try to full-back Chris Siale and after an unsuccessful conversion from Lyons, Australia led 11–0 after five minutes. In the 29th minute a sustained attack, in which possession was recycled quickly over many phases, saw the Ulster defensive line shattered. 'Seagulling' prop Chris Kennedy found himself in space out wide with no one in front and ran 20 metres to the line to score a well-taken try. The conversion from Lyons was successful and Australia were in control at 18–0. The visitors finished the game in style with inside centre Joel Slater crossing untouched out wide on 35 minutes and, with the conversion successful from Lyons, full-time was blown and Australia had come away with a 25–0 victory.

In an emotional conclusion to the game, the boys were introduced to, and addressed by, former Australian Schools and Wallaby prop Tony D'arcy, who is now coaching Ballymena. His eldest son, Chris, had been selected for the Queensland Schools team in August but tragically died from the meningococcal virus just days after his selection and never got to play for Queensland. Tony's words and involvement in the sheds after the match will be remembered by all members of the touring party for the rest of their lives.

Team Tufuga, Hoy, Kennedy, Potter, Hockings, Avei, Tomiki, Chapman, Maulio, Lyons, Siale, Slater, Graham, Collignon, Quinlivan.
Reserves Pearce, Holmes, Blake, McMeniman, Brown, Valentine, Dillon, Hunt.
Replacements Brown for Chapman (blood bin), McMeniman for Potter, Hunt for Graham, Valentine for Maulio.

GAME 7

Date	Tuesday 18 December 2001
Opponent	Leinster Schools
City	Dublin
Field	Donnybrook
Kick-off	7.00 p.m. local time
Temperature	5°C
Weather	Fine and cool
Ground	Heavy
Result	Australia 30 (Siale, Hockings, Massey tries; Dillon 2 penalties, Lyons 1 penalty, 3 conversions) defeated Leinster Schools 22 (Ross McCarron try; David Connellan 5 penalties, 1 conversion)

The Australian Schools team continued the Irish leg of their tour with a courageous 30–22 victory over Leinster Schools at Donnybrook in Dublin. The win came against a Leinster team that contained 13 of the 23 players selected for the Irish Schools squad to play Australia in Cork. Leinster were the reigning Irish Schools regional champions and prior to this match had gone 14 games without tasting defeat. This was their final fixture together for the season and given such circumstances they were always going to be tough opponents.

The early stages posed a particular challenge for the visitors as they worked to try to come to terms with local refereeing interpretations. The home team's enthusiasm and some curious refereeing combined to have the Leinster on the front foot early and pressing to establish superiority. This momentum was quickly transferred to the scoreboard, with a successful penalty from their scrum-half in the second minute for a 3–0 Leinster lead. Successful penalties to fly-half David Dillon in the seventh and ninth minutes had the visitors back on track and leading 6–3. The Australians then relaxed in defence from a scrum in their quarter and the home team took advantage to score through the midfield under the posts. It was a soft try and as the referee's whistle went for half-time the home team had secured a 13–6 advantage.

Leinster returned to the field after the break with a real sense of purpose and had obviously began to believe that victory was a very real possibility. After 10 minutes Australia trailed 6–16 but did not drop their heads and continued to chip away at the opposition. At the 12-minute mark, replacement fly-half Chris Lyons kicked a penalty goal to bring the margin back to seven points at 9–16. However, the home team were not letting up and two further penalties from their scrum-half at 18 and 25 minutes saw Leinster lead 22–9 with just 10 minutes remaining. Reinforcements were clearly needed and a triple substitution by the Australians saw prop Tufuga, flanker Avei and full-back Siale introduced, with almost immediate effect. A well-constructed try at 28 minutes by Siale was converted by Lyons and the score was suddenly back to less than a converted try at 22–16.

Although Leinster defended admirably in the shadows of full-time, their spirits were shattered on 34 minutes when lock Simon Hockings finished off a forward raid from long range to bring the visitors to within one point. The successful conversion by Lyons under pressure put the visitors in the lead for the first time in the match, with only one minute of time remaining. The Australians launched yet another attacking raid from long range that resulted in winger Kieran Massey crossing for the visitors' third try on 40 minutes, and another successful conversion to Lyons made it 30–22.

Team Pearce, Holmes, Blake, McMeniman, Hockings, Tomiki, Brown, Lilomaiava, Valentine, Dillon, Massey, Slater, Hunt, Collignon, Quinlivan.
Reserves Tufuga, Hoy, Kennedy, Chapman, Avei, Maulio, Lyons, Siale.
Replacements Lyons for Dillon, Chapman for Lilomaiava, Avei for Brown, Tufuga for Pearce, Siale for Quinlivan.

GAME 8

Date	Saturday 23 December 2001
Opponent	Irish Schools
City	Cork
Field	Temple Hill (Cork Constitution)
Kick-off	2.30 p.m. local time/1.30 a.m. Sydney time
Temperature	2°C
Weather	Clear but cold
Ground	Good
Result	Australia 47 (Mitchell, Hunt, Siale, Clements, Hoy, Avei tries; Lyons 3 penalties and 4 conversions) defeated Irish Schools 6 (David Connellan 2 penalties)

The Australians bustled well from the kick-off and immediately put their opponents under pressure. Australia lost their number 8 and captain, Mitch Chapman, with a painful hip injury at the 28-minute mark and things threatened to unravel as a long-range penalty against the run of play was converted well by Connellan on 30 minutes, which saw the locals trailing just 6–9. The final minutes of the half saw Australia showing great patience and continuity to put together their best passage in injury time. Excellent pick-and-drive from the forwards combined with good decision-making from the backs saw multiple-phase ball secured and significant inroads made. Ultimately, too many waves of attack left the Irish defence in disarray and winger Drew Mitchell strolled over unopposed out wide in the 37th minute for the first try of the match. Half-time: 14–6 to Australia.

The tourists returned to the field with a real sense of belief and purpose for the second half. The instructions were clear that with more discipline and patience the game could be broken wide open. The forwards needed to continue the close-in pick-and-drive work and the backs had to improve their ball handling with better concentration. The players carried these instructions out to perfection from the outset and a try similar to the one scored on the stroke of half-time was scored after just three minutes of the second half. Centre Junior Hunt carved through the undermanned defence to score beside the posts and Lyons converted for a 21–6 Australian lead. Australia came straight back with a sparkling try to the ever-elusive Chris Siale on six minutes and a great barging effort from lock Josh Clements in the 10th minute. Both tries were converted by Lyons and, with 25 minutes still remaining, Australia led 35–6.

With 15 minutes to go, the Australians built up more pressure with good lead-up play and hooker Jon Hoy went over for the team's fifth try, which was converted by Lyons to push the score out to 42–6. Flanker Ole Avei scored the final points of the match, crashing over for a try on 34 minutes. Lyons' conversion was unsuccessful and the final score read Australian Schools 47 Irish Schools 6.

This was a fitting climax to a great tour and an appropriate demonstration of the team's great ability to stay focused. That their last match on a long tour was their best was testimony to their work ethic and willingness to keep football as the main priority. The match saw many existing Australia v. Ireland Schools records shattered, including most points (47), most tries (6), biggest margin (41) and individual points scored (Chris Lyons 17).

Team Pearce, Hoy, Blake, Clements, McMeniman, Avei, Tomiki, Chapman, Valentine, Lyons, Mitchell, Slater, Hunt, Kome, Siale.

Reserves Tufuga, Holmes, Potter, Hockings, Brown, Maulio, Dillon, Massey.

Replacements Brown for Chapman, Hockings for Clements, Tufuga for Pearce, Massey for Hunt, Potter for McMeniman.

Laws of the game

We invited Australia's five test referees – Andrew Cole, Stuart Dickinson, Wayne Erickson, Peter Marshall and Scott Young – to comment in plain English on pertinent aspects of rugby's laws. The full version of the laws is available on the International Rugby Board web site at www.irfb.com.

LAW 1 – THE GROUND

DEFINITIONS
The **Ground** is the total area shown on the plan. The Ground includes:

- the **field-of-play** – the area (as shown on the plan) between the goal lines and the touchlines. These lines are not part of the field-of-play.

- the **playing area** – the field-of-play and the in-goal areas (as shown on the plan). The touchlines, touch-in-goal lines and dead-ball lines are not part of the playing area.

- the **playing enclosure** – the playing area and a space around it, not less than 5 metres where practicable, which is known as the perimeter area.

- **in-goal** – the area between the goal line and the dead-ball line, and between the touch-in-goal lines. It includes the goal line but not the dead-ball line or the touch-in-goal lines.

COMMENT: Peter Marshall

The ground should be inspected by a representative of each team prior to the commencement of the game. If either team has any objections about the ground or the way the ground is marked out, they must tell the referee before the game starts. The referee will try to resolve any problems, but will not start the game if any part of the ground is considered dangerous.

THE PLAYING AREA

INDICATES POST WITH FLAG (MAXIMUM HEIGHT 1.2 METRES ABOVE GROUND)

LAW 2 – THE BALL

Shape   The ball must be oval and made of four panels.

Dimensions   Length in line 280–300 millimetres
Circumference (end to end) 760–790 millimetres
Circumference (in width) 580–620 millimetres

Materials   Leather or similar synthetic material. It may be treated to make it resistant to mud and easier to grip.

Weight   400–440 grams

Air pressure at the start of play   0.67–0.70 kilograms per square centimetre, or 9½–10 lbs per square inch

COMMENT: Stuart Dickinson
The ball is the key ingredient that allows the game to be played. It is important that the shape, condition and air pressure of the match balls are checked prior to kick-off. Teams use correctly weighted rugby balls during training and become used to their flight and feel and it is therefore essential that they play under the same conditions.

LAW 3 – NUMBER OF PLAYERS: THE TEAM

DEFINITIONS
A **team** consists of 15 players who start the match plus any authorised replacements and/or substitutes.
Replacement: a player who replaces an injured teammate.
Substitute: a player who replaces a teammate for tactical reasons.

Maximum number of players on the playing area   Each team must have no more than 15 players on the playing area.

Team with more than the permitted number of players
Objection: At any time before or during a match a team may make an objection to the referee about the number of players in their opponents' team. As soon as the referee knows that a team has too many players, the referee must order the captain of that team to reduce the number appropriately. The score at the time of the objection remains unaltered.

When there are fewer than 15 players   A Union may authorise matches to be played with fewer than 15 players in each team. When that happens, all the laws of the game apply except that each team must have at least five players in the scrum at all times.

Players nominated as substitutes   For international matches a Union may nominate up to seven replacements/substitutes. For other matches, the Union with jurisdiction over the match decides how many replacements/substitutes may be nominated.

Suitably trained and experienced players in the front row
(a) The table below indicates the numbers of suitably trained and experienced players for the front row when nominating different numbers of players.

Number of players	Number of suitably trained and experienced players
15 or less	3 players who can play in the front row
16, 17 or 18	4 players who can play in the front row
19, 20, 21 or 22	5 players who can play in the front row

COMMENT: Wayne Erickson

Teams can nominate up to seven players as replacements, and most nominate four forwards and three backs. The four forwards usually comprise a specialist hooker, a prop who can play either side of the front row, a second row/number 8 and a specialist flanker. The back-line replacements usually contain a specialist scrum-half, someone to cover the fly-half/centre positions and a cover for wing/full-back. A player who is replaced because of an injury that is not a bleeding or an open wound cannot return to continue in the game, even as a replacement for someone else. Referees must be sure of the reason for players leaving the field and being replaced.

LAW 4 – PLAYERS' CLOTHING

DEFINITION
Players' clothing is anything players wear. A player wears a jersey, shorts and underwear, socks and boots.

Additional items of clothing

(a) A player may wear supports made of elasticated or compressible materials which must be washable.

(b) A player may wear shin guards worn under the socks with padding incorporated in non-rigid fabric with no part of the padding thicker than 0.5 cm when compressed.

(c) A player may wear ankle supports worn under socks, not extending higher than one-third of the length of the shin and, if rigid, from material other than metal.

(d) A player may wear mitts (fingerless gloves).

(e) A player may wear shoulder pads made of soft and thin materials, which may be incorporated in an undergarment or jersey provided that the pads cover the shoulder and collarbone only. No part of the pads may be thicker than

1 cm when uncompressed. No part of the pads may have a density of more than 45 kg per cubic metre.

(f) A player may wear a mouthguard or dental protector.

(g) A player may wear headgear made of soft and thin materials provided that no part of the headgear is thicker than 1 cm when uncompressed and no part of the headgear has a density of more than 45 kg per cubic metre.

(h) A player may wear bandages and/or dressings to cover or protect any injury.

(i) A player may wear thin tape or other similar material as support and/or to prevent injury.

(j) A player must not wear communication devices within that player's clothing or attached to the body.

COMMENT: Andrew Cole

There have been some changes in recent years, all with safety in mind. There is the double-edged sword of providing enough protection for players while ensuring that any protective equipment itself is safe for the contact that occurs. With any padding worn, the bottom line is that it must be soft and compressible. To make it easier for everyone, all recently manufactured protective equipment must bear the IRB logo as an indication that it has passed the safety standards. As far as studs go, it is important that the edges are not burred, sharp or pointed and the maximum length is 18 mm.

LAW 5 – TIME

Duration of a match   A match lasts no longer than 80 minutes plus time lost, extra time and any special conditions. A match is divided into two halves each of not more than 40 minutes' playing time.

Half-time   After half-time the teams change ends. There is an interval of not more than 10 minutes. The length of the interval is decided by the match organiser, the Union or the recognised body that has jurisdiction over the game. During the interval the teams, the referee and the touch judges may leave the playing enclosure.

Timekeeping   The referee keeps the time but may delegate the duty to either or both the touch judges and/or the official timekeeper, in which case the referee signals to them any stoppage of time or time lost. In matches without an official timekeeper, if the referee is in doubt as to the correct time the referee consults either or both the touch judges and may consult others but only if the touch judges cannot help.

Time lost   Time lost may be due to the following:

(a) **Injury**. The referee may stop play for not more than one minute so that an injured player can be treated, or for any other permitted delay. The referee may allow play to continue while a medically trained person treats an injured player in the playing area or the player may go to the touchline for treatment. If the referee believes that the player is feigning injury, the referee arranges for the player to be removed from the playing area, and restarts play at once. Alternatively, the referee may allow play to continue while a medically trained person examines the player in the playing area.

(b) **Replacing players' clothing**. When the ball is dead, the referee allows time for a player to replace or repair a badly torn jersey, shorts or boots. Time is allowed for a player to retie a bootlace.

(c) **Replacement and substitution of players**. Time is allowed when a player is replaced or substituted.

(d) **Reporting of foul play by a touch judge**. Time is allowed when a touch judge reports foul play.

COMMENT: *Scott Young*

The referee is sole judge of time but, as mentioned, may delegate this duty to others, including the touch judges. However, it is important to understand that should there be a discrepancy, for whatever reason, the referee will decide on the time remaining in the match. In the case of an injury, although the law states that only one minute should be allowed, the referee is again sole judge and would use his/her discretion in relation to the severity of the injury. Obviously in the case of a severe injury it may take more than one minute for a player to be taken from the field of play.

LAW 6 – MATCH OFFICIALS – LAW 6a

A. Referee – Before the match
DEFINITIONS

Every match is under the control of match officials, who consist of the **referee** and two **touch judges**. Additional persons as authorised by the match organisers may include the referee and/or touch judge reserve, an official to assist the referee in making decisions by using technological devices, the timekeeper, the match doctor, the team doctors, the non-playing members of the teams and the ball persons.

1. Appointing the referee
The referee is appointed by the match organiser. If no referee has been appointed, the two teams may agree upon a referee. If they cannot agree, the home team appoints a referee.

2. Replacing the referee
If the referee is unable to complete the match, the referee's replacement is appointed according to the instructions of the match organiser. If the match organiser has given no instructions,

the referee appoints the replacement. If the referee cannot do so, the home team appoints a replacement.

3. Duties of the referee before the match

(a) **Toss**. The referee organises the toss. One of the captains tosses a coin and the other captain calls to see who wins the toss. The winner of the toss decides whether to kick off or choose an end. If the winner of the toss decides to choose an end, the opponents must kick off and vice versa.

(b) **Players' clothing inspection**. The referee must inspect the players' clothing to ensure it is in compliance with Law 4. The referee may delegate responsibility for the inspection of players' clothing to the touch judges.

(c) **Touch judges**. The referee may instruct the touch judges as to their duties.

4. Limitation on the referee

The referee must not give advice to either team before the match.

COMMENT: Peter Marshall

This law outlines the authority and duties of the referee before and during the game. All players must respect the authority of the referee and must not dispute the referee's decisions. If a television match official has been appointed, the referee may seek their advice when there is doubt if a try or goal has been scored. In the case of a try, the referee should only refer incidents where there is doubt in the action of scoring the try (in goal or approximately 1 metre out from the goal line).

B. Touch judges – Before the match
1. Appointing touch judges

There are two touch judges for every match. Unless they have been appointed by or under the authority of the match organiser, each team provides a touch judge.

Driza-Bone: as Australian as the Wallabies

What do you do at the Rugby when it's cold or raining?

Throw on a Driza of course! The Driza-Bone coat has been part of the national uniform for as long as the Wallabies have been playing rugby. And when it's cold or raining at the game you can bet half the punters are wearing them. This famous oilskin has a uniquely Australian appeal associated with the bush and hard working rural life. It has evolved from the functional and weatherproof work coat to one that is worn in the city as a symbol of country living, and is synonymous with Austraila anywhere in the world.

Today, Driza-Bone is an internationally recognised brand that encompasses a wide range of coats, jackets, vests, hats and leathergoods used for both active and leisure outdoor activities.

There are even Driza-Bone coats for dogs!

The complete Driza-Bone range now totals 99 products including a collection of official ARU/Wallabies merchandise (pictured right).

To order your own Wallabies Driza-Bone, or to find your nearest stockist, give the folks at Driza-Bone a call on 1800 773 800

Driza-Bone products are available at all leading Australiana, saddlery, countrywear, camping/disposal, and department stores

Corporate enquiries are also welcome (Prizes, Gifts, Incentives, Promotion)

Driza-Bone is an official sponsor and licensee of Australian Rugby and the official off-field wet-weather apparel supplier to the Wallabies

See more about Driza-Bone at www.drizabone.com.au

AIS&P1579

The Spirit of Australia

No matter how far, or how wide we roam, we still call Australia home.

qantas.com

QANTAS

2. Replacing a touch judge

The match organiser may nominate a person to act as a replacement for the referee or the touch judges. This person is called the reserve touch judge and stands in the perimeter area.

3. Control of touch judges

The referee has control over both touch judges. The referee may tell them what their duties are, and may overrule their decisions. If a touch judge is unsatisfactory, the referee may ask that the touch judge be replaced. If the referee believes a touch judge is guilty of misconduct, the referee has power to send the touch judge off and make a report to the match organiser.

During the match
4. Where the touch judges should be

(a) There is one touch judge on each side of the ground. The touch judge remains in touch except when judging a kick at goal. When judging a kick at goal the touch judges stand in in-goal behind the goalposts.

(b) A touch judge may enter the playing area when reporting an offence of dangerous play or misconduct to the referee. The touch judge may do this only at the next stoppage in play.

COMMENT: Stuart Dickinson

The two touch judges are part of the team of three officials who control the match and they are also the reserve referees in case of injury. They perform three roles: primary – to adjudicate on touch, touch-in-goal and the scoring of goals; secondary – to adjudicate on foul play; and tertiary – to offer any other assistance to the referee where possible during the match, such as knock-on. The touch judges will at all times take up the best position to allow them to adjudicate on their primary, secondary and tertiary roles. This is usually done through leading and

371

trailing, where the leading touch judge is in a position where the play is coming towards them and the trailing touch judge will look at the back play for foul-play offences.

LAW 7 – MODE OF PLAY

Playing a match A match is started by a kick-off. After the kick-off:

- any player who is on-side may take the ball and run with it
- any player may throw it or kick it
- any player may give the ball to another player
- any player may tackle, hold or shove an opponent holding the ball
- any player may fall on the ball
- any player may take part in a scrum, ruck, maul or line-out
- any player may ground the ball in an in-goal.

Whatever a player does must be in accordance with the laws of the game.

LAW 8 – ADVANTAGE

DEFINITION
The law of advantage takes precedence over most other laws and its purpose is to make play more continuous, with fewer stoppages for infringements. Players are encouraged to play to the whistle despite infringements by their opponents. When the result of an infringement by one team is that their opposing team may gain an advantage, the referee does not whistle immediately for the infringement.

1. Advantage in practice

(a) The referee is sole judge of whether or not a team has gained an advantage. The referee has wide discretion when making decisions.

(b) Advantage can be either territorial or tactical.

(c) Territorial advantage means a gain in ground.

(d) Tactical advantage means freedom for the non-offending team to play the ball as they wish.

2. When advantage does not arise

The advantage must be clear and real. A mere opportunity to gain advantage is not enough. If the non-offending team does not gain an advantage, the referee blows the whistle and brings play back to the place of infringement.

3. When the advantage law is not applied

(a) **Referee contact**. Advantage must not be applied when the ball, or a player carrying it, touches the referee.

(b) **Ball out of tunnel**. Advantage must not be applied when the ball comes out of either end of the tunnel at a scrum without having been played.

(c) **Wheeled scrum**. Advantage must not be applied when the scrum is wheeled through more than 90 degrees (so that the middle line has passed beyond a position parallel to the touchline).

(d) **Collapsed scrum**. Advantage must not be applied when a scrum collapses. The referee must blow the whistle immediately.

(e) **Player lifted in the air**. Advantage must not be applied when a player in a scrum is lifted in the air or forced upwards out of the scrum. The referee must blow the whistle immediately.

The Australian Rugby Companion

COMMENT: Andrew Cole

This is one of the shortest laws in the book but probably the most important. The advantage law sets rugby apart from other sports and can create unpredictability that leads to scoring situations. The whole idea of the law is to minimise stoppages. It is compulsory for the referee to play advantage. The referee must take into account many factors in playing advantage, including what effect the infringement had on the subsequent play, the time, the score and the game situation. In other words, was the opposition denied space, time or options by the infringement? If the non-infringing team gains significant territory or plays the ball as they wish, then advantage has been gained. Just as teams enjoy the thrill of scoring a try, referees also gain satisfaction from knowing their playing of advantage has led to the subsequent try.

LAW 9 – METHOD OF SCORING

A. Scoring points

1. Points values

Try. When an attacking player is first to ground the ball in the opponents' in-goal, a try is scored. 5 points

Penalty try. If a player would probably have scored a try but for foul play by an opponent, a penalty try is awarded between the goalposts. 5 points

Conversion goal. When a player scores a try it gives the player's team the right to attempt to score a goal by taking a kick at goal; this also applies to a penalty try. This kick is a conversion kick: a conversion kick can be a place kick or a drop kick. 2 points

Penalty goal. A player scores a penalty goal by kicking a goal from a penalty kick. 3 points

Dropped goal. A player scores a dropped goal by kicking a goal from a drop kick in general play. The team awarded a free kick cannot score a dropped goal until after the ball next becomes dead, or after an opponent has played or touched it, or has tackled the ball carrier. This restriction applies also to a scrum taken instead of a free kick. 3 points

Goal. A player scores a goal by kicking the ball over an opponents' crossbar and between the goalposts from the field-of-play, by a place kick or drop kick. A goal cannot be scored from a kick-off, a drop-out or a free kick.

2. Kick at goal – special circumstances

(a) If after the ball is kicked, it touches the ground or any teammate of the kicker, a goal cannot be scored.

(b) If the ball has crossed the crossbar a goal is scored, even if the wind blows it back into the field-of-play.

(c) If an opponent commits an offence as the kick at goal is being taken, but nevertheless the kick is successful, advantage is played and the score stands.

(d) If an opponent illegally touches the ball as the kick at goal is being taken and the kick is not successful, the referee may award a goal if the referee considers that one would otherwise probably have been scored.

B. Conversion kick

DEFINITION

When a player scores a try, it gives the player's team the right to try to score a goal by taking a kick at goal; this also applies to a penalty try. This kick is a conversion kick. A conversion kick can be a place kick or a drop kick.

COMMENT: Wayne Erickson
At a kick for goal after a try, we often see defending players
running out in an attempt to charge the kick down. Even if they
are quick enough to touch the ball in flight, the goal is allowed
as long as it goes through the posts. Penalty tries are rarely
awarded, and often attract controversy when they are. Read the
definition – what does 'probably' mean? Something between
'possibly' and 'certainly'? What about 'more likely than not'?
Who'd be a referee?

LAW 10 – FOUL PLAY

DEFINITION
Foul play is anything a person does within the playing enclosure
that is against the letter and spirit of the laws of the game. It
includes obstruction, unfair play, repeated infringements,
dangerous play and misconduct.

1. Obstruction

(a) **Charging or pushing**. A player must not voluntarily move
    or stand in front of a teammate carrying the ball. *Penalty:*
    penalty kick

(b) **Running in front of a ball carrier**. A player must not
    voluntarily move or stand in front of a teammate carrying the
    ball thereby preventing opponents from tackling the current
    ball carrier or the opportunity to tackle potential ball carriers
    when they gain possession. *Penalty: penalty kick*

(c) **Blocking the tackler**. A player must not voluntarily move or
    stand in a position that prevents an opponent from tackling
    a ball carrier. *Penalty: penalty kick*

(d) **Blocking the ball**. A player must not voluntarily move or
    stand in a position that prevents an opponent from playing

the ball. *Penalty: penalty kick*

(e) **Ball carrier running into teammate at a set piece**. A player carrying the ball after it has left a scrum, ruck, maul or line-out must not run into teammates in front of the player. *Penalty: penalty kick*

(f) **Flanker obstructing opposing scrum-half**. A flanker in a scrum must not prevent an opposing scrum-half from advancing around the scrum. *Penalty: penalty kick*

(g) A player carrying the ball cannot be penalised for obstruction under any circumstances.

COMMENT: Scott Young

Dangerous play and misconduct include but are not limited to punching, striking, stamping or trampling, kicking, tripping and dangerous tackling, playing an opponent without the ball, dangerous charging, tackling the jumper in the air, and dangerous play in a scrum, ruck or maul. Dangerous tackling includes a player being tackled high (above the line of the shoulders), early or late or without the ball. Players must also tackle with their arms. A shoulder charge is not deemed a tackle and must be penalised. In all cases of dangerous play and misconduct the minimum sanction is a penalty kick at the place of infringement. Acts contrary to good sportsmanship and any form of misconduct while the ball is out of play are also included under this section of the law. Should the referee decide that the act of dangerous play or misconduct deserves a formal caution, he/she would show that player a yellow card. The player would then be temporarily suspended (sin-binned) for a period of 10 minutes in open matches or five minutes in U19 matches. In the case where a referee has decided that the act is worthy of a send-off, the red card would be shown to the player. Once a player has been sent off, they are unable to play for the remainder of that particular match.

LAW 11 – OFFSIDE AND ON-SIDE IN GENERAL PLAY

DEFINITION

At the start of a game all players are **on-side**. As the match progresses players may find themselves in an **offside** position. Such players are then liable to be penalised unless they become on-side again.

In general play a player is **offside** if the player is in front of a teammate who is carrying the ball or in front of a teammate who last played the ball. Offside means that a player is temporarily out of the game; such players are liable to be penalised if they take part in the game.

In general play, a player can be put **on-side** either by an action of a teammate or by an action of an opponent. However, the offside player cannot be put on-side if the offside player interferes with play; or moves forward, towards the ball, or fails to move 10 metres away from the place where the ball lands.

Offside in general play

(a) A player who is in an offside position is liable to penalty only if the player does one of three things:

  ● interferes with play, or

  ● moves forward, towards the ball, or

  ● fails to comply with the 10-metre law (Law 11.4).

  A player who is in an offside position is not automatically penalised.

  A player who receives an involuntary throw-forward is not offside.

A player can be offside in the in-goal.

(b) **Offside and interfering with play**. A player who is offside must not take part in the game. This means the player must not play the ball or obstruct an opponent.

(c) **Offside and moving forward**. When a teammate of an offside player has kicked ahead, the offside player must not move towards opponents who are waiting to play the ball, or move towards the place where the ball lands, until the player has been put on-side.

Putting on-side a player retiring during a ruck, maul, scrum or line-out

When a ruck, maul, scrum or line-out forms, a player who is offside and is retiring as required by law remains offside even when the opposing team wins possession and the ruck, maul, scrum or line-out has ended.

In this situation, no action of the offside player or teammates can put the offside player on-side. The offside player can be put on-side only by the action of the opposing team. There are two such actions:

- **Opponent runs 5 metres with ball**. When an opponent carrying the ball has run 5 metres, the offside player is put on-side. An offside player is not put on-side when an opponent passes the ball. Even if the opponents pass the ball several times, their action does not put the offside player on-side.
- **Opponent kicks**. When an opponent kicks the ball, the offside player is put on-side.

Loitering

A player who remains in an offside position is loitering. A loiterer who prevents the opposing team from playing the ball as they wish is taking part in the game, and is penalised. The referee makes sure that the loiterer does not benefit from being put on-side by the opposing team's action.
Penalty: penalty kick

COMMENT: Peter Marshall

The offside law gives players time and space to play the game. An offside player in general play (in front of a teammate who has the ball or who played it last) will only be penalised when they try to take part in the game.

LAW 12 – KNOCK-ON OR THROW-FORWARD

DEFINITION

Knock-on

A **knock-on** occurs when a player loses possession of the ball and it goes forward, or when a player hits the ball forward with the hand or arm, or when the ball hits the hand or arm and goes forward, and the ball touches the ground or another player before the original player can catch it.

'Forward' means towards the opposing team's dead-ball line.

Exception   Charge down. If the ball goes forward as in a knock-on while a player charges down an opponent's kick, but the player does not try to catch the ball, then play continues.

DEFINITION

Throw-forward

A **throw-forward** occurs when a player throws or passes the ball forward. 'Forward' means towards the opposing team's dead-ball line.

Exception   Bounce forward. If the ball is not thrown forward but hits a player or the ground and bounces forward, this is not a throw-forward.

COMMENT: Andrew Cole

A knock-on occurs when it contacts a player's hand or arm and travels forward. If the same player regathers before the ball hits the ground it is not a knock-on. If a player charges down a kick it is not a knock-on. If a player deliberately knocks the ball on, it is a penalty. Spectators often misunderstand the forward pass – lines on the field should never be used to judge whether a pass is forward or not. A forward pass relates to the **passing action**, i.e. if the hands move forward in a pass it is forward. Quite often, due the momentum of the player passing, the ball will travel forward before it is caught by a teammate. This is NOT a forward pass. This illusion is emphasised when the player passing has been stopped in a tackle just as he passes the ball. **Look at his hands as he passes, not where the ball goes!**

LAW 13 – KICK-OFF AND RESTART KICKS

DEFINITION
The kick-off represents the start of the match, or the restart of a match after half-time or after a score.

Where the kick-off is taken
The kick-off is taken at the centre of the halfway line. If the ball is kicked from the wrong place, it is kicked off again.

How a kick-off is taken
(a) At the start of the match and after half-time, a team kicks off with a place kick.
(b) The kicker may place the ball on sand, sawdust or a kicking tee approved by the Union.
(c) After a score a team kicks off with a drop kick, which must be taken at or behind the centre of the halfway line.
(d) If the ball is kicked off by the wrong type of kick, it is kicked off again.

Ball goes directly into touch

The ball must land in the field-of-play. If it is kicked directly into touch the opposing team has three choices:

- to have the ball kicked off again, or
- to have a scrum at the centre and they have the throw-in, or
- to accept the kick.

If they accept the kick, the line-out is on the halfway line. If the ball is blown behind the halfway line and goes directly into touch, the line-out is at the place where it went into touch.

COMMENT: Wayne Erickson

The kick-off must reach the 10-metre line unless it is played by an opponent. We often see opponents move inside the 10-metre line to catch the ball and then knock on or drop the ball, which is picked up by the kicking team. Everybody screams for the ref to play the original offence of 'Not 10, ref!', but as soon as the ball is touched by an opponent, play should go on.

LAW 14 – BALL ON THE GROUND – NO TACKLE

DEFINITION

This situation occurs when the ball is available on the ground and a player goes to ground to gather the ball, except immediately after a scrum or a ruck. It also occurs when a player is on the ground in possession of the ball and has not been tackled.

The game is to be played by players who are on their feet. A player must not make the ball unplayable by falling down. **Unplayable** means that the ball is not immediately available to either team so that play may continue. A player who makes the ball unplayable, or who obstructs the opposing team by falling down, is negating the purpose and spirit of the game and must be penalised. A player who is not tackled, but who goes to ground while holding the ball, or a player who goes to ground and gathers the ball, must act immediately.

1. Player on the ground
The player must immediately do one of three things:
- up with the ball, or
- pass the ball, or
- release the ball.

A player who passes or releases the ball must also get up or move away from it at once. Advantage is played only if it happens immediately. *Penalty: penalty kick*

2. What the player must not do
(a) **Lying on or around the ball**. A player must not lie on or near the ball to prevent opponents getting possession of it.
(b) **Falling over the player on the ground with the ball**. A player must not voluntarily fall on or over a player with the ball who is lying on the ground. *Penalty: penalty kick*
(c) **Falling over players lying on the ground near the ball**. A player must not voluntarily fall on or over players lying on the ground with the ball between them or near them. *Penalty: penalty kick*

DEFINITION
Near is within 1 metre.

COMMENT: Stuart Dickinson
The game of rugby is to be played by players on their feet. If you are on the ground as a result of legitimate play, you must comply

with the relevant law, i.e. pass or play the ball. Then you must get back to your feet immediately, otherwise you are out of the game and have no rights. It is also imperative that you do not voluntarily go to the ground over other players, for example, diving on a player after a tackle.

LAW 15 – TACKLE: BALL CARRIER BROUGHT TO THE GROUND

DEFINITION
A **tackle** occurs when a ball carrier is simultaneously held by one or more opponents and is brought to the ground and/or the ball touches the ground. That player is known as the **tackled player**. Any opponents of the tackled player who go to ground are known as **tacklers**.

Tackle – where
A tackle can only take place in the field-of-play.

When a tackle cannot take place
When the ball carrier is held by one opponent and a teammate binds on to that ball carrier, a maul has been formed and a tackle cannot take place.

Brought to the ground defined
(a) If the ball carrier has one knee or both knees on the ground, that player has been 'brought to ground'.
(b) If the ball carrier is sitting on the ground, or on top of another player on the ground, the ball carrier has been 'brought to ground'.

The tackler

(a) When a player tackles an opponent and they both go to ground, the tackler must immediately release the tackled player. *Penalty: penalty kick*

(b) The tackler must immediately get up or move away from the tackled player and from the ball at once. *Penalty: penalty kick*

(c) The tackler must get up before playing the ball. *Penalty: penalty kick*

Doubt about failure to comply

If the ball becomes unplayable at a tackle and there is doubt about which player did not conform to Law, the referee orders a scrum immediately with the throw-in by the team that was moving forward prior to the stoppage or, if no team was moving forward, by the attacking team.

COMMENT: Scott Young

Once a tackle has been effected there are a number of practices that are outlawed and liable to penalty. No player may prevent the tackled player from passing or releasing the ball or getting up and moving away from the tackle area. The only exception in which an opponent can legally pull the ball from the hands of the tackled player is if that player is on their feet. Players cannot voluntarily fall on or over the tackled player, even if the ball is between or near them. Any player on their feet may not charge or obstruct an opponent who is not near the ball. It is also important for the referee to recognise when a ball in all tackle occurs and either the tackled player has not met their obligations under law or they have been prevented from meeting the obligations. In this situation a pile could occur and dangerous play may happen if the referee does not whistle immediately.

LAW 16 – RUCK

DEFINITIONS
A **ruck** is a phase of play where one or more players from each team, who are on their feet, in physical contact, close around the ball on the ground. Open play has ended. Players are **rucking** when they are in a ruck and using their feet to try to win or keep possession of the ball, without being guilty of foul play.

1. Forming a ruck
Where   A ruck can take place only in the field-of-play.
How   Players are on their feet. At least one player must be in physical contact with an opponent.

Summary
Ruck: Ball on the ground; needs at least two players on their feet, one from each team.

2. Joining a ruck
(a) All players forming, joining or taking part in a ruck must have their heads and shoulders no lower than their hips. *Penalty: free kick*
(b) A player joining a ruck must bind onto the ruck with at least one arm around the body of a teammate, using the whole arm. *Penalty: penalty kick*
(c) Placing a hand on another player in the ruck does not constitute binding. *Penalty: penalty kick*
(d) All players forming, joining or taking part in a ruck must be on their feet. *Penalty: penalty kick*

COMMENT: *Andrew Cole*
In today's game you seem to get many mini-rucks where the ball

is delivered quickly. Therefore prolonged rucking for the ball is unlikely to occur. The main flashpoint occurs when, after a tackle, players competing for the ball on the ground meet players such as George Smith, who are expert at arriving at the breakdown quickly and getting their hands on the ball. There is a very short window of opportunity for them to play the ball because as soon as two opposing players make contact over the ball a ruck is formed. The referee should, if time permits, call 'ruck formed' when he no longer wants the players to play the ball with their hands. It is important that the referee maintains offside lines for the players not in the ruck to create space for the attack once the ball is won.

LAW 17 – MAUL

DEFINITION
A maul occurs when a player carrying the ball is held by one or more opponents, and one or more of the ball carrier's teammates bind on the ball carrier. All the players involved are on their feet and moving towards a goal line. Open play has ended.

1. Forming a maul
Where   A maul only takes place in the field-of-play.
How   Players must be on their feet.

Summary
Maul: At least three players; all on their feet, the ball carrier and one from each team.

2. Joining a maul
(a)   Players joining a maul must have their heads and shoulders no lower than their hips. *Penalty: free kick*
(b)   A player must be caught in or bound to the maul and not just alongside it. *Penalty: penalty kick*

(c) Placing a hand on another player in the maul does not constitute binding. *Penalty: penalty kick*

(d) Keeping players on their feet. Players in a maul must endeavour to stay on their feet. The ball carrier in a maul may go to ground providing the ball is available immediately and play continues. *Penalty: penalty kick*

(e) A player must not voluntarily collapse a maul. This is dangerous play. *Penalty: penalty kick*

(f) A player must not jump on top of a maul. *Penalty: penalty kick*

COMMENT: Wayne Erickson

Most referees will let the players know when a maul has been formed, by calling, 'It's a maul!' or words to that effect. This is an important piece of communication, because the players then know that if the maul stops moving forward, they have a chance to restart it and move it forward again. If they can't, or if it stops again after restarting, they know that the referee will blow it up and give the scrum put in to the team which was NOT in possession when the maul began. In most cases, that's usually the other team, so it's vital that they know where they stand. The referee usually communicates all this through the half-backs, who let their forwards know what to do.

LAW 18 – MARK

DEFINITION

To make a mark, a player must be on or behind that player's 22-metre line. A player with one foot on the 22-metre line or behind it is considered to be 'in the 22'. The player must make a clean catch direct from an opponent's kick and at the same time shout 'Mark!'. A mark cannot be made from a kick-off.

A kick is awarded for a mark. The place for the kick is the place of the mark.

A player may make a mark even though the ball touched a goalpost or crossbar before being caught.

A player from the defending team may make a mark in in-goal.

1. After a mark   The referee immediately blows the whistle and awards a kick to the player who made the mark.

2. Kick awarded   The kick is awarded at the place of the mark.

3. Kick – where   The kick is taken at or behind the mark on a line through the mark.

4. Who kicks   The kick is taken by the player who made the mark. If that player cannot take the kick within one minute, a scrum is formed at the place of the mark with the ball thrown in by the player's team. If the mark is in the in-goal, the scrum is 5 metres from the goal line, on a line through the mark.

COMMENT: Peter Marshall

Once a mark is awarded by the referee it is exactly the same as a free kick. The referee will be looking to ensure that the kicker kicks the ball correctly and that the non-kicking team are back 10 metres and do not charge prior to the kicker commencing his kick.

LAW 19 – TOUCH AND LINE-OUT

Touch

DEFINITIONS

Kicked directly into touch means that the ball was kicked into touch without landing on the playing area, and without touching a player or the referee.

The **22** is the area between the goal line and the 22-metre line, including the 22-metre line but excluding the goal line.

The **line-of-touch** is an imaginary line in the field-of-play at right angles to the touchline through the place where the ball is thrown in.

The ball is **in touch** when a player is carrying it and the ball carrier (or the ball) touches the touchline or the ground beyond the touchline. The place where the ball carrier (or the ball) touched or crossed the touchline is where it **went into touch**.

The **line-of-touch** is an imaginary line in the field-of-play at right angles to the touchline through the place where the ball is thrown in.

The ball is **in touch** if a player catches the ball and that player has a foot on the touchline or the ground beyond the touch line.

If a player has one foot in the field of play and one foot in touch and holds the ball, the ball is **in touch**.

If the ball crosses the touchline or touch-in-goal line, and is caught by a player who has both feet in the playing area, the ball is **not in touch or touch-in-goal**. Such a player may knock the ball into the playing area. If a player jumps and catches the ball, both feet must land in the playing area otherwise the ball is in touch or touch-in-goal.

COMMENT: Stuart Dickinson

The line-out is formed when two or more players from either team are lined up, and it may only take place in the field of play. When this formation has occurred, a player may throw the ball in at any time provided there is not an excessive delay. In all line-outs the throw must be straight and travel at least 5 metres, otherwise the opposition have the right to choose a scrum or another line-out. If a ball is kicked into touch or taken directly from an opponent, a player may take a quick throw-in when no line-out is formed provided the ball has not touched another person. This is often the case when a full-back or winger will throw into himself in order to restart play as quickly as possible.

Line-out

DEFINITIONS

The purpose of the line-out is to restart play quickly, safely and fairly after the ball has gone into touch, with a throw-in between two lines of players. **Line-out players** are the players who form the two lines that make a line-out. The **receiver** is the player in position to catch the ball when line-out players pass or to knock the ball back from the line-out. Any player may be the receiver but each team may have only one receiver at a line-out. Players taking part in the line-out are known as **participating players**. Players taking part in the line-out are the player who throws in and an immediate opponent, the two players waiting to receive the ball from the line-out and the line-out players.

All other players. All other players who are not taking part in the line-out must be at least 10 metres behind the line-of-touch, on or behind their goal line if that is nearer, until the line-out ends.

15-metre line. The 15-metre line is 15 metres in-field and parallel with the touchline.

Scrum after line-out. Any scrum ordered because of an infringement or stoppage at the line-out is on the 15-metre line on the line-of-touch

Beginning and ending a line-out

(a) The line-out begins when the ball leaves the hands of the player throwing it in.

(b) The line-out ends when the ball or a player carrying it leaves the line-out. This includes the following:

- when the ball is thrown, knocked or kicked out of the line-out
- when the ball or a player carrying the ball moves into the area between the 5-metre line and the touchline
- when a line-out player hands the ball to a player who is peeling off
- when the ball is thrown beyond the 15-metre line, or when a player takes or puts it beyond that line
- when a ruck or maul develops in a line-out, and all the feet of all the players in the ruck or maul move beyond the line-of-touch
- when the ball becomes unplayable in a line-out. Play restarts with a scrum.

COMMENT: Andrew Cole

Teams must not delay the forming of a line-out. This gives the opposition time to match numbers. Once the ball is thrown in, the players' safety in the air becomes a priority. This involves adequate support from their own team and no barging or pushing from the opposition. The line-out has become a source of innovation from teams in recent times. This should occur

Offside at the line-out

(a) When a line-out forms, there are two separate offside lines, parallel to the goal lines, for the teams.

(b) **Participating players**. One offside line applies to the players taking part in the line-out (usually some or all of the forwards, plus the scrum-half and the player throwing in).

Until the ball is thrown in, and has touched a player or the ground, this offside line is the line-of-touch. After that, the offside line is a line through the ball.

(c) **Players not taking part**. The other offside line applies to the players not taking part in the line-out (usually the backs). For them, the offside line is 10 metres behind the line-of-touch or their goal line, if that is nearer.

The line-out offside law is different in the case of a long throw-in, or in the case of a ruck or maul in the line-out.

Player throwing in

There are four options available to the player throwing in (and the thrower's immediate opponent):

(a) The thrower may stay within the touchline.

(b) The thrower may retire to the offside line 10 metres behind the line-of-touch.

(c) The thrower may join the line-out as soon as the ball has been thrown in.

(d) The thrower may move into the receiver position if that position is empty. If the thrower goes anywhere else, the thrower is offside.

Penalty: penalty kick on the 15-metre line

COMMENT: Scott Young

Put simply, if a ruck or a maul forms from a line-out the offside line is the hindmost foot of that player's team. For players not taking part in the line-out the offside line is still 10 metres from the line-out. The fact that a ruck or maul has formed does not constitute the end of the line-out. The line-out ends when the maul or ruck has moved from the line of touch. Once the line-out is over, players may join that ruck or maul providing they do so from their own side and from behind the hindmost foot of their

393

The Australian Rugby Companion

side. Players cannot join a ruck or maul from their opponent's side.

LAW 20 – SCRUM

DEFINITIONS
The purpose of the scrum is to restart play quickly, safely and fairly after a minor infringement or a stoppage. A **scrum** is formed in the field-of-play when eight players from each team, bound together in three rows for each team, close up with their opponents so that the heads of the front rows are interlocked. This creates a tunnel into which a scrum-half throws in the ball so that front-row players can compete for possession by hooking the ball with either of their feet.

The **tunnel** is the space between the two front rows.

The player of either team who throws the ball into the scrum is the **scrum-half**.

The **middle line** is an imaginary line on the ground in the tunnel beneath the line where the shoulders of the two front rows meet.

The middle player in each front row is the **hooker**. The players on either side of the hooker are the **props**. The left-side props are the **loosehead props**. The right-side props are the **tighthead props**. The two players in the second row who shove on the props and the hooker are the **locks**. The outside players who bind onto the second or third row are the **flankers**. The player in the third row who usually pushes on both locks is the **number 8**. Alternatively, the number 8 may shove on a lock and a flanker.

Binding in the scrum
DEFINITION
When a player binds on a teammate that player must use the

394

whole arm from hand to shoulder to grasp the teammate's body at or below the level of the armpit. Placing only a hand on another player is not satisfactory binding.

(a) **Binding by all front-row players**. All front-row players must bind firmly and continuously from the start to the finish of the scrum. *Penalty: penalty kick*

(b) **Binding by hookers**. The hooker may bind either over or under the arms of the props. The props must not support the hooker so that the hooker has no weight on either foot. *Penalty: penalty kick*

(c) **Binding by loosehead props**. A loosehead prop must bind on the opposing tighthead prop by placing the left arm inside the right arm of the tighthead and gripping the tighthead prop's jersey on the back or side. The loosehead prop must not grip the chest, arm, sleeve or collar of the opposition tighthead prop. The loosehead prop must not exert any downward pressure. *Penalty: penalty kick*

(d) **Binding by tighthead props**. A tighthead prop must bind on the opposing loosehead prop by placing the right arm outside the left upper arm of the opposing loosehead prop. The tighthead prop must grip the opposing loosehead prop's jersey with the right hand only on the back or side. The tighthead prop must not grip the chest, arm, sleeve or collar of the opposition loosehead prop. The tighthead prop must not exert any downward pressure. *Penalty: penalty kick*

COMMENT: Peter Marshall
The scrum is a very competitive part of the game, where eight forwards are bound together and engage with eight opponents in a contest for possession. The referee will ensure the players are correctly bound and that the scrum is square and stationary prior to the ball being fed. The feeding half-back and his immediate opponent may follow the ball through the scrum,

providing they are on the same side of the scrum as the ball was fed and they remain behind the ball. Players in the back line must remain behind the last feet of their players in the scrum.

LAW 21 – PENALTY AND FREE KICKS

DEFINITIONS
Penalty kicks and **free kicks** are awarded to the non-offending team for infringements by their opponents.

1. Where penalty and free kicks are awarded
Unless a law states otherwise, the mark for a penalty or free kick is at the place of infringement.

2. Where penalty and free kicks are taken
(a) The kicker must take the penalty or free kick at the mark or anywhere behind it on a line through the mark. If the place for a penalty or free kick is within 5 metres of the opponents' goal line, the mark for the kick is 5 metres from the goal line, opposite the place of infringement.

(b) When a penalty or free kick is awarded for an infringement in in-goal, the mark for the kick is in the field-of-play, 5 metres from the goal line, in line with the place of infringement.

Penalty: Any infringement by the kicker's team results in a scrum at the mark. The opposing team throws in the ball.

3. How the penalty and free kicks are taken
(a) Any player may take a penalty or free kick awarded for an infringement with any type of kick, punt, drop kick, or place kick. The ball may be kicked with any part of the lower leg or the foot, excluding the knee and the heel.

(b) Bouncing the ball on the knee is not taking a kick.

(c) The kicker must use the ball that was in play, unless the referee decides it was defective.

Penalty: Any infringement by the kicker's team results in a scrum at the mark. The opposing team throws in the ball.

COMMENT: Stuart Dickinson

When the referee has made a mark for the free kick, the opposition team must be at least 10 metres opposite on the offside line prior to their opponent's tapping or kicking the ball. This offside line is an imaginary line that extends across the field parallel to the touchlines. If the opponents take a quick tap, all the players not back 10 metres are offside and liable to penalty. If those players continue to move back and do not interfere with the opposition, they can be put on-side by a teammate who has come from an on-side position behind the 10 metres. This is why you see players running back 10 metres and looking at the touch judge and putting their hand up so they know they are on-side.

LAW 22 – IN-GOAL

DEFINITIONS

In-goal is part of the ground, as defined in Law 1, where the ball may be grounded by players from either team.

When attacking players are first to ground the ball in the opponents' in-goal, the attacking players score a **try**.

When defending players are first to ground the ball in in-goal, the defending players make a **touchdown**.

A defending player who has one foot on the goal line or in the in-goal who receives the ball is considered to be **in in-goal**.

Grounding the ball

There are two ways a player can ground the ball:

(a) **Player touches the ground with the ball**. A player grounds the ball by holding the ball and touching the ground with it, in in-goal. 'Holding' means holding in the hand or hands, or in the arm or arms. No downward pressure is required.

(b) **Player presses down on the ball**. A player grounds the ball when it is on the ground in the in-goal and the player presses down on it with a hand or hands, arm or arms, or the front of the player's body from waist to neck inclusive.

Other ways to score a try

(a) **Grounded on the goal line**. The goal line is part of the in-goal. If an attacking player is first to ground the ball on the opponents' goal line, a try is scored.

(b) **Grounded against a goalpost**. The goalposts and padding surrounding them are part of the goal line, which is part of in-goal. If an attacking player is first to ground the ball against a goalpost or padding, a try is scored.

(c) **Pushover try**. A scrum or ruck cannot take place in the in-goal. If a scrum or ruck is pushed into the in-goal, an attacking player may legally ground the ball as soon as the ball reaches or crosses the goal line and a try is scored.

(d) **Momentum try**. If an attacking player with the ball is tackled short of the goal line but the player's momentum carries the player in a continuous movement along the ground into the opponents' in-goal, and the player is first to ground the ball, a try is scored.

(e) **Tackled near the goal line**. If a player is tackled near the opponents' goal line so that this player can immediately reach out and ground the ball on or over the goal line, a try is scored.

(f) This player must not infringe the tackle law. The tackle law

Laws of the game

requires a tackled player to play the ball immediately.
However, the tackled player may place the ball on the
ground in any direction provided it is done immediately.

(g) In this situation, defending players who are on their feet may
legally prevent the try by pulling the ball from the tackled
player's hands or arms, but must not kick the ball.

(h) **Player in touch or touch-in-goal**. If an attacking player is
in touch or in touch-in-goal, the player can score a try by
grounding the ball in the opponents' in-goal provided the
player is not carrying the ball.

(i) **Penalty try**. A penalty try is awarded if a try would probably
have been scored but for foul play by the defending team.
A penalty try is awarded if a try would probably have been
scored in a better position but for foul play by the defending
team.

(j) A penalty try is awarded between the goalposts. The
defending team may charge the conversion kick after a
penalty try.

COMMENT: Andrew Cole

Infringements in-goal are treated the same as in the field of play.
If a defending player commits an offence that prevents a try
being scored, it will result in a penalty try, which is awarded
under the posts. If an attacking player commits an offence in-
goal, the mark for the penalty is 5 metres out from the goal line.
If an attacking player grounds the ball against the goalpost
padding and the ground, it is a try. If an attacking player is
responsible for the ball being in-goal and a defender grounds it,
it is a 22-metre drop-out. If a defender takes the ball back into
in-goal and a defender grounds it, it is a 5-metre scrum. If a
player kicks the ball dead from the field of play, the opposing
team has an option of 22-metre drop-out or scrum back where
the kick was from.

Referee signals

Simplifying the laws of rugby is an ongoing challenge for the game's administrators. Here Australian Test referees Stuart Dickinson and Wayne Erickson join forces to demonstrate the full gambit of signals that can occur in a game of rugby.

Penalty kick

Shoulders parallel with touch line. Arm angled up, pointing towards non-offending team.

Free kick

Shoulders parallel with touch line. Arm bent square at elbow, upper arm pointing towards non-offending team.

Try and Penalty try

Referee's back to dead-ball line. Shoulders parallel with goal-line. Arm raised vertically.

Advantage

Arm outstretched, waist-high, towards non-offending team.

Scrum awarded

Shoulders parallel with touch line. Arm horizontal, pointing towards the team to put in the ball.

Throw-forward/Forward pass

Hands gesture as if passing an imaginary ball forward.

The Australian Rugby Companion

Knock-on

Hand above head motioning forward and then back through a small radius.

Not releasing ball immediately

Both hands close to the chest, as if holding an imaginary ball.

Voluntarily falling over on a player

Curved arm makes gesture to imitate action of falling player. Signal is made in direction in which offending player fell.

Diving to ground near tackle

Straight arm gesture, pointing downwards to imitate diving action.

Prop pulling down opponent

Clenched fist and arm bent. Gesture imitates pulling opponent down.

Prop pulling opponent on

Clenched fist and arm straight at shoulder height. Gesture imitates pulling opponent on.

Wheeling scrum more than 90 degrees

Rotating index finger at shoulder height.

Foot up by front-row player

Foot raised, heel touched.

403

Throw-in at scrum not straight

Hands at waist level imitate action of put-in not straight.

Failure to bind fully

One arm outstretched as if binding. Other hand moves up and down arm, to indicate the extent of a full bind.

Voluntarily collapsing ruck or maul

Both arms at shoulder height as if bound around opponent. Upper body is lowered and twisted as if pulling down opponent who is on top.

Handling ball in ruck or scrum

Hand at ground level making sweeping action as if handling the ball.

Throw-in not straight

Shoulders parallel with touchline. Hand above head indicates the path of the ball, not straight.

Closing gaps at line-out

Both hands at eye level, pointing up, palms inward. Hands meet in squeezing action.

Barging in line-out

Arm horizontal, elbow pointing out. Arm and shoulder move outwards as if barging opponent.

Leaning on player in line-out

Arm horizontal, bent at elbow, palm down. Downward gesture.

Pushing opponent in line-out

Both hands at shoulder level, with palms outward, making pushing gesture.

Lifting player illegally in line-out

Both fists clenched in front at waist level, making lifting gesture.

Obstruction in general play

Arms crossed in front of chest at right angles to each other, like open scissors.

Offside at line-out

Hand and arm move horizontally across chest, towards offence.

Offside at ruck or maul (fringing)

Arm outstretched, fingers pointing downwards. Hand makes a circle.

Offside at scrum, ruck or maul

Shoulders parallel with touch line. Arm hanging straight down, swings in arc along offside line.

Offside choice: penalty kick or scrum

One arm as for penalty kick. Other arm points to place where scrum may be taken instead of kick.

Offside under 10-metre law

One hand moves in line above head.

High tackle (foul play)

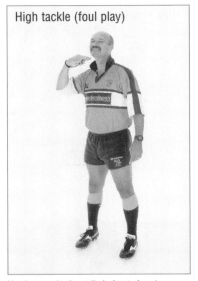

Hand moves horizontally in front of neck.

Stamping (foul play – illegal use of boot)

Stamping action or similar gesture to indicate the offence.

Punching (foul play)

Clenched fist punches open hand.

Dissent (disputing referee's decision)

Outstretched arm with hand opening and closing to imitate talking.

Award of drop-out on 22-metre line

Arm points to centre of 22-metre line.

Forming a scrum

Elbows bent, hands above head, fingers touching.

Ball held up in-goal

Space between hands indicates that ball was not grounded.

Unplayable maul

Arm out to award scrummage to side not in possession at maul commencement. Other arm out as if signalling advantage and then swing it across body with hand ending on chest.

409

The Australian Rugby Companion

Non-release of tackled player by tackler(s)

'Hugging' action.

Blood bin

Arms crossed above head indicates player has bleeding injury and may be temporarily replaced.

Index

Index

Index

414

Index

Index

418